THE TRAGEDY OF CHILD CARE IN AMERICA

EDWARD ZIGLER,
KATHERINE MARSLAND,
AND HEATHER LORD

The Tragedy
of Child Care
in America

YALE UNIVERSITY PRESS   NEW HAVEN & LONDON

Set in FontFont Scala and Scala Sans by Duke & Company, Devon, Pennsylvania.
Printed in the United States of America by Sheridan Books, Ann Arbor, Michigan.

ISBN 978-0-300-12233-6 (hardcover : alk. paper)

A catalogue record for this book is available from the Library of Congress and the
British Library.

This paper meets the requirements of ANSI/NISO Z39.48-1992 (Permanence of Paper).
It contains 30 percent postconsumer waste (PCW) and is certified by the Forest Stewardship Council (FSC).

10 9 8 7 6 5 4 3 2 1

This book is dedicated to John Brademas and Elliot Richardson, two brilliant and caring public servants (one a Democrat and one a Republican) who came very close to providing our country with a high-quality child care system.

CONTENTS

PREFACE

I ASKED MY FORMER STUDENTS and now colleagues to join me in writing this book because I consider the failure to establish a uniformly high-quality child care system available to all America's children to be the greatest shortcoming of my career. I am writing this preface because, while an early reader of the manuscript advised that our title, "The Tragedy of Child Care in America," was too negative, I still think the status of child care in America is a tragedy. But now that I am pressed, I also think that our nation must, can, and will do something about it. My hope is that this book will serve as a starting point for discussions about how we can remedy the child care problem and better address the needs of both working parents and their children.

There is much to bemoan. Too many of our children spend a significant part of their growing years in poor to mediocre child care that does little to stimulate their optimal growth and development. The magnitude of this crisis was made clear over thirty years ago when the National Council of Jewish Women published its first survey of child care in America, *Windows on Day Care*.[1] The organization conducted a follow-up survey nearly three decades later and found that the quality of child care had not improved.[2] The famous Cost, Quality and Child Outcomes Study Team reported that 40 percent of children in infant and toddler centers in the four states they studied were encountering such poor-quality care that their health and safety were at risk.[3]

It is not hard to figure out why. Gail Collins, an authority on child and family issues, points out, "You need certification in this country to be a butcher, a barber, or a manicurist, but only twelve states require any training to take care of children. Only three require comprehensive background checks."[4] She notes the cases of Iowa, where there is one inspector for 591 child care programs, and California, where centers are inspected only once every five years.

The tragedy is not just that this sorry state of affairs has lingered for so long. It is also tragic to consider the fate of what are now generations of children exposed to poor-quality care. We know that good-quality care supports optimal cognitive, social, and emotional development, school readiness, and academic achievement. Poor-quality care does not. Economists like the Nobel Laureate James Heckman have emphasized how important early-childhood learning experiences are to the later quality of the workforce and hence the economic strength of our nation. If the child care setting holds such great potential for enhancing the development of the child, it is a shame that we are not capitalizing on it as a significant socialization and learning environment.

Why not? A major stumbling block to any progress on the child care front is a deeply held view in the American ethos that the family sphere is sacrosanct. Families are responsible for raising their children, and government should never intrude unless children are in great danger—abused or deprived of the essentials of life. Shpancer is correct in arguing that "non-parental daycare in the U.S. is a controversial issue, as the cultural ideal still strongly favors maternal care of young infants and children."[5] Indeed, the rallying cry that led to President Nixon's veto of a 1971 bill that would have established a national child care system was that parents, not government, should raise children. (I will return to this sorry tale.) To prove just how ingrained this view is, Shpancer noted that even statistics showing that children are more likely to be abused in the home than in child care has not altered in any way the view that home rearing is inherently superior to even part-day rearing in child care settings.

The American Academy of Pediatrics recognized in 1973 that this debate was not an either/or situation and recommended the expansion of high-quality child care programs. These physicians properly viewed child care as a supplement to the primary child rearing by parents. Child care providers do not replace parents any more than public schools do. Ideally, child care is a strong partnership between a supplemental caregiver and the parents, who are always the senior partners.

Another reason for our failure to act on the child care crisis is that child care is widely viewed as a service that permits parents to enter the job market, not as a critical learning environment for children. What child care policies we do have were enacted for workforce development or welfare reform, not for children's education and well-being. Too many people envision child care as a container. Before parents go to work they drop their child into the container, where he or she is kept safe. The parents then retrieve the child at the end of the day (hence the term "day care"). This perception is, of course, not shared by the child. Child development is not put on hold until Mommy or Daddy returns. Think for a moment about what occurs in a good preschool classroom. Children learn, play, socialize, and rest. There is no real distinction between high-quality child care and high-quality preschool education except for the lengths of the day and the year. This fact has not been grasped by voters or policy makers. Indeed, a comprehensive analysis of children's political issues by Kirp and Kong shows that decision makers view early-childhood education as a winning issue and child care as relatively unimportant.[6]

America actually came very close to establishing a good-quality, affordable child care program available to all families who wanted to enroll their children. In 1971 Congress passed the Comprehensive Child Development Act, a somewhat flawed piece of legislation that would have put into place a national child care system much like that already in place in many industrialized nations. An earlier version of the bill would have created an excellent child care system that guaranteed both good management and good quality. Although it enjoyed wide political and popular support, the bill was vetoed in a stinging message by President Nixon. The counterproductive changes to the earlier bill and the veto were the result of the actions of a strange mixture of far-left liberals and far-right conservatives. I was a member of the Nixon administration at the time and helped to draft the original legislation. It still pains me that we came so close to the goal and lost it. The 1971 bill will be discussed at length in this book, in the hope that it will provide some direction for the future.

After Nixon's veto message, which compared child care to the communal raising of children, policy makers were loath to touch the issue again. One brave exception was a conservative Republican, Senator Orrin Hatch, who drafted his own child care bill after hearing that working mothers in his home state of Utah were having difficulty obtaining child care. He did so not only in the face of the defeat of the earlier bill but in opposition to the leader of his own Mormon church.

A glimmer of hope appeared in 1997, when President and Mrs. Clinton hosted the White House Conference on Child Care. Many advocates expected Hillary Clinton, the author of *It Takes a Village,* to take a leading role in addressing the nation's child care problem, which she had referred to as a "silent crisis." Kirp and Kong describe the enthusiasm surrounding the event: "After wandering in the desert for years, advocates had finally gotten the attention they craved, a day-long White House Conference on Child Care."[7] I attended the conference and agree with Kirp and Kong that it was more than a gabfest. There was every indication that child care was "becoming the next big idea on the domestic policy front" and that "there was reason to anticipate concrete results."[8] Unfortunately, no real action came out of this conference. Kirp and Kong explain that the Monica Lewinsky scandal broke shortly afterward, and the remainder of the Clinton years' policy development was trumped by the pressures of impeachment. Again we came close but failed to grasp the brass ring.

As this book goes to press, there is hope that we are emerging from a dark period during which there has been almost no discussion in Washington about improving the quality of care experienced every day by millions of our nation's children. We now face an economic crisis more severe than any since the Great Depression and are compelled to reexamine fundamental values. Despite these daunting times, however, there are indications that the Obama administration may turn fresh eyes toward child care policy in this country. Thus, perhaps a moment of great opportunity is at hand to finally effect real change in the area of child care.

The moribund nature of any discussion of child care as an issue demanding serious attention in Washington was highlighted in an October 2007 op-ed piece in the *New York Times* written by Collins. She notes that the one exception to this vacuum is Senator Chris Dodd of Connecticut, "who talks about child care all the time." She points out that Dodd has reaped little political capital from being "the issue's champion of the Senate forever."[9] Dodd himself is aware that child advocates "aren't inclined to be the kind of people who engage in the political process" and adds, "They don't have the money." I have been one of those advocates who have engaged in the political process and have had the privilege of working closely with Dodd for a couple of decades. I can speak from personal knowledge of Dodd's great commitment to improving the child care situation in America. We need more legislators like him.

With the exception of the nonrefundable income tax credit for child and dependent care, the only piece of national legislation directed at helping families pay for care is the Child Care and Development Block Grant (CCDBG). This bill passed with bipartisan support in Congress and was signed into law in 1990 by Republican President George H. W. Bush. Because of its importance, this law will be discussed at length in this book. Getting the law on the books was a major achievement. Much of the credit goes to Marian Wright Edelman, founder and president of the Children's Defense Fund, who led the coalition supporting the bill. On the other side, far-right thinkers opposed the bill just as vigorously as they did the 1971 bill. The best explanation for their failure is that by the late 1980s so many women were in the out-of-home workforce that it was impossible to assert that mothers should stay at home with their children, thus eliminating the need for child care.

The law that was finally passed was much weaker than the original version. At the outset it was called the Act for Better Child Care, or ABC. As the title implies, the bill contained guarantees of quality improvement, but these measures became less and less prescriptive as the bill wended its way through Congress. The final legislation permitted up to 4 percent of child care funds to be spent on improving quality. As a comparison, when it became obvious that the quality of the Head Start program was not what it should be, Senator Edward Kennedy led an effort in Congress to set aside 25 percent of new Head Start appropriations (after adjusting for inflation) for quality improvements.

Indeed my biggest complaint about the CCDBG is that it does little to assure the quality of child care purchased with federal funds. The law allows states a great deal of flexibility in how they design their programs, within minimal federal guidelines. The only quality standard is that the child care provider must meet minimal health and safety standards, but states have not always complied with even these extremely weak rules. CCDBG funds are largely spent on vouchers that income-eligible parents can use to purchase any type of care they choose. The subsidy is too small to pay for high-quality child care, which is generally more expensive than care of lower quality, so parents do not have true choice over caregiving arrangements for their children. The bulk of recipients rely on what is called kith and kin care, meaning relatives, boyfriends, and neighbors. None of these providers are required to have any training or experience in caring for children.

While I continue to support increases in the appropriations for CCDBG, I take little satisfaction in the fact that the money is being used to purchase care of unknown quality for our most vulnerable children. This situation has become even more desperate with the 1996 welfare reform plan, which concentrates on getting people off the welfare rolls and does not address the type of care their children receive while they are at work. Further, the CCDBG gives the false impression that the problem of accessing child care is limited to the poor. CCDBG subsidies are restricted to low-income working families and families receiving or transitioning away from welfare. (As poor as most of these families are, they are required to make a co-payment.) Yet for decades the child care problem has also bedeviled middle-class parents, who also find it hard to afford the quality care they want their children to have.

On the positive side, 1.7 million children received child care through this law in 2005 alone. CCDBG funds have been increased at the state level after states were allowed to add Temporary Assistance for Needy Families funds to their CCDBG money. However, even with the added resources, the money doesn't begin to meet the need. Ewen and Matthews report that fewer than 14 percent of eligible children are being served.[10] Even the limited value of the CCDBG is being further compromised. The National Center for Children in Poverty reported that over the past six years half of the states have cut child care subsidies.[11] At the same time, twenty-six states increased their spending on preschool programs, only confirming that there is great momentum at both the state and national levels to increase the supply of preschool education for children of all income groups. There is next to no momentum at either level to improve the child care mess. Policy makers do not seem to realize that quality child care can contribute as much to school readiness as good preschool programming.

Of course, something is better than nothing. The CCDBG does provide many poor and near-poor families with some desperately needed support to purchase child care so parents are able to work. Over my forty-plus years in the policy arena, I certainly have experienced more losses than victories. In the world of policy you can lose a hundred times, but you have to win only once if a piece of overarching legislation completely addresses the problem. I await that legislation, but I realize that one can also make progress by eking out small victories. The CCDBG and other small victories are described in this book.

Credit for what progress has been made goes to the many individuals and organizations who have worked tirelessly to improve the child care situation in this nation. My description of child care as a tragedy is not a criticism of their efforts. At the federal level, they have helped secure child care subsidies, a child care tax credit, and a nonpaid family leave policy—all building blocks to better policies in the future.

When the federal government drags its feet on issues, states sometimes take the lead. In some states there are exemplary models of system building and quality improvement. The advocates and decision makers in these states should be congratulated for their progress. In this book we discuss two large national projects that provide demonstrably high-quality care to children. Both systems began with a genuine commitment by all the stakeholders to provide good-quality care. Mechanisms were built to ensure that caregivers are well-trained and paid a decent wage, which lowers turnover. Quality control involves regular monitoring and follow-up to correct any weak spots discovered.

These successes bring me to one further reason why I consider the child care situation in America to be a tragedy. If we did not know how to provide good-quality child care to children of all ages, then it would be understandable that our nation has not moved forward to solve the problem. However, as the examples of successful programs noted in our book make clear, we have all the knowledge that is needed. As a scholar who strongly believes that our knowledge base should be used to inform sound public policy, I find it tragic that policy is not incorporating what we know.

The tragedy plays out in the daily lives of millions of America's children and families. Despite volumes of research and valiant efforts on the part of experts and advocates, progress toward creating a system of supports that addresses the needs of both working adults and their children has been woefully insufficient. As we go to press, the United States is one of only a few industrialized nations with no paid parental leave after the birth or adoption of a baby. We are one of only a few nations with no coordinated system of affordable, good-quality care for children during their first, most formative three years of life. And we are falling behind other nations in the provision of good-quality care for preschoolers and school-age children.

The purpose of this book is not just to convince readers that our nation desperately needs a much more comprehensive effort to end the child care tragedy. I have been working to create policies for accessible and affordable quality child care for four decades. This book contains the solutions gleaned from my studies and those of my students, two of whom are my coauthors. The book not only highlights how bad we believe this situation to be, but also gives our ideas about how to improve the child care experienced by the majority of children in America today. We remain optimistic that one day our nation's decision makers will perceive child care, appropriately, as an environment that has an important impact on the child's current and future growth and development.

I close with an explanation. I am much older than my young co-authors and have been working on the child care crisis since before they were born. Many descriptions of historical events in this book derive from my personal experiences. To avoid the awkwardness of using the third person or constantly identifying me as "Zigler" or "the first author," we decided to use the first person. In the following pages, "I" means Zigler, even though my coauthors did a great deal of the thinking and writing. As a graduate student, Dr. Katherine Marsland collaborated with me on child care issues, particularly on documenting state child care regulations. (While many have faith in the power of regulation, we found the rules in many states almost guarantee that the quality of care will be somewhere between poor and mediocre.) Dr. Heather Lord was also my graduate student. She, too, is amazingly talented and has great knowledge about both child care and social policy. The recommendations in this book are as much the conclusions reached from these professionals' reviews of the literature as mine. Thus, while "I" is used to aid readability, this book is very much the work of the three of us.

ACKNOWLEDGMENTS

THE AUTHORS ARE DEEPLY INDEBTED to a group of leading workers who have labored diligently in the trenches to improve the quality of child care in America. They include Shannon Christian, Jamie Gottesman, Joan Lombardi, Susan Muenchow, Linda Smith, Matia Finn-Stevenson, and Garrit Westervelt. These worker-scholars were kind enough to share views and recommendations with the authors, who take complete responsibility for the final views presented in this book.

The authors are also grateful for the research assistance provided by Leigh Esparo, Beth Lapin, Julie Linden, Andrew Martinez, Kate Sejourne, Heather Friess, and Heather Weh. We offer a special note of thanks to Sally Styfco for her editorial assistance and to our families for their invaluable support.

This book was made possible through the financial support of the following foundations: the Smith Richardson Foundation, the William T. Grant Foundation, the A. L. Mailman Family Foundation, and the Foundation for Child Development.

CHAPTER ONE

The Challenge of Child Care

Child care is in crisis. No matter what measures are used—access, quality, or affordability—we know that the child care system is failing working parents and their children. Worse yet, it is failing even as families in every income bracket are becoming more reliant on it.

National Council of Jewish Women

IN 1970 FINDING AFFORDABLE, good-quality child care was identified as the number one challenge facing America's families.[1] Despite a growing body of knowledge about the developmental needs of young children and the valiant efforts of advocates and policymakers, the subsequent forty years have been marked by pitifully little progress toward the creation of a coherent child care system. Consequently, the United States continues to experience what has aptly been referred to as a "silent crisis" in child care.[2] Although the problem is common, its nature is as diverse as the population itself. In fact, the term "child care" means different things to different people. To some, it refers to a place where children are watched while their parents work. To others, it refers to any group setting in which children are cared for by a paid provider. To still others, it refers to care by anyone other than a parent—regardless of whether that person is paid. What all of these conceptualizations share is an emphasis on the adults involved—the needs of working parents; the employment status of the caregiver; the type of person doing the caregiving.

In contrast, I view child care as a context in which children develop. Indeed, second to the family, child care is the most influential developmental context for many children. Although the specific context can range from care by friends or relatives to care provided in formal settings, what matters most are the child's experience of the caregiving environment and

1

the extent to which the child's physical, social, emotional, and cognitive needs are met. At its most optimal—when the quality of care is good and children's needs are met—child care is synonymous with early education. Unfortunately, not all child care is of good quality—thus not all child care is necessarily educational. In fact, poor-quality child care can jeopardize children's health and safety and actually compromise children's development, putting them at risk for poor school readiness and educational outcomes. From this perspective, the child care problem is far more than a challenge for adults. It is a serious threat to the well-being of our children. In turn, to the extent that children's school readiness and academic achievement are compromised by poor child care experiences, it is also a problem for society, which ultimately relies on the human capital embodied in our children.

It is from this ecological perspective that I describe child care in America as tragic. Despite close to four decades of increasing knowledge about and attention to this issue, we continue to allow children to be raised in environments that fail to address their developmental needs. In this book I explore how and why America arrived at this shameful state and how the lessons learned can inform the development of effective child care solutions. I begin with an overview of the enormity of the problem and what the now voluminous research base tells us about how child care influences children's development. I then examine the history of child care policy since 1969, discuss why these efforts have failed, and identify the issues that persist. I conclude with recommendations for a policy agenda that is informed by research and what we have learned through efforts at the federal and state levels.

WHY CHILD CARE BECAME AN EVER-GROWING SOCIAL POLICY ISSUE

Although child care in America has a long history, economic and social changes during the past four decades have significantly altered the structure of families in America and have contributed to an unprecedented rise in the reliance on nonparental care.[3] Most notably, the number of children with mothers in the workforce has increased substantially. According to the most recent data available from the U.S. Bureau of Labor Statistics, between 1975 and 2004, workforce participation of mothers with children age six and under climbed from 39.0 to 62.2 percent. In particular, mothers of very young children have joined the workforce in growing numbers. Whereas only 34.3 percent of mothers with infants under age three were employed in 1975, 57.3 percent were employed in 2004. Further, the participation of mothers with school-age children (ages six to seventeen) has also increased dramatically, rising from 54.9 percent in 1975 to 77.5 percent in 2004. Importantly, while the proportion of children with employed parents is larger among single-parent households, according to a 2004 study by the Employment Policy Foundation, 51.5 percent of children under age eighteen now live in families in which *both* parents are in the labor force, largely due to economic necessity.[4]

The number of single-parent households has increased concurrently, particularly those headed by single mothers. Although the majority of children under the age of eighteen continue to live with two married parents, as of 2005, 23 percent of children lived with only their mothers, the majority of whom must work to support their families. Between 1970 and 2001, among single mothers with children under age eighteen, the proportion who were employed rose from 36.4 percent to 65.5 percent. Notably, the largest increase in workforce participation during this time was among single mothers with children under age three.[5]

The increase in households headed by single women is closely tied to high rates of child poverty, as families headed by single mothers are much more likely to live in low-income conditions (71 percent) than those headed by single fathers (46 percent) or two parents (27 percent). Moreover, between 1997 and 2001, among children of single mothers, 78 percent had working mothers, compared to 64 percent a decade earlier.[6] This trend may be, in part, a function of increased work requirements tied to welfare reform in the 1990s. Specifically, the 1996 Personal Responsibility and Work Opportunity Reconciliation Act (PRWORA) replaced Aid to Families with Dependent Children (AFDC), which was an entitlement program, with Temporary Assistance for Needy Families (TANF), a block-grant program that established time-limited assistance and imposed work requirements on recipients. In subsequent years, workforce participation of unmarried mothers increased by 12 percent, with 75.5 percent of unmarried mothers with children under age eighteen employed in 2000.[7]

Another trend that has influenced the demand for child care has been the growth in the number of adults working nontraditional or "shift" hours. While most still work during the traditional 6 AM to 6 PM hours, approximately 20 percent of all full-time workers now work evening shifts (for example, 2 PM to midnight), night shifts (9 PM to 8 AM), rotating shifts (changing periodically from days to evenings or nights), split shifts (part days and part evening or nights), or weekends. According to the most recent census data available, between 11 and 18 percent of parents with children under age eighteen work one or another type of nontraditional shift. Among dual-income parents of children under age six, the rates are slightly higher, with roughly 35 percent of couples reporting that one or both parents work nontraditional shifts.[8] These parents often piece together "split-shift" parenting in order to minimize the use of nonparental child care, particularly during the years before school entry.

Together, these demographic changes have prompted a surge in demand for child care that meets the needs of a wide range of working parents' schedules. According to the most recent analysis of census data available, 60 percent of children under age six receive care on a regular basis from someone other than their parents.[9] Roughly 65 percent of three-year-olds and 79 percent of four-year-olds participate in nonparental child care arrangements on a regular basis. Among infants and toddlers, 40 percent of children under age one and 59 percent of two-year-olds are cared for in nonparental settings. Reliance on nonparental care for children age five and older is even greater, with school serving as a part-day child care setting for roughly 80 percent of the school-age children with employed mothers.[10] In total, approximately 32 million children are cared for in nonparental settings on a regular basis.[11] These settings vary in type, quality, affordability, and accessibility. The absence of a coordinated infrastructure or unified system creates a chaotic hodgepodge of care that is stressful for parents, negatively impacts family life, and has serious ramifications for children's development, school readiness, and educational achievement.

THE PATCHWORK OF CHILD CARE

Where and by whom are all of these children cared for? Child care in America is enormously diverse; thus the answer to this question varies according to the age of the child, family characteristics, and the availability of care. In this section we discuss the two core dimensions along which child care settings vary: type of care and age of child (table 1).

Table 1

4 (Child Care Type) × 3 (Age of Child) Matrix of Child Care Typology

AGE OF CHILD	KITH & KIN	BABYSITTER/NANNY	FAMILY CHILD CARE	CENTER CARE	
				FOR-PROFIT	NONPROFIT
Infants and Toddlers (0–3)					
Preschool-age children (3–5)					
School-age children (5–14)					

CHILD CARE TYPE

Types of Child Care

While some differentiate among type of care based on their location (in or out of home) or formality (the degree to which settings are subject to quality oversight), in this section we will focus on four basic types of care: (1) kith and kin care; (2) babysitter or nanny care; (3) family child care; and (4) center-based care.

Kith and Kin Care

Kith and kin or "informal" care includes child care provided by grandparents, aunts or uncles, and other relatives of the child, as well as care by friends and neighbors. These caregivers may provide care in the child's home or in their own home, and they are typically exempt from state licensing requirements, depending on the state and the specific circumstances. One benefit of informal arrangements is that the caregivers usually share the parents' child-rearing values. Additionally, the flexibility of the arrangement makes it attractive to parents who work nontraditional or inconsistent hours. Further, kith and kin care tends to be less expensive than more formal arrangements. However, the experience that kith and kin caregivers bring to their duties varies tremendously, and not all caregivers are happy in their caregiving roles. Consequently, the quality of such care is highly variable and not always reliable.[12]

Babysitter or Nanny Care

Babysitter or nanny care refers to formal or informal care by one unrelated, paid caregiver. This type of care can range from occasional babysitting by teenagers to care by professional nannies. One benefit of these arrangements is that they tend to be flexible, enabling parents to tailor care to their needs. A second benefit is that good-quality babysitter or nanny care tends to be more individualized than care in group settings. The quality of these arrangements varies greatly, however, largely due to differences in the experience and training that caregivers bring to their roles. Caregivers may be totally lacking in skill and experience, or they may be highly trained and able to supply good references. Further, this type of care tends to be the most expensive, and—like kith and kin care—is vulnerable to breakdowns when the caregiver is ill or otherwise unavailable. Moreover, in most cases, this type of care is subject to almost no quality oversight. Though some agencies that supply nannies, babysitters, or au pairs check references, in general they require only that the provider be bonded, which protects property but does not ensure good-quality caregiving.

Family Child Care

Family child care is one of two major types of formal nonrelative child care. In these arrangements, providers are essentially small entrepreneurs who typically care for a small mixed-age group of children in their own home.[13] The exact definition of a family child care home varies from state to state, but all are private residences where care is provided to a limited number of children—typically four to six. The caregiver may or may not be related to the child or have children of his or her own at home. The small group sizes and residential environment of this type of care appeal particularly to parents of infants and toddlers, although there is no guarantee that such settings will actually resemble the child's own home aside from being a private residence. In fact, the quality of these caregiving environments is highly variable and subject to very uneven and lax oversight.[14]

In family child care, some children may experience excellent care while others are subjected to care that endangers their physical safety. Indeed, a recent study found that child fatalities were sixteen times higher in family child care homes than in formal child care centers.[15] Because the quality of family child care varies so dramatically—from the very best of care to the very worst—choosing this setting is a high-stakes gamble. While testifying before a congressional committee in 1987, I was asked what I thought of family child care and immediately responded, "It is a cosmic crapshoot." When asked what I meant, I pointed out that a mother seeking family child care could knock on a door and encounter a kind, caring, and knowledgeable individual who would provide excellent care for the child and be so involved as a partner in raising the child that the mother feels she has obtained a new family member. By the same token, this mother could knock on a door a block away and leave her child, and the child could be dead by night. The day after this testimony, the *New York Times* ran an editorial titled "The Cosmic Crapshoot" in which the paper supported my views by noting the hundreds of children burned to death in family child care in New York City.[16]

Center-Based Care

Unlike kith and kin care, babysitter care, and family child care, center-based care occurs in a nonresidential setting. In this type of care, children are generally grouped by age and developmental stage. Center-based care is the most popular form of child care for children age three to five and is often chosen because it tends to be the most reliable option.[17] Although some centers specialize in infant and toddler care, the majority do not serve children under the age of three, in part due to the higher labor costs entailed in caring for very young children.

Child care centers differ from family child care homes in several structural respects as well. In many states, directors are required to have training in child development or early-childhood education. Although not all states require caregivers to have such specialized training, caregivers in center-based settings are more likely to have preservice education and to pursue professional development than are their counterparts in family child care settings. The two settings also tend to differ in structure and atmosphere, with family child care usually being more "homey" but child care centers offering more organized group activities, such as circle time, art and music activities, and field trips. Although the philosophy, curriculum, materials, space and facilities, and caregiver characteristics differ from provider to provider, good-quality child care centers resemble good-quality preschools or nursery schools. Both cultivate children's development across social, emotional, physical, and cognitive domains. However, studies indicate that only 10 to 15 percent of child care centers provide care rated by trained observers to be of good quality.[18]

There are two subcategories of center-based child care: for-profit and nonprofit centers. For-profit centers include large national or regional chains, such as KinderCare and Knowledge Learning Corporation, and also smaller mom-and-pop businesses. Nonprofit centers may be operated in churches, synagogues, or community centers, or by employers for the benefit of their employees. Although larger for-profit centers benefit from economies of scale, their decisions regarding factors such as caregiver salaries and caregiver-to-child ratios are often guided by financial concerns rather than by the interests of children. For example, one study found that for-profit centers allocated only 41 to 49 percent of their budgets to staff salaries and benefits compared to the 62 percent allocated by nonprofit centers.[19]

Age of Child

The second dimension along which child care settings vary is the age of the children served. According to this categorization, there are three types of care: (1) infant and toddler care for children from birth to age three; (2) preschool-age child care for children ages three and four; and (3) school-age child care for children ages five to fourteen. Because the developmental needs of children in these three age groups differ so dramatically, the challenges to policy development also vary along this dimension. In chapters 5 through 7 of the book I examine the challenges specific to each of these age groups in more depth.

QUALITY, AFFORDABILITY, AND ACCESSIBILITY PROBLEMS

The heterogeneity of child care would not be an issue if children were experiencing good-quality care and families were not so consumed by the necessity of piecing together often less-than-optimal solutions on their own. In fact, given the enormous diversity in family needs, a variety of care types is a necessity. In the absence of a comprehensive system, however, child care in America tends to be low-quality, expensive, and difficult to access.

Safety and Quality of Child Care

Research over the last three decades has significantly advanced our definition and understanding of what constitutes quality child care and the importance of child care as a context for children's development.[20] Numerous small- and large-scale studies of the relation between child care quality and children's development have demonstrated that quality care is characterized by "safe and healthful care, developmentally appropriate stimulation, positive interactions with adults, encouragement of the child's individual emotional growth, and promotion of positive relationships with other children."[21] Such care meets children's social, cognitive, physical, and emotional needs.

The research in this area has shown that good-quality child care—particularly during the first four years—promotes children's school readiness and long-term educational success.[22] This connection is particularly true for children who are at risk of school failure due to factors associated with growing up in poverty. Moreover, as Heckman and Masterov discuss in a recent policy brief from the Committee for Economic Development, high-quality early care and education is a sound economic investment. In the short term it promotes improved educational outcomes. In the long term it reduces social costs to society and, more important, cultivates a better-prepared workforce, which in turn bolsters economic productivity. In fact, these authors estimate that, for children living in poverty, the economic rate of return on investments in good-quality early care and education is 16 percent.[23]

Nevertheless, the quality of child care in America remains woefully inadequate, averaging somewhere between poor and mediocre.[24] My best estimate and that of other experts is that 12 percent of care is so poor that it compromises the development of participating children.[25] Of course, one way to interpret this figure is to focus on the roughly 88 percent of care that meets at least basic quality standards. However, this approach disregards the plight of four million children jeopardized by care that fails to address their developmental needs at the most basic levels.

Affordability

As any working parent knows, child care is expensive. According to one recent analysis, the annual cost of center-based child care for a four-year-old in an urban area is higher than the average annual cost of public college tuition in all but one state.[26] The cost of infant and toddler care is an even heavier financial burden, with the average annual cost of center-based infant care consuming almost 20 percent of average take-home pay.[27] Thus, out of necessity, cost is the feature that parents weigh most heavily when they select care for their children. And because good-quality care costs more, the emphasis on containing costs affects both the quality of care that children experience and the dynamics of the child care market. This effect is particularly important with respect to infant and toddler care, which is the most expensive form of care due to the high labor costs associated with smaller group sizes and lower caregiver-to-child ratios. In addition, this expense occurs when young families are least able to afford high-quality care or the opportunity costs associated with staying home.

These market dynamics have important implications for the child care labor force and in turn for the quality of care children receive. Largely in response to the consumer emphasis on costs, child care providers seek to minimize the costs of inputs into care, the largest of which is labor.

Consequently, child care is among the most poorly compensated professions, with average wages lower than those of locker room attendants, bicycle repairers, and animal trainers. In 2004, caregivers earned an average of only about $8.37 per hour, with half of all caregivers earning less than $7.90 per hour.[28] In contrast, the mean hourly wage for kindergarten teachers was $20.38 per hour. Moreover, wage increases in the early care and education field have not kept pace with inflation, averaging less than 2 percent per year. Alarmingly, over 25 percent of center-based caregivers and 35 percent of home-based providers have incomes below 200 percent of the poverty line. In addition to being poorly compensated, child care workers often lack benefits, such as health insurance and pension plans. The most recent data indicate that only 33 percent of center-based caregivers have health care benefits through work, and only 21 percent participate in an employer-sponsored pension plan.[29]

This compensation problem has a damaging ripple effect on child care quality in at least three respects. First, poor compensation and limited career opportunities discourage entry into the field, making recruitment of qualified caregivers extremely difficult. According to a recent report from the Foundation for Child Development, the proportion of center-based caregivers with at least a four-year college degree dropped from 43 percent in 1983–85 to 30 percent in 2002–04, and new hires increasingly have only a high school degree or its equivalent.[30] Among home-based providers, educational attainment is even lower, with more than 45 percent having a high school degree or less and only 11 percent having a four-year college degree.[31] Recent trends suggest that caregivers with more training and education are more likely to enter the education workforce than the child care workforce, largely due to compensation differences.[32]

Second, poor compensation and lack of career advancement opportunities contribute to low morale and discourage caregivers from pursuing ongoing training. This is important because studies have shown that ongoing training contributes to higher-quality classrooms.[33] Third, even when experienced and well-qualified providers enter the field, they are unlikely to stay given the opportunity to move into better-compensated fields. Recent data indicate that the average annual turnover rate among caregivers is 30 percent. This instability further erodes the quality of care experienced by children by compromising their relationships with caregivers, which are essential to the development of social and cognitive competencies. Moreover, hiring patterns suggest that when caregivers with more education and training leave the child care workforce, they are being replaced with caregivers who have far lower levels of education and training.[34]

As Hertzenberg, Price, and Bradley note, "Parents can't afford to pay, teachers can't afford to stay, there's got to be a better way."[35] In chapters 8 and 9 I will discuss policy options to address this critical dimension of the child care problem.

Accessibility

As of 2002, there were more than 113,000 licensed centers and 300,000 regulated family child care homes across the nation, reflecting increases over 1979 numbers by 500 and 200 percent, respectively.[36] However, *access* to child care—both formal and informal—is uneven. Pockets of unavailability of licensed care exist, particularly for infants and toddlers, children with special needs, school-age children, and children whose families work nontraditional hours. Formal child care is less frequently available in low-income neighborhoods, and informal care may be less readily available than previously thought. A 1995 study found that nearly two thirds of families receiving welfare had no friend or relative who could provide child care and that their access to formal arrangements was limited by cost and transportation.[37]

In sum, child care is a problem that has been researched, discussed, debated, and written about for decades now. One thing is certain: we do not lack knowledge about the breadth, scope, and nature of the problem. Tragically, we do appear to be unable—or unwilling—to apply what is known toward a solution that will adequately address the needs of children and their families. Consequently, parents struggle to cobble together feasible solutions with inadequate knowledge, support, and resources; families are stressed; and far too many children fail to receive good-quality care. As author Betty Holcomb aptly notes, "The fragility of child care casts a shadow over the lives of both parents and their children."[38] I would argue that it also casts a shadow over our nation and our nation's future.

In the next two chapters, I review the history of child care policy since 1970 and examine how and why America has failed to meet this challenge.

CHAPTER TWO

A Golden Moment Squandered

THE INSIDE STORY OF THE CRITICAL 1971
COMPREHENSIVE CHILD DEVELOPMENT ACT

In the rearing of our children, we are handing on life like a torch
from one generation to another.

Aeschylus

Greater than the tread of mighty armies is an idea whose time
has come.

Victor Hugo

IN THE UNITED STATES, child care has traditionally been perceived as
a private responsibility.[1] While other nations, including much of Western
Europe, have systems of child care starting at infancy, the U.S. government generally restricts its intervention into this realm of the family to
cases of abuse and neglect or disputes of child custody. When it comes
to the care of children before they enter kindergarten, families are left to
struggle with minimal guidance or assistance. Ross Thompson, an expert
on early development, argues, "Society's commitment to ensuring the
healthy development of every child requires far more than standing on the
sidelines and wishing parents the best in their efforts to benefit their off-
spring."[2] Until greater social commitment is a reality, parents experience
this period as a vacuum, devoid of services and support when they need it
most. However, once children reach their fifth birthday, the responsibility
for providing formal care and education for them during the school day
is shifted to the government. Almost every child in our country is thrust
into an education system that encompasses 15,000 school districts with

nearly 100,000 schools and more than 2 million teachers.[3] This apparent contradiction begs the question: Why is our system of public education children's only entitlement while our lack of a child care system is our nation's greatest tragedy for its children?

This question can be answered by considering the strong values attached to perceptions of the role government should play in the lives of children and families. The family has long been seen as responsible for child rearing and is the major determinant of a child's development. Far-reaching changes in the social and economic climate during the twentieth century, however, have led to the new reality that 65 percent of mothers with a child under age five are in the workforce, fueling the need for child care outside the home.[4] Good-quality care, sensitive to children's needs, can improve and strengthen families and, research shows, allows parents to work with less guilt and stress. To understand why child care has been seen as a private problem we must explore basic American values and how they find their way into policy.

Many people see the purpose of child care, especially for children under age three, as enabling mothers to work. Despite widespread support for the early education of our nation's preschoolers—75 percent of voters support making preschool available to all three- and four-year-olds—a mother's decision to work is considered a private one, and thus it is generally assumed that child care is also a private responsibility.[5]

In 1970, the White House Conference on Children identified affordable, reliable, comprehensive child care programs of good quality as the most pressing need of American families and children. At the time, advocates pointed to the labor force participation of women with children under age six, which grew from 11.9 percent in 1950 to 30.3 percent in 1970. (One can only imagine their reaction if they were told that in 2004 the figure would reach 64.1 percent.[6]) The Comprehensive Child Development Act (CCDA), passed by Congress in 1971 but later vetoed by President Nixon, answered this call with legislation that would have created a voluntary, universally available system of child care in the United States. Tragically, the nation came tantalizingly close to a solution but fell short at the last moment. Instead, thirty years later we have a dizzying array of federal and state funding streams and a hodgepodge of programs, constituting a nonsystem.[7] It is impossible to calculate the damage our failure to systematically address this problem has exacted on the lives of American children and families.

MAKING CHILD CARE POLICY

Experts typically agree on three necessary circumstances for changing or creating policy: (1) a pervasive sense that a real problem exists; (2) an effective lobby that advocates for action to address the problem; and (3) receptive individuals in the legislative and executive branches to enact policy change. Leading political scientists studying child care conclude that for "value-ridden issues such as child care," rational analyses fall short because they cannot adequately determine what the problem is and what solutions might follow. Instead, "questions of what values, and whose values, ultimately are to count, inherently must be answered through political process, not rational analysis alone."[8] Gilbert Steiner, a senior fellow at the Brookings Institution, reaches similar conclusions in his book *The Futility of Family Policy*. Steiner argues that for "intractable problems" like child care, the conflicting values and goals make it impossible to create one neat package with universal appeal.[9]

The deeply held values regarding the relationship of the family to the state perpetuate child care's status as a private problem to be resolved within the family. President Carter, who in 1976 first developed the notion of "pro-family policy," stated that "government steps in by necessity when families have failed."[10] This viewpoint reflects an American ethos of personal responsibility and sanctity of the family that dates back to the colonial era. In the 1830s the French observer Alexis de Tocqueville, with great acumen, identified individualism as a hallmark of American society in his classic study *Democracy in America*. These values of sanctity of the family and rugged individualism lead to policies that are limited to children whose families cannot afford care or children whose families place them at risk of harm.[11] The vast majority of parents are left struggling with little assistance to balance work and care for their children.

Mona Harrington, in *Care and Equality*, contends that liberals and conservatives alike tend to perceive care as an issue of private morality. Indeed, research supports her hypothesis that individual responsibility is rooted in American family ideologies.[12] In a comparison of American and European policy, child care scholar Sheila Kamerman notes that "this country has chosen individualism as a central value. It has sustained its complex multicultural and multireligious diversity, and avoided value confrontations by separating church from state and keeping national government out of the family, unless it can define a particular family as dangerous or endangered."[13]

Research finds that parents strongly endorse the notion that they alone bear responsibility for the care of their children.[14] This belief appears to have been internalized even by low-income working mothers, who in focus groups coordinated by the National Organization for Women's Legal Defense and Education Fund frequently invoked the phrase, "Nobody asked us to have these kids." This line of thought reflects the societal expectation that the responsibility for care of children rests squarely on the back of parents.[15] Furthermore, public opinion data collected by Public Agenda, a nonpartisan research organization, identifies child care as "an area that parents expect to struggle with and resolve for themselves"—60 percent of parents with children under age five say it is a family responsibility to ensure they have child care when they need it.[16]

Parents of young children strongly endorse a variety of measures to improve child care policies when they are specifically asked about them. A 1969 Gallup poll found that 68 percent of women and 59 percent of men favored "having the Federal Government provide funds to set up these [day care] centers in most communities." Today, by margins "of 80 percent or more the public supports programs that are affordable, accessible, and of high quality."[17] Despite this support, there is little call for action by the public for government assistance. How do we explain this ambivalence? Harrington contends that "basic confidence in the private institutions—market and family—sets up the assumption that trouble anywhere in these systems is not caused by uncontrollable events but wrongdoing."[18] It is no surprise that parents claim full responsibility for child care, since admitting anything less in a system where "government steps in by necessity when families have failed" would be tantamount to conceding an inability to care for one's own children.

The Policy Agenda
Policy is changed or created in reaction to a pervasive sense that a real problem exists. At any given time, the problems that legislators, advocates, members of the media, and other people inside and outside government are paying serious attention to are termed the policy agenda. This agenda represents the issues for which policy can be made or changed.[19] For any interest group or coalition working to push an agenda for child care, "gain-

ing attention alone" is not the issue: "The real battle is over whose interpretation, whose framing of reality, gets the floor."[20] In reviewing child care
policy in the late 1960s and early 1970s, Kimberly Morgan, noted child care
historian, writes, "Activists on both sides of these [child care] issues were
polarizing into two hostile camps, one that pushed on the ideals of the Great
Society, the other clinging to an older version of American society, that of
the traditional family, traditional gender roles, and segregated schools."[21]

Right-Wing Conservatives

In the late 1960s and early 1970s the radical New Right movement of
American conservatism was defining itself with a platform of sexual,
reproductive, and family issues.[22] Adherents saw themselves as "defend-
ers of morality," upholding family values and individual responsibility.
Child care policy dredged up the moral and social questions surrounding
families and children that appealed to many who felt disaffected by the
platforms of the Republican and Democratic parties.[23] The New Right de-
monized nonparental caregiving as perverse and dangerous for children,
opposed the Equal Rights Amendment, clung to traditional gender roles,
and harbored disdain for middle-class women who left the home for the
workforce.[24] The New Right was deeply opposed to publicly funded child
care because it enabled middle-class women to work. In the late 1970s,
the Reverend Jerry Falwell founded the Moral Majority as a conservative
Christian advocacy group and championed a similar stance on many of
the same issues. Along with groups like the John Birch Society and Eagle
Forum, these organizations represent a loose confederacy now considered
the voice of the far right spectrum of the Republican Party.[25]

George Lakoff, professor of cognitive linguistics at the University of
California, Berkeley, and consultant to liberal candidates and politicians,
argues that "because conservatives understand the moral dimensions of
our politics better than liberals do, they have been able not only to gain
political victories but to use politics in the service of a much larger moral
and cultural agenda for America."[26] James Pierson, then director of the
John M. Olin Foundation (which financed leading think tanks on the far
right), concurred in a *New York Times* article: "The ideas have to be tended
to—only after that can you tend to the policies."[27]

Effective Lobby

The second precondition for policy change is a lobby that advocates for a solution to a problem and shapes public will. There never has been an effective lobby for child care. A great irony in this story is that the right wing abhorred the child care legislation for its association with women's employment, when in fact the women's movement never materialized into a powerful player in the final child care debates. Despite moments of strength, the women's movement provided an insufficient counter to a right wing that was deeply opposed to federal involvement in the lives of middle-class Americans.

Consider, in contrast, the strong public and political will behind the issue of prescription drug coverage for the elderly. According to estimates from the Tax Policy Center, if the Medicare changes and tax cuts enacted between 2001 and 2004 were made permanent, the estimated present value of reduced federal revenues and increased expenditures is greater than $34 trillion, or more than three years' worth of our gross domestic product.[28] One study found federal spending for the elderly at three times the level of spending for children. Further, despite an increase in real per capita income and a drop in the poverty rate for both the overall and elderly populations, the same proportion of children, one in six, were in poverty in 1967 and 2002. These Medicare policies have economists scrambling to make sense of how to balance the budget and avoid national bankruptcy. Why did this happen? Lobbyists, including AARP, helped propel prescription drug coverage for the elderly as the issue of the moment, and this became an issue about which "Congress had to do *something*."[29]

Ad Hoc Coalition for Child Development

So, if children don't have AARP on their side, what do they have? Since 1971, there has been a loose coalition of labor leaders, liberal think tanks, organizations such as the National Association for the Education of Young Children and the Children's Defense Fund, and academics working for child and family programs. For the 1971 bill, though, the Ad Hoc Coalition for Child Development was the primary advocacy group. This group was composed of twenty-one labor, education, welfare, women's, civil rights, and children's advocates headed by Marian Wright Edelman.

Edelman was a child advocate who embodied the spirit of the civil rights movement and was the most powerful voice in the Ad Hoc Coalition for Child Development. As a child growing up in South Carolina, she had been the target of racial discrimination but believed deeply that redress of these social ills was possible through education, community, family, and faith. She began her career as a civil rights lawyer in Mississippi. In 1965, when the governor of Mississippi threatened to refuse federal Head Start funds because the law required integrated classrooms, Edelman led a group of private, public, and religious organizations called the Child Development Group of Mississippi to win a $1.5 million federal grant to create Head Start centers sponsored by local universities, which were exempt from the governor's review.[30] A highly effective and able leader, Edelman went on to create the Children's Defense Fund (CDF), the premier advocacy organization for disadvantaged children, particularly children from minority groups.

In the late 1960s Edelman saw the child care legislation being debated in Congress as an opportunity to protect Head Start, noting, "There was a separate section near the end of the bill that protected Head Start, which was my primary agenda."[31] Harboring distrust of state governments because of the southern states' reluctance to implement civil rights reforms, she passionately argued for localities to play a primary role in implementing and administering child care. Some who were close to the debates attribute the bill's demise to Edelman's unwillingness to compromise on the issue of local control. Indeed, in 1971 her reliance on the community organization techniques that were successful in the War on Poverty contributed to an unwieldy piece of legislation and branded her a radical in the eyes of an increasingly powerful conservative movement.[32]

Inconsistent Involvement of Women's Groups
The feminists of the early 1970s, as today, were not of one opinion when it came to child care. Radical feminists envisioned child care as a great equalizer of wealth between the sexes, challenging the traditional division of labor between female caregiver and male breadwinner and freeing women from dependency on men. To achieve these ends, "radical feminists had to engage in party politics, belying the view that these women stood determinedly outside the political mainstream." Other liberal feminists, committed to a strict, sex-blind conception of equality, refused to respond to women's need for child care because doing so would signal an acceptance that biological differences and societal responsibilities necessitated

more or different social services for women than for men.[33] This division plagued the 1970s movement and is still alive—discussions today of the Family and Medical Leave Act include concerns that women would be seen as costlier and riskier employees and thus the target of employment discrimination.

In the 1970s, organizations including the National Organization for Women (NOW), the National Council of Negro Women, and National Council of Jewish Women were proponents of federal child care bills. NOW even went as far as to change its 1966 Statement of Purpose to call for "a nationwide network of child-care centers."[34] These groups were aligned with civil rights activists who saw child care as a way to socialize children into a culture of tolerance and unite the social classes. NOW representatives expressed the need for making child care centers "economically and racially integrated" and argued for child care as a "right for all children." Representative Bella Abzug (D-NY) and other feminists in the early 1970s believed that "by creating high-quality institutions that would serve all children" society could achieve the goals of both the civil rights and women's movements.[35] The underground feminist journal *Old Mole* stated at the time that "as women try to understand their own oppression, they keep coming up against one central thing: our society says a woman's first job is to take care of her children—alone, in her own house. All the time . . . that is why she is taught to be passive and self-sacrificing, . . . paid less, educated less, torn by guilt, isolated, and harassed."[36] Betty Friedan, the godmother of the women's movement and author of *The Feminine Mystique,* organized the Women's Strike for Equality on August 26, 1970, whose demands included "free, twenty-four-hour universal child care." Men and women in nearly fifty cities participated, with estimates of almost fifty thousand striking in New York City alone.

Despite the success of Friedan's strike and early rhetoric from women's groups, most reviews of the women's movement in the 1960s and 1970s allow only a few pages to feminists' role in creating publicly available child care arrangements.[37] In some respects, feminists' silence and divisiveness on the issue made a more powerful statement than any advocacy they undertook.

So, if child care is often considered a women's issue, why were the women silent during the rapid social changes of the 1960s? Simply put, the women's movement had problems of its own, and child care "brought together some of the most difficult questions for feminists: the role of the state; significance of motherhood; differences between women, especially class differences; and how all these relate to strategies for short or long term change."[38] For many feminists the "family was seen as an overwhelming oppressive institution and in so far as motherhood was the means through which women were subordinated within the family, it too was rejected." Internal policing led NOW and other women's organizations to soften their demand for universal care, as they found it necessary to avoid this lightning rod in order to appeal to a wide constituency of women.[39]

Feminists were also battling rising right-wing conservatives determined to impose a family structure epitomized by the 1950s television sitcoms. In this fantasy, the father starred as provider and CEO of the family, and mom costarred as a full-time at-home caregiver. After all, Title VII of the 1964 Civil Rights Act, which provides the only federal protection from discrimination at work, was the unexpected outcome of a larger effort to sabotage civil rights legislation. Sex was absent from the original bill, which forbade workplace discrimination on the basis of race, color, religion, and national origin. At the last minute, sex was inserted by southern House members opposed to civil rights. They reasoned that inclusion of sex would be so controversial as to generate enough opposition to destroy the act. Fortunately, they were wrong, and the bill narrowly passed the House of Representatives. It was so close to the end of debates, though, that "sex" wasn't even defined in the final language of the bill. Clearly, exerting a right for women to work outside the home, free of discrimination, was task enough for many women's groups.

Misplaced Efforts

Perhaps more disappointing than women's groups' overall silence on child care were instances in which they did exert their force but misplaced their efforts. When I was revising the Federal Interagency Day Care Requirements (FIDCRs), which would later become the backbone of the proposed national child care system, several feminists requested a debate. Their concern was that I failed to include regulations requiring centers to use only sex-neutral dolls. They had missed the point. By myopically focusing on symbolic issues of gender-neutral dolls they lost sight of the important issue, the quality of care available to millions of mothers and children.

Regulations are about staffing ratios and teacher education—not the type of doll with which a child can play. This instance of divisiveness was not the only time that part of the group was caught in issues of symbolism over substance. At a famous Houston conference, one faction took up a symbolic debate over the civil rights of lesbians rather than the "bread and butter" problems like the child care problem facing the majority of American women.

The feminist movement never materialized into a powerful player in child care, and to this day, unlike farmers experiencing a drought or the elderly facing high prescription drug costs, those in need of child care have no lobby to effectively and consistently advocate for a realistic solution to their problem.

A NATION'S ATTEMPT AT CHILD CARE

A Receptive President and Congress
The third necessary circumstance for policy creation or change is a receptive legislature. We could tell a story of voting records, congressional bills, opinion polls, and vetoes to explain America's closest attempt at creating a child care system. But watching policy being made is like watching sausage being made insofar as watching the process is sure to spoil your appetite. Since the child care issue stems from values, its history is the story of individuals: their personalities, relationships, conspiracies, and principles. There are two parallel stories about receptive audiences for child care policy: one about Congress working on the CCDA to provide a voluntary, universal system of child care; the other about President Richard Nixon, who needed a child care delivery system to make his welfare reform plan (the Family Assistance Plan) a reality. The stories are told as I lived them from my post as director of the Office of Child Development, which became the nexus of these two efforts. Within the Nixon administration I was the point person on all children's issues.

Leading Up to the 1971 Child Development Act
Child care was thrust onto the national agenda by the 1960 National Conference on the Day Care of Children, cosponsored by the Women's Bureau and the Children's Bureau. The conference sought to rally public opinion around "what a tremendous force for national well-being a full

program of day-care services for children could be." Conference speakers argued that an increased number of mothers had entered the workforce, demanded an end to the stigmatization of working mothers, and expressed the sentiment that working mothers could actually be better mothers than those who stayed home and were restricted by their role as "nothing more exciting than a housewife." Child care historian Elizabeth Rose notes that conference participants "were fighting an uphill battle, for they had to contend with the mixed legacy [of ideas] . . . that day care is bad for children and . . . that educationally oriented care can be beneficial for children; that children always need their mothers and that children need to gain independence . . . that mothers should devote themselves to caring for children and that mothers should work to support their children."[40]

The 1960s can be characterized as a period of gradually growing acceptance of mothers' employment and expanding interest in early childhood education, and in that decade there was a drive to reduce the welfare rolls. Thus, in the absence of a universal program, child care continued to be bundled with welfare reform.

In 1965, President Johnson launched the War on Poverty with unbridled optimism and created the Office of Economic Opportunity (OEO) to oversee these programs. This action embodied the hope that American poverty could once and for all be eliminated by empowering the poor to take control of their lives and communities. Sargent Shriver, the director of the OEO, called for the development of a preschool intervention program.

Shriver's program would be a revolutionary two-generation approach to eliminating poverty and remedying the educational inequalities borne by impoverished children.[41] A planning committee of fourteen experts, including me, was convened. This group recommended the development of a pilot program with the following goals: improving physical health; fostering social, emotional, and cognitive development; engendering social responsibility; building self-confidence; supporting relationships with family and others; and creating a sense of dignity and self-worth for both child and family. In February 1965, Shriver selected Dr. Julius Richmond, a pediatrician and one of the few people in the country with experience operating a program for disadvantaged children, as director.[42] The Johnson administration was eager to start, and Congress was willing to increase the budget, so Head Start was launched not as a pilot program but with a collection of six- to eight-week summer sessions that served over 500,000 children in the summer of 1965. The speed with which this huge program was mounted earned Head Start the nickname Project Rush Rush in Washington.

As Head Start was getting off the ground, Congress was confronted with the unexpected expansion of the country's welfare rolls by 214 percent between 1960 and 1968.[43] In response, Congress enacted the Work Incentives Program (WIN) in 1967 and, for the first time, imposed a dictum—get a job or lose all benefits—on women with young children receiving aid under the Aid to Families with Dependent Children (AFDC) program. Child care was a necessary component of the program, and under WIN the federal government paid 75 percent of child care costs for welfare mothers. Joseph Reed, executive director of the Child Welfare League of America (CWLA), argued that in the absence of universally available care, the quality of care provided to welfare mothers was custodial at best and amounted to the "ghettoiz[ing] of day care centers for children from welfare families."[44] In the late 1960s, a wave of optimism rose from the early indications of success and popularity of Head Start, motivating legislators and the public to articulate that all children could benefit from enriched early development environments. Thus began a groundswell of support to make these services available to middle-class families.

Walter Mondale, a Democrat from Minnesota and chair of the Subcommittee on Children and Youth of the Senate Committee on Labor and Public Welfare, introduced the Head Start Child Development Act in May 1969. This bill proposed a massive expansion of the Head Start budget from $325 million to $5 billion over a five-year period. The act would have expanded eligibility and improved quality, but its primary objective was to ensure a role for OEO's Community Action Programs in administering Head Start. In August of the same year, John Brademas of Indiana, chair of the Select Subcommittee on Education of the House Committee on Education and Labor, introduced the Comprehensive Preschool Education and Child Day Care Act, which would have coordinated child care, Head Start, and preschool programs at the federal level. Neither bill made it out of committee, but they laid the groundwork for debates to come.

THE NIXON WHITE HOUSE: CHILD CARE AS A TOOL FOR THE FAMILY ASSISTANCE PLAN

Richard Nixon's narrow win in the 1968 presidential election brought Republicans to the Oval Office for the first time in eight years. Nixon wanted approval of the Republican Party's major constituencies, including its growing conservative arm, but at the same time needed to work with the Democrats who controlled Congress.[45] When Nixon took office he buoyed everyone's spirits with proclamations of bipartisan support for children's issues, especially those affecting children under age five. While he appeased conservatives by vowing to respect the "sacred right of parents to rear their children according to their own values and understanding," he declared in a February 1969 message to Congress, "So crucial is the matter of early growth that we must make a national commitment to providing all American children an opportunity for healthful and stimulating development during the first five years."[46] Like many Americans, I was encouraged by this statement, and it was a critical factor in my decision to join the Nixon administration as a presidential appointee.

At the top of Nixon's agenda was a sweeping and enlightened proposal for welfare reform, the Family Assistance Plan (FAP), devised by Daniel Patrick Moynihan. (Moynihan went on to become a well-known Democratic senator who wrote the Family Support Act of 1988.) FAP, a testament to Moynihan's prescient thinking, would be a two-generation approach to breaking the cycle of welfare dependency—mothers would work for a guaranteed minimum wage, and children would get a start in life that set them on a course to self-sufficiency. This necessitated a vastly expanded role for the federal government in child care.

The Office of Child Development and FAP

In April 1969, Nixon announced the creation of the Office of Child Development (OCD; now the Administration on Children, Youth, and Families) in the Department of Health, Education, and Welfare (HEW). Nixon's HEW secretary, Robert Finch, announced that OCD would provide a "single focal point within HEW for child care and preschool programs."[47] In 1968, programs for children were being administered by multiple agencies, and the secretary sought interagency coordination. Jule Sugarman, a brilliant liberal out of OEO with a background as a civil servant in the U.S. Post Office, was charged with writing the regulations that would govern federal day care programs. He produced the 1968 FIDCRs—a set of ambitious standards popular with advocates because they championed comprehensive services similar to Head Start. These standards were so unrealistic and unenforceable, however, that Sugarman had already cut a deal with relevant agencies decreeing that they would never be enforced. Sugarman also arranged the transfer of Head Start into OCD from OEO. Nixon wanted to dismantle OEO and eliminate many of its War on Poverty social action programs, and he put Donald Rumsfeld and his newly hired assistant Dick Cheney in charge of OEO. The political and public popularity of Head Start necessitated its transfer to another federal agency.[48]

In August 1969 a director had yet to be named for the OCD, and a Nixon assistant reminded Moynihan that "OCD needs to get moving . . . Nixon promised day care for 450,000 more children as part of FAP, but . . . no one was thinking about how to deliver it."[49] Reflective of this void, the first version of the FAP paid little attention to child care—in the hundred-page bill that passed the House in April 1970 only three pages focused on child care. The bill stipulated that HEW was to receive "such sums as may be necessary" to arrange for "various types of child care needed in light of the different circumstances and needs of children involved."[50] This vacuous language outlined only the shell of a child care program.

In April 1970, I was appointed chief of the Children's Bureau and first director of OCD. My initial responsibilities included administering Head Start, revising the unworkable 1968 FIDCRs, acting as the president's point person on child care before Congress, and designing a system of child care for the FAP welfare reforms. As chief of the Children's Bureau, I was to keep abreast of all issues related to children.

I quickly took up the issue of child care. The demographics indicated that an increasing proportion of women were employed outside the home and would need child care services. Further, FAP clearly needed a child care delivery system: for welfare reform to work, at least 450,000 children would need care. Nixon said of child care within FAP, "The day care that would be part of this plan would be [of] a quality that will help in the development of the child and provide for its health and safety, and would break the poverty cycle for the new generation."[51] These statements reflected Moynihan's conviction, formed out of the arguments put forth by Secretary of HEW Elliot Richardson and me, that any successful welfare reform effort absolutely necessitated a two-generation program. Such an approach would both move mothers off the welfare rolls and keep their children off the rolls in the future by providing development-enhancing child care. Further evidence of the power of Moynihan's arguments for a two-generation FAP came one afternoon in the Oval Office. I was standing in the Oval Office when I complimented Nixon on his speech about the first five years of life, highlighting the congruency of it with my own views on child development. Nixon's response to me was, "You should tell that to Pat Moynihan—he wrote it."

I was an academic at heart and continued to pay close attention to relevant child care scholarship. Mary Keyserling of the National Council of Jewish Women (NCJW) had just completed the first national study of child care in America, entitled *Windows on Day Care*. Keyserling found that "growth in services available has failed to keep pace with rapidly rising need. Large numbers of children are neglected; still larger numbers now receive care which at best, can be called only custodial and at worst, is deplorable. Only a relatively small proportion are benefiting from truly developmental quality care."[52] Through the Children's Bureau, I sponsored the publication of the study and took up the issue of getting the nation ready for child care with a clear emphasis on development. I started the Child Care Office within OCD and named Sam Granato as its head. This office later evolved into the Child Care Bureau under President Clinton and was headed by Joan Lombardi.

With the support of HEW Secretary Richardson, I set out to create a set of child care requirements that would provide a "developmental" level of care necessary to protect a child's healthy development and that could be enforced, ensuring a threshold level of quality for any services bought with federal funds. Achieving this goal would require a revision of the unworkable 1968 FIDCRs, a project that was rolled into parallel efforts within Congress, later producing what was to become the NAEYC standards.

The 1970 White House Conference
I chaired a three-day conference, which convened approximately one thousand experts to discuss child care issues. The goal of the conference was to produce manuals—"cookbooks" on the principles of quality care that would outline key components of infant, preschool, and school-age care and serve as a guide for family child care providers.

Windows on Day Care had revealed that "in the nation as a whole, as many as 2 million children may be receiving care in homes other than their own while their mothers are at work. Fewer than 5 percent of these homes, it is estimated, are licensed or supervised . . . 11 percent were regarded as 'poor' or 'very poor.' Some of the latter provided the worst horror stories encountered."[53] Each year without action meant another quarter of a million children could be reliving these horror stories. This report didn't even consider the quality of more commonly used centers.

The White House Conference on Children, gathered once a decade, was an opportunity for experts and representatives from all states to put the issues facing America's children in the public eye. In 1970, unlike at previous conferences that had generated a laundry list of problems, the more than four thousand attendees were forced to vote on their priorities. The need for child care was identified as the number one problem facing the American family.[54] *Newsweek* reported in 1971 that there existed only 640,000 licensed day care slots for the 4.6 million working mothers of children under age six.

FAP and Child Care

Nixon's FAP plan set aside $750 million in its first year for child care services. A logistical problem was how to spend this money—should the government build its own facilities, subsidize existing ones, or directly pay providers of care? In addition, there was a debate within the White House on who would run child care under FAP—the Department of Labor or OCD within HEW.

I took a novel approach to winning child care for OCD and HEW. I defined a continuum of care and positioned the HEW proposal in the middle, such that it was likely to be taken as the most attractive option. At one end, "custodial care" was the type of care proposed by the Department of Labor—in essence providing a container to keep a child safe while a parent worked. This approach was favored by the Department of Labor because of its low cost. At the other end, "comprehensive care" was based on the Head Start model and provided a range of services for the child's physical, social, emotional, and mental health. Comprehensive care was favored by child care advocates. In the middle I positioned "developmental care," which is age-appropriate care delivered by a sufficient number of trained staff. Developmental care, including early education but not social services, would provide the best care for the most children with the fewest dollars.[55] Further, different standards were introduced for infants and toddlers, preschoolers, and school-age children. Because infants need much lower child-to-staff ratios, their care is significantly more expensive than care for older children.

Evidence of controversy quickly surfaced. In 1971 Harold Stevenson was president of the Society for Research in Child Development and decided to do something completely unprecedented at the biennial meeting in Minneapolis. When a president of SRCD finishes his term, he delivers a presidential address. Stevenson decided instead to have a symposium featuring three prominent child developmentalists from Washington—Senator Mondale, Representative Orval Hansen (R-ID), and me—to start a conversation about child development and social policy. Religious right-wing agitators showed up at the conference and picketed the bill and its supporters including Mondale and me.

At the SRCD business meeting that year, Urie Bronfenbrenner took the lead in recommending that SRCD go on record endorsing the passage of the CCDA. So, with the chants of right wingers lingering in the background, they voted. This action was very unusual for SRCD, which at that time was extremely reluctant to take any position on public policy issues. Their positive vote put the imprimatur of the leading child research organization on the bill that Mondale and I were trying to make law. SRCD represented one of the few countervailing forces against the right wing.

At that same time, the Office of Management and Budget argued that developmental care was too costly and was unnecessary for moving mothers off the welfare rolls, preferring the Department of Labor's cheaper custodial model. I calculated the cost of custodial and developmental levels of care based on the revised FIDCRs. OCD staff broke down the costs of staffing, transportation, equipment, and other expenditures necessary for developmental care. They estimated that two thirds of the children would be of school age and in need of only part-day care, which would be significantly less expensive. Using these projections, I was able to demonstrate that good-quality developmental care for nearly one million children was within the administration's $750 million budget.

Richardson, a real hero for America's children, took this figure to the White House and won child care for OCD. This decision had clear implications for the quality of care to be delivered. Richardson was one of the few Nixon officials who saw the need for high-quality, universal child care. He would later act as a broker between Congress and White House staff, going to great lengths to salvage a system of child care.

THE COMPREHENSIVE CHILD DEVELOPMENT ACT

Brademas and Mondale had turned insight from the White House Conference on Children into foresight and introduced the CCDA to the House and Senate, respectively. Brademas, with characteristic prescience, saw FAP as an opportunity to gain Nixon's support for his child care bill and had already initiated discussions with Richardson and me. The Nixon administration generally endorsed the CCDA. The bill, at least in its early form, appeared to be a ready-made solution for the child care problem under FAP. Both this bill and the companion Senate bill introduced by Mondale initially enjoyed broad bipartisan support. In the House, the bill was cosponsored by 120 members, one third of whom were Republicans.

The CCDA included $700 million for federal funding of high-quality child care for welfare recipients and $50 million for purchasing new child care centers. Fees for child care services were to be based on a sliding scale, with poor families covered for free. The bill applied the FIDCR standards I wrote, provided funds for the professionalization of the child care workforce, and placed this child care system within OCD. The model was based on the best thinking at the time concerning the nature of the child care environment that was conducive to fulfilling children's developmental needs. The plan included incorporating Head Start centers into the network and mandating the Head Start model for at-risk children. Most revolutionary, the bill declared in its preamble a goal "to establish the legislative framework for the future expansion of such programs to provide universally available child development services."

Once debate began in Congress two major challenges arose: establishing the ceiling for income eligibility and determining the level of government responsible for implementing and delivering the program.

Universality

Most legislators in both houses agreed that there needed to be socioeconomic diversity in the programs but disagreed about the minimum income at which families should pay for child care services. The universality of the program was a strategic decision because successful legislation needs a strong constituency, which the poor are not. A *New York Times* editorial on July 18, 1971, cited improved quality of care as another benefit: "Giving all mothers, including those with educational sophistication and political influence, a stake in truly imaginative child development centers is a way of creating an instant support force to fight for high quality and expert staffing."

The final House bill provided free care to families earning less than a specified yearly income (for a family of four, $4,320). This income level was also the cutoff for FAP assistance. The Senate bill provided free care to families of four with an income of up to $6,960. The White House was willing to consider some assistance for families just above the House eligibility cutoff for welfare. The budget office was concerned with the $13 billion four-year price tag on the bill and wanted to restrict funds to families eligible for welfare.[56]

While policy makers saw efforts to reach the middle class as necessary to maintain the political viability of this massive investment, there were murmurs of opposition and equivocation rising from various groups on both sides of the aisle. Universal services touched a nerve with right-wing groups, including the John Birch Society, fundamentalist church groups, and other coalitions that sent thousands of letters claiming that CCDA represented an invasion of the family by the federal government. In the House, Chairman of the American Conservative Union John Ashbrook (R-OH) warned that the worst element of this legislation was that the "socioeconomic and race mix of students would reach its greatest potential" and referred to it as the "child control act" and "parental replacement act."[57] On the other side, Edelman was concerned primarily with poor children and less interested in obtaining a socioeconomic mix. Beyond the ideological differences, other conservatives were concerned with the cost.[58]

Prime Sponsorship Was the Linchpin

Prime sponsorship refers to the level of government, or size of the entity, that would be responsible for implementing, monitoring, and administering the child care programs under CCDA. The Nixon administration originally proposed to have fifty prime sponsors—the fifty states. This method is how large-scale programs are conventionally administered.

As the person who would ultimately be responsible for administering the program through OCD, I saw small prime sponsorship (high local control) as a logistical nightmare. Brademas, a Rhodes Scholar with a doctorate in political science who went on to become president of New York University, shared my worry that a federal program directly involved with thousands of community organizations would be intractable and inefficient. Brademas was a political realist and perceived that the Republican support, necessary for passage of the bill, was in part dependent on devolving some of the federal government's role to the states. Above all, Brademas was a pragmatist committed to maintaining a large bipartisan coalition in the House, and he was willing to compromise. Brademas's original 1971 bill limited prime sponsorship of a child development program to cities and states with populations of more than half a million people. Smaller communities would submit applications through a local council to the prime sponsor, who would then submit an application to the federal government. Gradually, through subcommittee debates, the population requirement was whittled down to 100,000, a number that the Nixon administration could live with.

In the Senate, there was no minimum population required of a community to submit an application for federal funding. Mondale argued, "It is terribly important that we make money available directly to community groups and local government," and he made no restriction on the number of sponsors.[59] Edelman's politics mixed well with Mondale's. She had Mondale's ear and held a deep belief that state governments could not be trusted with these funds. Drawing on her experiences with Head Start in Mississippi, she demanded that any unit of local government or nonprofit agency be eligible to be a prime sponsor. Edelman worked so closely with Mondale that an aide to Senator Jacob Javits, a liberal Republican who initially supported the bill, quipped to me, "Do you think Sid Johnson [Mondale's chief aide on this legislation] can go to the john without Marian's okay?"

FAP and the Administration's Support for CCDA

The differences between the House and Senate approaches to program sponsorship were also evidenced in debates about Nixon's welfare reform plan. The House had passed FAP, and Brademas saw FAP as a chance to win Nixon's support for his child care bill. I had worked closely with Brademas to help develop a pragmatic approach to CCDA that would satisfy the administration. I kept Richardson informed through frequent briefings, as Richardson was my immediate supervisor and it was important that he and Brademas advanced the same position. Richardson and I shared a similar vision, and Brademas was accommodating to the administration's requests and strived to create a bill that wouldn't be vetoed. The Senate, on the other hand, was divided about FAP. Mondale, in particular, was less committed to the FAP plan, as it would force mothers to put their children in full-day child care while they worked, and he worried the administration would not provide sufficient funds to ensure high-quality care for these vulnerable children.[60]

As debates in Congress continued, Stephen Kurzman, assistant secretary for legislation, and I were sent to Capitol Hill to deliver testimony confirming the administration's support of CCDA pending modifications in the area of cost, prime sponsorship, and income eligibility. The White House proposal set a minimum population for prime sponsors at 500,000, provided free care to families of four with incomes up to $4,320 (the same figure as the House bill), and authorized the bill at $1.2 billion, approximately half of the Mondale-Brademas bill authorization of $2.5 billion. Based on experiences administering Head Start to over 1,000 grantees, the administration reasoned it was safest to deal with fewer than 100 prime sponsors, thus arriving at a population requirement of 500,000 persons. This was a compromise from the White House's original position of fifty state-level prime sponsors.

Time Was Running Out
The child care advocates, especially Edelman, were not willing to compromise on the size of prime sponsors. During the fall of 1971, I heard rumblings from the White House that if prime sponsorship wasn't brought in line with Nixon's parameters the bill would be vetoed. I attended a secret gathering of advocates assembled in the home of Terry Lansburgh, Baltimore socialite and President of the Day Care and Child Development Council of America. My goal was to convince the advocates to compromise on prime sponsorship, but I was immediately dismissed. Edelman was the strong holdout, adamant that Nixon would never issue a veto in an election year and determined to hold out for small areas of prime sponsorship. Fearing that the bill might be destroyed in a veto, I took Edelman aside and pleaded with her to support the administration's proposal of prime

sponsorship at 500,000 inhabitants. After all, if it was unfair to smaller groups it could always be amended the next year by Congress. I will never forget Edelman's words: "Ed, you don't understand politics—Nixon will never veto this bill in an election year." I responded, "Marian, you know a lot more about politics and what's possible and what isn't, but there is nothing wrong with my hearing, and what I'm hearing out of the White House is veto."

The Right Flexes Its Muscle

While the act was being debated on the congressional floor between September and November, right-wing activists from the John Birch Society and fundamentalist Christian organizations formed a coalition and were working hard behind the scenes. Within the White House, Patrick Buchanan, who controlled the news summary presented to Nixon each day, leveraged his relationship with the conservative newspaper *Human Events* and columnist James Kilpatrick to shape Nixon's opinion. Buchanan would arrange to have someone write a conservative column on the CCDA, and then he would slip it into the daily news summary shared with Nixon.[61] Kilpatrick, ever the willing conspirator, obliged and wrote a 1971 editorial titled "Child Development Act—to Sovietize Our Youth." A 1971 front-page article demanding a veto claimed, "This sounds dangerously like the kind of eugenics and thought control the civilized world learned to revile when practiced in Nazi Germany and in the Soviet Union."[62]

This engineering of Nixon's opinion had the added bonus of galvanizing right-wing conservatives. Intent on sending a clear message, they sent as many as 5,000 letters a week to the White House, and up to another 7,000 a day to Walter Mondale, claiming that the CCDA constituted a large-scale "invasion of the family" and must be stopped.[63] This letter writing was for all intents and purposes a smear campaign. The right arm of the Republican Party was strangling the little outstanding support for the bill. Congressional conservatives began to mobilize for a veto and circulated a "Dear Colleague" letter to make sure enough congresspeople would vote in favor of sustaining a veto. (The Senate can vote to override a presidential veto with a two-thirds vote.) They wanted a guarantee that Nixon wouldn't hesitate in issuing a veto. What was at one point an issue with wide bipartisan support had become a lightning rod for controversy.

Senator William Buckley claimed proposals for federal child care "threaten the very foundation of limited government and personal liberty."[64] In the House, John R. Rarick (D-LA) characterized the bill as "replacing U.S. parents with the Federal Government and the home with a national institution" and claimed that "this power grab over our youth is reminiscent of the Nazi youth movement; in fact, it goes far beyond Hitler's wildest dreams or the most outlandish of the Communist plans."[65] Thomas Pelly (R-WA) argued that psychologists desired "a giant laboratory to tinker with children's minds." Although most legislators, even conservatives, didn't share them, these extreme views marked a growing momentum of opposition to the bill.

As the population necessary for prime sponsorship dropped lower, more and more of the original supporters withdrew their support. At a conference committee meeting about the prime sponsorship issue, Representative Al Quie (R-MN), an original cosponsor, announced that he opposed the bill because the area eligibility limits for sponsorship were so low as to make the program totally unmanageable. In an address to the House floor he stated, "I wish I could come before you and urge you to support the conference report but I cannot . . . this report is an administrative monstrosity. It is impossible for it to work out properly."[66]

Quie's opposition was a turning point. Many who worked on the bill during this time claim that Edelman's unwillingness to compromise made the bill unpalatable even to politicians who were originally among the supporters. Trouble was ahead. Brademas, with full knowledge the White House could veto, worked tirelessly to sustain the 100,000 population requirement. At one point he even publicly disagreed with Carl Perkins, a senior-ranking committee chairman from Kentucky. Perkins wanted a smaller population requirement, only 10,000, because Kentucky was largely rural and Perkins himself was from a county with a population of 60,000. His own county wouldn't have qualified as a prime sponsor under Brademas's plan. Perkins won the debate on the floor of the House and exacted tough revenge against Brademas, kicking him off the committee that would resolve outstanding issues on the bill. To add insult to injury, Perkins reduced the population figure to 5,000 and inserted the unworkable 1968 FIDCRs (rather than the set I wrote) into the final bill.

The final conference report was issued on November 29, 1971, allowing prime sponsors to be as small as 5,000. The bipartisan support for the bill had unraveled—it passed the Senate by a 63–17 vote and the House by a slim margin.

Signs of Trouble at the White House

The letters and warnings from conservatives fell on friendly ears within the White House. In October 1971, Patrick Buchanan began circulating internal memos outlining the reasons for a veto. He identified cost, involvement of the government in "massively and directly raising children," and an apparent disjunction between the bill and Nixon's FAP, which was "designed to help bring the family together." He argued that the CCDA amounted to "an incentive for the family to break apart, for each to pursue separate careers—while the State takes over the children."[67]

Simultaneously, conservative opposition to the bill launched a full assault—Jeff Bell, the Capitol Hill director of the American Conservative Union affirmed, "We wanted to drive a stake through its heart."[68] James Kilpatrick, the conservative columnist, warned that "if Rich Nixon signs [the CCDA], he will have forfeited his last frail claim on Middle America's support."[69] As much as this opposition was about child care, it was also about feminism, women's rights, and civil rights. The CCDA was antithetical to the conservative agenda of keeping private the social relations between women and minorities and the state.

Eleventh-Hour Efforts by Richardson

Richardson, hopeful he could reach a compromise, tried to schedule an appointment with Nixon, finally being granted one on November 15, 1971. It was clear before that meeting that the die was cast and that Nixon planned on vetoing the bill. Richardson lobbied hard, though, and with great stalwartness opposed a veto in a memo to White House staff: "It is my belief that a Presidential veto would be a major error. The credibility of the President's commitment to the first five years of life is certainly at stake, as is the integrity of our relationship with those Members of Congress who have done so much to bring about the result [a child care system for FAP] we have repeatedly claimed we wanted." At the November meeting, Richardson briefed the president on the bill, including the "exceedingly embarrassing position" Richardson would be placed in if the bill were vetoed, having negotiated and given testimony with Nixon's apparent approval.[70] Richardson made little headway with Nixon. This is not surprising given that conservative forces had the upper hand within the White House and had been conspiring against the bill for the previous two years.

I was in San Francisco when Richardson called and told me the news. "Ed, I know how long you've been working on this and how much this bill means to you, and I wanted you to hear it from me and not on TV or in the news—the president has decided to veto the bill." I asked to write the veto, hoping to identify the problems in the current bill, make clear the great need for a system of child care, and offer assurance that when a better bill came along, the administration would consider it. Richardson said he would check with the White House and call me back. He did, and related the answer: "No, you can't write it—they said no."

Not Just Any Veto Message

Nixon tapped Patrick Buchanan to write the veto message and, according to preserved notes, told him to "put in what the right wing wants to hear."[71] Buchanan delivered and, not surprisingly, used some of the very same language Kilpatrick used when he warned that Nixon would have "forfeited his . . . claim on Middle America's support." Nixon delivered one of the most vitriolic veto messages in history, declaring: "For the Federal Government to plunge headlong financially into supporting child development would commit the vast moral authority of the National Government to the side of communal approaches to child rearing over the family-centered approach." The message included the assertion that "the Federal Government's role wherever possible should be one of assisting parents to purchase needed day care services in the private, open market, with Federal involvement in direct provision of such services kept to an absolute minimum."[72]

ANALYZING HISTORY

The Rising Power of the Right Wing

Self-defined "pro-family" groups destroyed proposals that would have extended the federal role in making child care services available to middle-class families and further enabled what they saw as perverse changes in gender roles. The bill was an attempt by Congress to address the needs of America's parents and children, reflect a growing awareness that the ecology of most children's development included nonparental care, and write into law the conviction held by policy makers that this environment should be of good quality. The New Right, using the same tactics it would employ to drive the Republican Party to the right, mobilized its constituency all the way from grassroots up to Presidential advisors to ensure that no universal child care legislation would be seriously considered at that time or the near future.[73]

President Nixon vetoed the 1971 Comprehensive Child Development Act under the pretext that it mimicked communist approaches to child rearing. Ironically, the bill would have provided services and resources to families such that they could make real choices about the care of their children. The allusions to communist child rearing are mystifying when one reads the original intent of the bill.

The right-wing attack was vehement, powerful, and indicative of the polarization of politics generated by both sides of the aisle during this period. The President's FAP was crumbling in the absence of its creator, Patrick Moynihan, who had left the White House. Since Nixon had decided to veto the bill anyway, why not frame it as a victory for the right wing that questioned his politics at that point, especially after his diplomacy in China. Others believe the veto was a means to dampen competition from potential conservative rivals in the 1972 primaries. Jack Duncan, who was staff director of Brademas's subcommittee on education, reasoned that congressional Republicans withdrew support out of frustration with "politics-as-usual" and were so angry with the unwillingness of advocates and specific members of Congress to compromise that they thought it better to wait for another chance.[74]

In the end, this stubbornness of both the left and right, combined with a lack of countervailing force to the thousands of letters coming in from right wingers, made many question whether a system of public child care was worth the effort. As is true so much of the time, for the advocates it appears the vision of the perfect became the enemy of the good. Child care historian Kimberly Morgan concludes: "In sum, the passions of both the left and the right jointly defeated an attempt to form a national, unified day-care policy."[75]

Waffling in Washington

Nixon's veto offered a stark conclusion to this chapter of federal child care policy: "Federal involvement in direct provision of such services [must be] kept to an absolute minimum." I concluded that my time in Washington might also be best kept to a minimum and planned on returning to Yale. I told Richardson of my intention to resign. Richardson said, "I wouldn't blame you if you went back to Yale and your hour-long lunches—but look, we're still going to get FAP through and you are the only person in Washington who is concerned with the quality of child care in that bill." I knew that if I left Washington, the administration of child care would certainly have gone to the Department of Labor, which would have welcomed the chance to use low-cost custodial care. Richardson implored, "Stay." I told Richardson I was in a very awkward position—there was no way I could defend Nixon's veto. Elliot asked me for some time while he went to White House to discuss this matter.

Elliot returned with a solution. He had cut a deal: I didn't have to support the veto, but couldn't attack it. How? "Waffle." This Washington term is quite simple. Talk in an obfuscating manner without clearly saying anything. I did just that during my remaining days within the Nixon administration, all the while licking the wounds of the greatest loss of my professional life. When it became clear in mid-1972 there would be no FAP and therefore no accompanying child care component, I left. Upon returning to Yale I immediately geared up to continue the battle to improve the quality of American child care. Unsurprisingly, Richardson and I remained colleagues and friends until his death. At the end of his life, Richardson and I both worked closely with a Washington organization called Fight Crime: Invest in Kids, which continues to effectively advocate for high-quality children's programs of all kinds.

CHAPTER THREE

An American Child Care Policy

THIRTY-FIVE YEARS OF FAILURE

Even if you're on the right track, you'll get run over if you just
sit there.

Will Rogers

IN THE TWO DECADES following the veto of the 1971 Comprehensive
Child Development Act, no major piece of child care legislation became
law. Finally, in 1990 the Child Care and Development Block Grant was authorized at $750 million for its first year—a relatively small sum compared
with the $2 billion authorized for the CCDA in 1971.[1] Surprisingly, the
CCDBG was signed by a Republican president amid outcry from a right
wing even more powerful than it was in 1971. This turn of events, it seems,
was yet another twist in the tangled history of American child care policy.

In this chapter, I explore the impact of a divided child care constituency and an increasingly powerful right wing, still deeply opposed to
public funding of child care, on our nation's ability to address the child
care crisis. The opposition stemmed from a basic tenet of the far right,
namely that women should not work outside the home. This chapter pre-
sents a discussion of the unfinished FIDCRs and the rising right wing,
telling the story of events as they unfolded across the intervening decades.
This approach reflects the reality that values were central in defining the
scope and content of child care debates in 1970s, are pertinent today, and
by all appearances will be so in the future.

The National Council of Jewish Women, whose initial evidence of the
deplorable conditions of child care helped usher in the national debates
and generate momentum for the 1971 bill, published a followup report

in 1999. In their 1972 landmark study, *Windows on Day Care,* the NCJW documented alarming inadequacies in the American child care delivery system, including filthy and unsafe settings with untrained staff.

Nearly three decades later, the follow-up report revealed that while a virtual social revolution had occurred as ever growing numbers of women took jobs outside the home, little had changed in child care centers, and "many of the conditions revealed in *Windows on Day Care* remain at a crisis level." This report detailed the lack of progress in the affordability, availability, and quality of child care and noted, "The only equitable feature of our child care problem today is that many children are treated with the same relative neglect." Sadly, the authors concluded, "many of the recommendations included in the original study are still relevant."[2] At the turn of the millennium, the American child care system continued to fail children, parents, and society.

NEARLY FORTY YEARS OF PITIFUL PROGRESS: A LONG LUNCH BREAK?

At the end of chapter 2, I shared the conversation in which Elliot Richardson told me I could either return to academia to enjoy hour-long lunches or stay in Washington to make child care happen under FAP. He informed me in no uncertain terms that I was the strongest voice in Washington for championing quality care over custodial care. I stayed in Washington because I was committed to the principle that we, as a nation, should not be spending federal tax dollars to buy child care below a reasonable threshold of quality. We should not be buying the neglect of children. Richardson argued that I should stay to provide a voice within the administration to protect quality child care under FAP. I turned my immediate attention to answering the pile of letters from right-wing conservatives that had accumulated as CCDA was being pushed through Congress. The veto was enough to send a clear message that right-wing conservatives were a contentious force, and the thousands of letters sent during the 1971 fight underlined that point. What wasn't immediately clear was that the power of the right was sufficient to shape child care policy making and to dictate the terms of the debate through the new millennium.

By the spring of 1972 I had finished answering the letters and completed the new day care requirements. The 1972 requirements revised the

1968 Federal Interagency Day Care Requirements to be more specific on virtually every aspect of a center's operation. The 1968 FIDCRs were ambiguous and impossible to enforce, while the 1972 FIDCRs were designed to be enforced. This revision was no easy task. The 1972 FIDCRs required the approval of Richardson, who worked closely with me in writing the final version and took a personal interest in the regulations. Richardson, like me, was opposed to overregulation and refused to include any regulation that went beyond establishing a desirable threshold of quality. Richardson and I went through draft after draft in an attempt to achieve this goal.

I was caught between Richardson and the child care experts, some of whom preferred to regulate the minutiae of child care. For example, before Richardson signed off on the FIDCRs in June 1972, he insisted that I remove a requirement that drinking fountains in child care centers be a certain number of inches from the floor. This change presented no problem to me, as I was primarily interested in regulating structural features of child care, including child-to-adult ratios and caregiver qualifications. The final regulations expanded the regulatory scope of the FIDCRs to family child care and detailed age groupings, meal requirements, provider responsibilities, minimums for staff competency levels, and a minimum wage for center employees. The requirements increased the child-to-adult ratios but specified that only caregivers, not clerical or janitorial staff, could count in the ratios. The revised ratios for children under three years old included 3:1 (0 to 18 months) and 4:1 (19 to 38 months).[3]

The 1972 FIDCRs were intended to be "realistic, enforceable child care standards."[4] As rigorous and enforceable standards these constituted a major advance over the original 1968 FIDCRs, which specified neither requirements for care of children under age three nor appropriate staffing ratios. Richardson and I believed that the revised FIDCRs would affirm the administration's commitment to providing good-quality day care to children in the wake of the CCDA veto. The revisions renewed the cost-quality battle: proponents of cost-effectiveness lamented the more stringent changes, while advocates of quality bemoaned the weakening of staff-child ratios for preschoolers.

OMB, not surprisingly, challenged the content of the standards. In a confidential white paper OMB staff assessed the HEW proposals and opposed them on the grounds that they would: (1) commit the federal government to directly define the nature of child care, (2) raise the quality of care in centers to unnecessarily high standards, (3) increase FAP's day care allocation, (4) establish a prime sponsor system similar to that proposed by Mondale and Brademas (but with fewer sponsors), and (5) make an overall policy declaration in support of developmental child care. Overall, the staff, in the characteristically understated language of OMB, decided this policy "would be undesirable."[5]

Some of the most vocal opponents to the revised FIDCRs, though, were the advocates of comprehensive child care. From the perspective of the Child Welfare League, Children's Defense Fund, and others, HEW and the administration had conspired to undermine the quality of federally funded day care by endorsing cost-effective developmental care. They believed that the FIDCR revisions, though now practical and enforceable, destroyed the idealistic standards of the 1968 FIDCRs. Indeed, loyalty to the 1968 FIDCRs became a test of one's commitment to the proper care of children. Pragmatically, the 1968 FIDCR was worthless, as it contained ephemeral, unenforceable language. (Indeed, to placate opponents within the Nixon administration, the designer of these standards had already agreed not to enforce them.) Politically, though, the advocates' withdrawal of support for the 1972 FIDCRs meant the administration had nothing to gain from endorsing the revised requirements. Perfect became the enemy of the good.

By fall 1972, it became clear that FAP was dead. And without FAP there was no child care to protect. Believing that I could do more good outside of government than in it, I returned to Yale. This was neither the end of my involvement in Washington nor the end of the FIDCRs—I will revisit both in the context of further congressional efforts to address the child care crisis.

One political consequence of the 1971 veto was that for years child care bills were something of an albatross in Washington.[6] Why? Consider what happened when Brademas and Mondale tried to introduce legislation that included only a fraction of what the 1971 bill covered.

In 1972, Brademas and Mondale introduced bills into the House and Senate, respectively, but failed to recapture the momentum generated for the 1971 bill. Members in both houses sang a refrain about the family-weakening implications of federal child care policy. Mondale responded by calling a series of hearings strategically entitled "The American Family: Trends and Pressures." His goal was to alleviate conservative concerns about undermining families so that child care legislation could be passed.

In July 1974, Mondale and Brademas introduced the Child and Family Services Act. This bill contained lower authorization levels than the 1971 bill, lacked any population requirement for prime sponsorship, and framed child care as a means of fostering family cohesiveness in the face of economic and social change, rather than child care as a universal right.[7] Notably absent were the words "child development," as the far right had somehow taken umbrage at this term. This mystified me. As a developmentalist I always had viewed "child development" as neutral nomenclature for a well-accepted field of study.

The legislation languished in committee as the Watergate scandal captivated the nation's attention, and it appeared unlikely that the bill would materialize into law that year.[8] Nevertheless, the right wing perceived a threat and launched a devastating attack. In 1975, an anonymous smear campaign inundated congressional offices with thousands of letters and misinformed pamphlets. Mondale and Brademas bore the brunt of this assault.

Mondale stated in the *Congressional Record,* "A vicious and totally inaccurate propaganda campaign is currently being waged against the child and family services legislation pending before Congress . . . [It] is being subjected to one of the most distorted and dishonest attacks I have witnessed in my fifteen years of public service."[9]

Each day, between two thousand and six thousand incensed and hysterical letters poured into congressional offices. A woman from Liberty, Michigan, concluded in one such letter, "It's the most disgusting and revolting piece of literature I have ever read."[10]

In addition to the letters, thousands of pamphlets filled with emotional and wildly misinformed allegations circulated in Washington. The pamphlets misleadingly attributed to the legislation the claim that "as a matter of the child's right, the government shall exert control over the family." Mondale noted that those "allegations are totally false, and I believe that the individuals or organizations making the allegation know it is false. I say that because the materials containing these allegations are unsigned—a clear and significant sign that the organizations or individuals circulating these allegations know that they cannot defend or document them."[11]

Further, right wingers aired a television program in John Brademas's hometown of South Bend, Indiana, that vaguely attributed this statement to him. While stations quickly offered a retraction and an apology, Brademas said, "Never in my seventeen years as a representative in Congress have I seen a more systematic, willful attempt to smear both me and my work in the House of Representatives."[12]

The campaign was executed so quickly that Mondale had to hire two extra staffers to answer the thousands of letters coming in each day. Mondale took stock of the spread of the attack: "It started down in Oklahoma and Texas, then it came north like the hoof-and-mouth disease." Then, with a note of resignation, Mondale reflected, "This is my first massive experience with the 'big lie' and it's not much fun."[13]

CONSERVATISM: VOICES AND VALUES

A clear pattern emerges from the actions and reactions of the right during the course of the 1971 CCDA and subsequent efforts by Mondale and Brademas. The right framed child care within an ideology of the family and was deeply opposed to providing child care services that would enable a middle-class mother to abandon her responsibility to child, family, and society. They indicated through welfare reform policies, however, that they were in favor of requiring poor mothers to abandon their children for the out-of-home workplaces and, as a result, to place their children in child care of questionable quality. The story of the right's reaction to child care is emblematic of the rise of right-wing conservatism and its newfound voice. The right gained the ability to define the terms of the political debate and the scope of possible child care solutions.

The 1970s witnessed a coordinated, strategic, well-disciplined, and well-financed effort by the right wing to push its values and its policy agenda forward, to reclaim control of the political landscape, and to realign the Republican Party. Conservatives recognized the power of ideas to shape the political landscape and directed vast resources into think tanks and research organizations that would disseminate their public policy ideas.[14] The Olin Foundation, for example, between its founding in 1953 and its closing in 2005, poured more than $370 million into this effort. Its pet projects included early financing for the Federalist Society and support for two then-little-known scholars, Charles Murray and Richard J. Herrnstein, to write *The Bell Curve*. James Pierson, longtime director of the Olin Foundation, shared his grant-making strategy: "The ideas have to be tended to . . . only after that can you tend to the policies."[15]

A loose coalition of right-wing think tanks that identified ideas as their weapon of choice formed. The Heritage Foundation, created in 1973, explicitly sought to formulate and promote conservative public policies and took on child care policy as an early priority. Between 1977 and 1979 its budget grew from $2 million to $18 million. Other conservative organizations emerged during this period: Phyllis Schlafly's Eagle Forum in 1972, Concerned Women for America in 1979, and the Family Research Council in 1980.[16]

The New Right leveraged its culture of ideas to distinguish itself from a traditionally moderate Republican ideology based in limited government and epitomized by Nelson Rockefeller and Elliot Richardson's wing of the party. A defining feature of the New Right was a focus on "family values," specifically the politics of sexuality, family, and reproduction, including such issues as child care. The right sought to win over the middle class by positioning itself as pro-family, juxtaposed with feminists and others seen as out-of-touch upper-class elites.[17] Family values became the dominant rhetoric of conservative politics in America, and the New Right was outspoken, even in proclaiming a notion of the family that was largely inconsistent with the realities of America during the 1970s and 1980s.[18] It worked—the right wing mainstreamed what was originally considered fanaticism.

Populist Thomas Frank begins his 2004 bestseller "What's the Matter with Kansas?" by sharing a pattern of facts that puzzled him: "The poorest county in America isn't in Appalachia or the Deep South. It is on the Great Plains, a region of struggling ranchers and dying farm towns, and in the election of 2000, George W. Bush carried it by a majority of greater than 80 percent."[19] How?

Frank quickly arrives at the conclusion that New Right conservatism (he terms it Backlash Conservatism) is enabled by a "critical rhetorical move: the systematic erasure of the economic."[20] By trumping economic concerns with its double aces of family values and religious rhetoric, the New Right manages to win over Middle America, once the hotbed of the populist movement.

Right Wing Takes on Child Care: It's All in the Delivery

In a 2005 *New York Times* bestseller, *Freakonomics*, Chicago economist Stephen Levitt argues, "An expert must be bold if he hopes to alchemize his homespun theory into conventional wisdom. His best chance of doing so is to engage the public's emotions, for emotion is the enemy of rational argument. And as emotions go, one of them—fear—is more potent than the rest."[21] The right takes full advantage of this idea, suspending rational argument by invoking emotional arguments and bullying dissenters.

Day Care Deception

Brian C. Robertson, a fellow in the Center for Marriage and Family at the Family Research Council, a conservative Washington think tank dedicated to establishing a "Christian standard of morality in all of America's domestic policy," wrote *Day Care Deception: What the Child Care Establishment Isn't Telling Us.* As his title suggests, he argues that two major deceptions currently exist: (1) a continued "cover-up" of social scientific findings on the risk of nonparental group care for preschoolers; and (2) a continued attempt to falsely portray public investment in organized groups that care for children as something working parents want. Much more powerful than his argument, though, was the fear-evoking language he chose to plead his case against public child care.

In this book, popular with the extreme right, Robertson introduces his case by transforming the April 1999 Columbine High School massacre, one of our nation's tragedies, into an argument against public child care. Following the shootings, in Littleton, Colorado, the media scurried to identify the causes of such an unthinkable crime. The explanations from media and scholars at the time included inadequate gun control, violent culture and media, bullying, and cliques. Robertson finds a completely different reason: child care. Apparently, not long before the massacre, Dylan Klebold, one of the two Columbine perpetrators, wrote an essay that depicted Satan opening a day care center in Hell. Robertson used this finding—hardly up to the standard of evidence required by most scholars—to warn us that "we are just beginning to see the consequences of this enormous, unprecedented shift toward a new and basically untested way of rearing and socializing young children."[22]

Sociologist Barry Glassner, in the national bestseller *The Culture of Fear: Why Americans Are Afraid of the Wrong Things,* observes: "By failing to provide adequate education, nutrition, housing, parenting, medical services and child care over the past couple of decades we have done the nation's children immense harm. Yet we project our guilt onto a cavalcade of boogeypeople—pedophile preschool teachers, preteen mass murderers, and homicidal au pairs, to name only a few."[23] Robertson, it seems, is guilty of this projection.

Robertson and others on the far right fear that freeing women from their family responsibilities will disrupt social order, and they conceptualize any deviation from their family ideology—based on a nostalgic and outdated model of the family with a breadwinner father and homemaker mother—as perverse. Indeed, much of their success is derived from their extraordinary ability to put their finger on the pulse of American anxiety about women's expanded roles. Betty Holcomb observes that right-wing conservatives "challenge the stubborn and ingrained habits of thinking, the well-worn 'commonsensical' explanations of men's and women's behavior. Instead they offer up the formulas that come to mind first—the stereotypes of gender, the shared assumptions about men and women, fathers and mothers, parents and workers, that Americans have held for the past century."[24] While many Americans may disagree with a value system so extreme, many are equivocal about working mothers and cling to a "traditional" image of the family. In his latest book on this topic, *Forced Labor: What's Wrong with Balancing Work and Family*, Robertson frames it as an uncompromising choice: "We either favor the family or we favor the forces that are working for its destruction." Finally, if you're not scared yet, E. Ray Moore, a proponent of the home schooling movement, warns us all, "As we look at modern trends, with millions both in daycare and in nursing homes, we are compelled to conclude that the earlier you institutionalize your children, the earlier they will institutionalize you."[25]

WHAT WERE THE CHILD CARE ADVOCATES DOING?

The 1976 presidential election brought Jimmy Carter, a Democrat, and Walter Mondale, an author of the original 1971 CCDA and the 1974 Child and Family Services Act, into the White House. Many believed that the timing was right for child care legislation. In 1977 and 1978, Senator Alan Cranston (D-CA) held hearings on "future federal legislation involving child care and child development." At the same time, compelling demographics emerged from the Department of Labor indicating for the first time that the majority of mothers with children under eighteen worked outside the home. At the hearings, mum was the word when it came to anything controversial enough to ignite the right. Initially, advocates encouraged Cranston not to enter into the fray over what would constitute a prime sponsor, lest he risk repeating the 1971 disaster.[26] Mondale graciously kept his distance for fear his support would rekindle the right—and maybe because he found his "first massive experience with the 'big lie' . . . not much fun."[27]

The following February Cranston introduced the Child Care Act of 1979. Almost immediately the letters started coming in, and James Kilpatrick's syndicated columns warned of "Launching Another Disaster."[28] Surely this bill was not sneaking by the right, but advocates hoped that with enough will and a friendly Congress and executive branch, they could finally address the impending child care crisis. The first blow came when Arabella Martinez, assistant secretary in HEW, testified against the bill. The second came when there was no clear force to counter that opposition.

Herding Cats: The Child Care Act of 1979

In March 1979, Cranston asked staffer Susanne Martinez to call in the power players. They pulled the child care experts, advocates, and policy makers into one room to discuss and flesh out the specific features of the bill. By the end of the meeting, it was clear that the only thing this group shared was a desire for child care legislation. When it came to exact features of the bill, everyone had a different hobby horse. One of the most vocal opponents was the powerful Children's Defense Fund (CDF), headed by its founder, Marian Wright Edelman. Martinez, in an interview with child care historian Sally Cohen, noted that most people were supportive of Cranston's bill, but "without CDF's support, we could not be productive on the bill."[29] Cranston, becoming more and more frustrated with the lack of cohesion, finally blurted, "You people can't agree on anything." That was the end of it.

Cranston cancelled the final day of hearings, withdrew the bill, and proclaimed at a press conference, "What was needed was not more hearings but more unanimity."[30] This sequence of events had a lasting impact on me. To this day, whenever there is a meeting with an important decision at stake, I gather the stakeholders in one room and form a consensus on a common position to sell. Indeed, this drove my approach to dealing with the divisiveness among academics on the effects of child care.

FIDCRs Resurface

While a federal child care system was out of the cards, in part precluded by the divisiveness of its advocates and the power of the right, there were still millions of children that would need to receive services from someone. By March 1981 a record 8.2 million children below age six had working mothers.[31] After periodic debate throughout the 1970s, the FIDCR controversy came to a boil when HEW was faced with the familiar quagmire of funding child care that would both protect children and satisfy OMB leadership. OMB was keen on keeping costs low and reducing the federal government's regulatory role. Child care advocates, including me, NCJW, and NAEYC, pressed HEW to adopt the proposed 1972 regulations as the "minimal requirements to preserve the safety of children in federally funded care." We argued that the 1972 standards were not lofty best practices or goals but rather the baseline for cost-effective developmental care. The major purpose of the FIDCRs was to provide a floor of quality below which federal funds would not be used to defray costs. Conservatives and proprietary providers opposed the regulations on philosophical and financial grounds, respectively.

Stuart Eizenstat, Carter's domestic policy staff director, pressured HEW Secretary Patricia Harris to send the 1972 FIDCRs to Congress to be legislated. She did so, and all signs for passage appeared positive. After twelve years of protracted debate, beginning with Jule Sugarman's 1968 effort, the FIDCRs finally would be implemented.[32]

It was not going to be that easy. At that point, lobbying groups representing big child care chains and mom-and-pop providers started a letter-writing campaign opposing the FIDCRs, citing the high costs that staffing ratios would impose on providers. Another surprising player, the National Governors Association, weighed in against the FIDCRs because it opposed federal government meddling in the control of state-funded programs. Congress agreed to suspend implementation of the new standards for one year—just enough time for Ronald Reagan to take office.

The FIDCRs became a casualty of the Reagan Revolution. Legislatively, they were buried. The guidelines remain to this day in the Federal Register as an appropriate model for states, and they influenced the NAEYC licensing standards.[33] It is unlikely that the FIDCRs will ever be put into effect on a national scale. Although it is a dead issue, the federal government, through the states, persists in buying care that may be detrimental to children's development.

Quiet before the Storm

Conservatism swept through Washington with the election of Ronald Reagan in 1980. In the face of Reaganomics, child care advocates were left trying to minimize losses and position themselves for future efforts at legislation. Throughout the 1980s the government's role in child care did not expand in proportion to the growing need, but rather declined in significant ways.[34] Federal child care subsidies took two major forms in the 1980s: tax credits for those earning enough money to have tax liabilities, and direct subsidies. The Child and Dependent Care Tax Credit was the major tax policy, and by fiscal year 1988, the expenditures for the tax credit were $3.9 billion.[35] Although this figure includes care for dependents other than children, the tax credit was the federal government's largest commitment to direct child care assistance, but poor families with little taxable income did not benefit from the credit because it was not refundable.

Throughout the 1980s the tax credit increased, but direct subsidies distributed under Title XX of the Social Securities Act were greatly diminished. Even with increases in the tax credit, it fell short of parents' needs: the ceiling was too low to compensate for actual costs of care, an annual tax credit does little to help parents cope with the reality of weekly child care bills, and it was not refundable. In short, changes in the tax credit in most cases did not help poor or working-class families, and changes in Title XX reduced the available subsidies.

Child Care Advocates

There have really been only two major organizations devoted exclusively to child care. Unfortunately, neither could maintain itself financially. The first was the Day Care and Child Development Council of America, which was active during the fight for the 1971 CCDA. The second was launched in 1983 by Elinor Guggenheimer. The Child Care Action Campaign (CCAC) was an advocacy organization devoted to achieving high-quality, affordable child care for all families and had as one of its early goals the attraction of popular media attention. The results were powerful—thousands of supportive letters poured into congressional offices after CCAC convinced leading magazines to run features on child care.

The Children's Caucus

In the same year, 1983, Senators Christopher Dodd (D-CT) and Arlen Specter (R-PA) initiated the Children's Caucus. They knew that any effort to introduce child care legislation would need a platform or leverage point within Congress. Dodd, a key advocate for children, wanted to address issues facing the nation's children, but the Republicans were in control of the Senate. He teamed up with Specter to create a thirty-member bipartisan group that would act like a regular committee and hold hearings on issues that affected children, including child care. They needed an outside expert to identify the pressing issues, so they turned to me. Their first hearing, on school-age child care, was dramatic and attracted significant media attention (see chapter 5).

Reality of Maternal Employment Demands Policy Action
While advocates and policy makers were positioning themselves, families were recovering from the inflation of the 1970s and finding that a second income was a necessity. In 1987, 67 percent of women with children under the age of eighteen were in the out-of-home workforce, as compared to 39 percent in 1970.[36] Further, by 1988, there were 13.5 million single-parent families headed by women—nearly double the 7.5 million in 1970.[37] New Right activists Phyllis Schlafly and Jerry Falwell were still preaching that the mother's proper place was in the home, but there were fewer and fewer mothers at home to hear them.

Why were these mothers working? The same reasons fathers do: to adequately feed, clothe, and shelter their children. Despite popular perceptions that feminists were responsible for sending women into the workplace, the real growth in need for supplementary child care was not among welfare mothers only, but all mothers, including well-educated professional women. In a 1983 *New York Times* poll, 71 percent of working mothers responded that they worked "not for something interesting to do, but to support their families."[38]

By 1987, 8.2 million children under age five had mothers who worked outside the home and needed care services. The Congressional Research

Service estimated that there were fewer than 3 million regulated child care slots in 1986–1987.[39] In the absence of the FIDCRs, regulation had been abdicated to the states, and there was massive variation in quality, with much of child care at the lower end of the quality scale. A poll released that year showed that 73 percent of Americans were willing to pay higher taxes for better child care programs.[40]

ACT FOR BETTER CHILD CARE

The relative silence on child care policy was broken in 1988 when more than one hundred child care bills were introduced. Child care was pushed to the top of the policy agenda by the reality of increased maternal employment outside the home, business leaders who clamored for child care as a solution to labor shortages, and children's advocates concerned about the quality of available child care.

Among the bills introduced in the 1987–88 congressional session was the Act for Better Child Care (ABC). This was sponsored by Dodd and had nearly 200 cosponsors in the House and Senate. The bill was created by the Alliance for Better Child Care, a coalition of more than one hundred education groups, including child advocates, labor unions, child care scholars, and other interest groups led by the Children's Defense Fund. The ABC bill called for $2.5 billion to be spent annually to improve quality, affordability, and availability of child care through federal grants to the states. The authors of the ABC bill navigated around the issues of universality and prime sponsorship. Only families with incomes below 115 percent of their state's median income would be eligible, and all funds would be distributed to states to provide to families through vouchers. (Federal control was out of the question under Reagan's New Federalism.)[41]

Even with this cautious approach, the ABC bill ignited debates over the use of vouchers in child care and the provision of funds to providers with religious affiliations. Helen Blank, director of child care at CDF and Edelman's delegate, led the Alliance for Better Child Care and lobbied its members to agree on a compromise that would require centers to cover or remove religious symbols as a condition for receiving federal child care dollars. In the end, despite the plethora of plans, or perhaps because of it, no major child care legislation was passed that year.

Conservative Brio

The demographics, the powerful advocacy group pushing for the ABC bill, and support from legislators did not stop conservatives. Conservatives claimed that the ABC bill discriminated against families in which one parent stayed home to care for children and families that preferred religiously based child care. Robert Rector of the Heritage Foundation was a leading opponent, testifying before congressional committees that the bill should address the needs of "traditional families." Phyllis Schlafly, president of Eagle Forum, focused on the limitations placed on religiously affiliated child care providers, arguing the bill contained the "most bigoted, anti-religious sections ever proposed in any legislation."[42] Republicans introduced tax credits as an alternative to ABC and emphasized their support of federal funding for religiously affiliated care.

Conservatives, the National Governors Association, and the National Council of State Legislators (NCSL) opposed the idea of unifying standards across states, no matter how minimal these requirements were, and thus expressed apprehension over the ABC bill.[43] The NGA and NCSL lamented "unfunded mandates" and the federal government's involvement in state expenditures—not unlike their opposition to the FIDCRs. Tom Kean, the Republican governor of New Jersey, testified before the Senate on behalf of the NGA that "day care is not like socks or pantyhose—one size doesn't fit everybody."[44] Conservatives wanted to limit the "intrusiveness" of such standards and called for small government.

In 1989, the Senate passed a modified version of the ABC bill, but the House was deeply divided about standards and religiously affiliated care. Augustus Hawkins (D-CA), one of the most senior members of Congress, introduced the Child Development and Education Act. This act was based on my School of the Twenty-First Century model, which relied on public schools to provide services, including preschool care and before- and after-school care to older children. This bill was more comfortable for groups, such as the National Education Association and the Parent Teacher Association, that were opposed to the use of vouchers. An interesting footnote is that I offered the School of the Twenty-First Century proposal to Blank, leader of the ABC alliance, over lunch. I offered to give it to the alliance to present as its own. She was not interested—the alliance had the ABC bill.

Defectors

The debate raged on within the House, and Representatives Thomas Downey (D-NY) and George Miller (D-CA), concerned that ABC would never pass, introduced a new bill. Their bill was more modest and included expanded tax benefits, increases in other funding streams (such as Title XX) earmarked for child care, and minimum health and safety standards. Alliance members opposed this bill, which was more palatable to conservatives. More important than the content of the bill, however, was that its introduction came as a shock to Edelman and other members of the alliance.[45]

An outraged Edelman attacked and castigated leading Democrats. In a memo to Downey and Miller she wrote: "This memo is for the record . . . Its purpose is to let thousands and thousands of child care advocates, women, and working parents all around the country—who have worked unceasingly for years . . . know that if child care legislation is not enacted this year, the two of you will deserve the full blame for this tragic and unnecessary outcome . . . [The recent committee decision] is only the latest in a series of efforts you have engaged in to sabotage groundbreaking child care legislation all year for petty jurisdictional and power reasons."[46] The memo surprised many on the coalition, who feared that this political maneuvering could be perceived as childish, provide another excuse for legislators to vote against the bill, and give conservatives a leverage point.[47] For those outside the child care arena it was extremely odd to find Edelman, a well-known children's advocate, in disagreement with Miller and Downey, two strong child care advocates who consistently battled for enlightened legislation. After all, CDF had elected Miller its "man of the year" only months earlier.[48] Some observers of this battle came to the conclusion that for Edelman it would be "my way or the highway." Unsurprisingly, no agreement was reached in 1989.

Advocates Battle

By 1990 conservatives had time on their side and were able to develop alternative bills. The Alliance for Better Child Care, on the other hand, was splintering. The Family Research Council activated its grassroots network and flooded Congress and the media with its message. Phyllis Schlafly, bullhorn in hand, led parades of women pushing baby carriages around the Capitol. CDF launched its largest publicity campaign. Advocates stretched paper chains from the Capitol to the White House and flooded newspapers with editorials in support of the bill.

In 1990 the Child Care and Development Block Grant (CCDBG) passed. It was authorized at $750 million for its first year—a small sum next to the $2 billion authorization proposed for the 1971 Comprehensive Child Development Act and the $2.5 billion proposed for the ABC bill.[49] The CCDBG was a barely recognizable shadow of the original ABC bill. Of the new block grant, 75 percent was set aside for child care vouchers for families with incomes below 75 percent of the state median income. The remaining 25 percent was reserved for quality improvements and before- and after-school care. Licensing and regulating was abdicated to the states.

ABC Becomes a Pyrrhic Victory

Who won? Edelman and CDF claimed victory for breaking the silence on child care and getting a bill passed. They proclaimed CCDBG to be a success. But Schlafly recalled to Betty Holcomb, author of *Not Guilty! The Good News for Working Mothers,* that "we were fighting government bureaucrats, the marshmallow politicians, and all of their so-called experts and we won. We beat them."[50]

Why did a Republican president in 1990 sign *any* child care bill amid so much opposition? Demographics had driven child care onto the policy agenda—*something* had to be done. For advocates and politicians a lot was at stake. Whoever controlled the terms of the debate framed the problem. That frame then determined, in part, the appropriate solution.

Social conservatives distinguished between working mothers and career mothers. Working mothers are the poor single mothers who need to work in order to be self-sufficient. Social conservatives believe that these women should work: recall the 1996 welfare reform debates. Career mothers, according to social conservatives, are middle-class and upper-middle-class women who work for selfish reasons.[51] So, the two alternatives for framing the debate had powerful implications for support from conservatives and for the degree of universality: Was the rising number of employed mothers made up of women who needed to put children in child care while they worked to support their families? Or were they career mothers abandoning their child care responsibilities for the workplace? In reality, this is a false dichotomy: the inflation of the 1970s made dual income central to maintaining a decent quality of life for many families. Further, not all single mothers were impoverished—rising divorce rates had pushed many middle-class women into this category.

Nonetheless, conservatives leveraged this dichotomy to reframe the nature of the debate, creating a CCDBG that was much weaker than the original ABC championed by the alliance. The proliferation of conservative think tanks in the 1980s and strategic positioning by right wingers gave Republicans the intellectual capital to frame the debate in their terms and offer alternative proposals to the ABC bill at every turn. By the time the bill reached President Bush, it was essentially a Republican bill that provided a way to quickly achieve a domestic priority. The CCDBG pleased conservatives because it emphasized parental choice through the mandated use of vouchers and devolved nearly all decisions, including regulation, to the states.

More Money into a Broken System

The CCDBG was clearly an important step in the history of child care, which had been legislatively deadlocked since the early 1970s. Further, the CCDBG, along with a second program called the At-Risk Child Care Program (targeted to families at risk of becoming welfare dependent and authorized at $300 million annually), and tax credits significantly expanded the amount of money in the child care system. However, the legislation was inadequate to address the child care needs facing families, and it proved counterproductive to the optimal development of children. Insofar as the CCDBG fails to raise the quality of child care, it only increases the availability of low-quality care, which puts at risk the positive development of young children. We cannot support a policy solution that compromises the quality of care and development of children.

The low funding levels of CCDBG led to long waiting lists within states. A 1995 Government Accountability Office (GAO) survey of seven states found that five had waiting lists ranging from 3,000 to 36,000 families. Schlafly appeared to relish that unfortunate fact. She noted to Holcomb, "The fight was to make sure that day care was not going to become a middle-class entitlement . . . and we won."[52] Further, the distribution of money through vouchers, within a system that allowed states to control the minimal health and safety regulations, essentially poured money into care of questionable quality. Vouchers can legally be used for anything from NAEYC-accredited centers to kith and kin care, from sisters and mothers to drunken boyfriends. It's an open secret that desperately poor women can cut deals with family members: "You keep $37.50, and I'll keep $37.50." It is up to states to make laws to prohibit this corruption. Worse yet, following enactment of this act, members of Congress believed that the child care problem in the United States had been solved and no further action was needed.[53] While CCDBG may have overcome a twenty-year impasse on child care, it amounted to little more than a shadow of a solution. A few lucky working mothers received assistance while millions of children and families waited for a real answer.

In 1996, child care was again pushed onto the policy agenda, but this time by new welfare reforms block-granting federal welfare dollars to the states under Temporary Assistance for Needy Families (TANF). A discussion of the 1996 welfare reforms is outside the scope of this chapter, but there were important implications for child care. TANF eliminated multiple funding streams for child care and combined funds under a revised CCDBG. The revised CCDBG was called the Child Care and Development Fund (CCDF). The major changes were an increase in total funding for child care and a decrease in the minimum required set-aside for quality improvements to 4 percent of funds. Generally, child care debates after the 1990 CCDBG and 1996 TANF bill have been limited to debates over annual appropriations, technicalities of funding streams, and quality set-asides.

Child Care within Welfare Reforms

Insofar as child care is provided within the larger framework of welfare reform, efforts to improve the quality of care clash with efforts to increase supply and reduce costs so that more low-income families can move off of the welfare roles.[54] By 2000, more than half of federal CCDF funding came from TANF. This is important because the purpose of TANF is to facilitate employment (just as the Labor Department had argued for under the Family Assistance Plan, motivating its championing of a low-cost custodial approach). Child development was not a goal of the 1996 welfare legislation. Compared to Moynihan's FAP, a two-generation approach to welfare, the most recent welfare policies largely neglect the needs of children and constitute a real regression from where America was in the 1970s. Legislation that aligns child care funds with welfare dollars focuses the limited amount of care support on some of our most vulnerable families: those transitioning onto and off of public assistance. But what about the millions of other children? If facilitating employment is the goal of child care under welfare reform, our measures of success are the number of children served and the employment rate of their parents. Indeed, the 1996 welfare reform has been declared a success when the key consideration is the number of mothers moved off the welfare roles. Children's experiences within this welfare reform have been relatively neglected.

Who Lost?

The losers of the 1990 CCDBG debates, the victims of our failure to adequately address the child care crisis in this country, are the tens of thousands of children on waiting lists and the millions of children who did receive vouchers but were pushed into care that was of poor to mediocre quality. Without a federal system of child care, states determine the licensing and regulation standards, which makes a profound impact on the quality of care. Some care is good; most is poor or mediocre. Vouchers maximize parental choice but present serious problems. In a nonsystem, largely devoid of universal regulation and accountability, there is no way of even ensuring the availability of good-quality care for parents to choose. Surely a system in which individuals with no training in child development qualify for a voucher is problematic. While some advocates consider securing more money for CCDBG a success, we cannot possibly have success until we create a revolution in the way we frame the problem and evaluate solutions to it. We need to fully shift our approach from conceptualizing child care as a container to recognizing child care as an important developmental context. Children lost in 1971. Children lost in 1990.

MOTHERS FAIL TO STEP UP TO THE PLATE

Where were the advocacy groups for these employed mothers? Child care waned as a political priority for feminist groups during the late 1970s and into the 1980s. Betty Friedan, in her 1981 book *The Second Stage,* urged women to "move beyond prizing work above family" and focus on issues such as improving child care. But this was not a popular notion in feminist circles.

In the 1980s and 1990s, as in previous decades, many women's groups distanced themselves from child care because it reinforced the role of women as caregivers. Other women's groups were concerned foremost with women's employment and feared that raising issues suggesting that women had gender-specific needs would prejudice employers against them. Further, the issues of class conflict raised by child care may have discouraged rather then encouraged other feminists from engaging in child care advocacy. The abysmal wages of child care providers means that child care often entails the exploitation of low-income women by another group of affluent and middle-class women. More recently, some women's groups have begun to increase their involvement in advocating for child care as a necessity for women's career advancement. One interesting aspect of this new insurgence is some of the dialogue between twenty- to thirty-year-old women and the women who experienced feminism in the 1970s. In June of 2003, a program called Family Initiative: Better Child Care, Preschool, and Afterschool was launched by Legal Momentum (previously known as the NOW Legal Defense and Education Fund). At a nonpartisan congressional briefing organized by Legal Momentum, Jane Smith, the CEO of Business and Professional Women/USA, testified on behalf of their grassroots members that "top on their list of concerns is the issue of quality, affordable child care." The irony should not be lost that this is virtually identical to the conclusion emerging out of the 1970 White House Conference on Children.

Recent demographic trends demonstrate that some women today with higher levels of income and education are choosing to stay at home with their children, creating a dip in the rate of maternal employment for the first time since 1960.[55] In 2000, the Bureau of Labor Statistics identified the first ever drop-off in workforce participation by married mothers with a child less than one year old, from 59 percent in 1997 to 53 percent in 2000. Analyses revealed that the drop was driven by women who were white, over thirty, and well educated. Subsequent scholarship questioned whether the drop was real or an artifact of data collection.[56]

Whether this effect was real or not, the firestorm response by the media made it into an issue. Conservatives jumped on it as proof that they were correct all along and that the brightest, most well-educated Americans were finally seeing it their way. Liberals, for their part, argued that the time bind had gotten so great and child care costs so high that mothers were without options.

Arlie Hochschild, author of *The Time Bind: When Work Becomes Home and Home Becomes Work* contends that America is "now the workaholism capital of the world." Susan Douglas and Meredith Michaels take on the issue of "new momism" in their book *The Mommy Myth*. They argue that a mother's job has actually expanded over the past thirty years and that "to be a remotely decent mother, a woman has to devote her entire physical, psychological, emotional, and intellectual being, 24/7, to her children." This requirement creates a standard of success they argue that is "impossible to meet." Men and women are now leaving work only to face a "second shift" of work in the home and then the third and most difficult shift: recovering from the damage and stress created by the first two.[57]

The relative silence of the women's movement on child care issues in the 1980s and early 1990s is further evidence of the capacity of child care to be a lightning rod for controversy about family, religion, the role of the federal government, and gender. The cost of their collective inaction is higher than many will ever know. Joan C. Williams argued in the *Harvard Women's Law Journal* that many women never get near the glass ceiling in the workplace because "they are stopped long before by the maternal wall."[58]

The available data supports Williams's insight, indicating that women are twice as likely to leave an employer when they have inadequate access to child care. The most recent estimate of the long-term gender earnings gap shows that women earn 62 percent less than men earn over a fifteen-year period, well over twice as large as the 23 percent gap previously derived from the federal Current Population Survey. Dr. Heidi Hartmann, President of the Institute for Women's Policy Research and coauthor of the report, stated that previous estimates were misleading because they "ignore the labor market experiences of over half of working women, who either work part-time or take time out of labor force for family care," and that the newer estimate captured "the cumulative effect on women's earnings of balancing family and work responsibilities."[59] Reliable child care is clearly indispensable to gender equity.

Recent court rulings are sending a clear message to employers that lack of support for their employees' child care responsibilities is a basis for discrimination claims. Despite this, "discrimination against parents and other caregivers in employment is becoming a new battleground," and an "increasing number of employees are suing employers because they . . .

were treated unfairly based on their responsibilities to care for children or others," according to Joan C. Williams, director of American University's Program on WorkLife Law. Over 50 percent of legal challenges to employers involved male employees who were fired or disciplined for work/family conflicts arising from providing care for their children.[60] Child care is no longer "just" a women's issue.

HOW'D THEY DO THAT? FRAMES AND THE CHILD CARE DEBATE

The ability of the right wing to spread their message has highlighted the effects of framing on proposed solutions. If the current state of child care policy is so costly to social progress, is it possible that we have all been duped into ignoring the crisis? Research indicates that how we perceive the goals, philosophies, and purposes of child care influences how we understand policy and what we demand. Much of this body of research is based on the currently popular Frame Theory.

Frame Theory proposes that each of us organizes the world around us by using preexisting scripts, frames, and metaphors to guide our thinking on an issue.[61] This mental shortcut is necessary to deal with the vast amounts of information coming in from the environment. A societal characterization of child care as a "kiddy container" or "child storage" means that children are seen as precious objects requiring little more than being kept safe and warm. Specifically, research reveals that most Americans see child care through the frames of child safety and parental employment.[62] These frames lend themselves to the storage container metaphor. When parents are asked what they believe characterizes good-quality care, most indicate that they would be happy with a provider who is affectionate and responsible in a safe and orderly environment.[63] Framing helps to explain why society would be willing to pay for low-quality "storage container" care rather than high-quality early care and education.

Media Influence on Child Care Frames

Media coverage is a powerful force for pushing a problem onto the policy agenda. One of the best-known examples is how the national newspaper coverage of the tragic 1911 fire at the Triangle Shirtwaist Company in New York City, which killed more than 140 young women and children, served to focus public attention on child labor and unsafe factory conditions.

Combined with the investigations of the National Child Labor Committee and the documentary photography of Lewis Hines, media accounts of the Triangle fire galvanized the public against child labor and have been credited with contributing to the passage of the 1916 Keating-Owen Act.[64]

Shanto Iyengar, a Stanford professor of political communications and expert in the effects of mass media, identifies two types of frames employed by the media: episodic and thematic. Episodic news frames are the type we most often see on the evening news and take the form of specific stories about individuals at specific times: for example, the nightly crime report, or the Triangle shirt factory story. On the other hand, thematic frames contextualize a public issue within a broader context, as do reports on the need for child care in the United States. Iyengar concludes that "episodic framing tends to elicit individualistic rather than societal attributions of responsibility while thematic framing has the opposite effect."[65]

What does the most memorable media coverage of child care look like? In the fall of 1995, ABC's Diane Sawyer ran a story in which a hidden camera was placed in the infant-toddler room of a New Orleans child care center. As a part of the segment, ABC invited me and two other child development experts to watch the tape in the studio at the same time as the national audience and provide comments during the broadcast. The tape showed children strapped into car seats scattered around the floor, children stepping on each other, a child in the corner playing with matches. At one point, one of the caregivers (if you could call her that) picked up an eighteen-month-old and threw the baby headfirst into a crib. The force could have easily broken the baby's neck. She then picked up the baby, slapped it three times . . . I couldn't control my reaction and blurted, "That's child abuse!"

There was huge outcry against the program. Not an outcry about the child care center, mind you, but the program. The American public didn't want to see this—it didn't want to deal with this. Angry viewers claimed that this wasn't child care and insisted the program visit other centers. They were right, in a sense. This was one (atrocious) center, in one city. So, the next week they visited a second site in another city. It was absolutely beautiful and of exceptional quality. Where was that site? It was in the Senate office building in Washington, DC. If it's good enough for a senator, then it's good enough for all of us. (See chapter 7 for a discussion of the child care available to members of Congress.)

Often the news stories related to child care that gain the most attention are sensationalistic and episodic, thus imposing blame and guilt on
families. While the real crisis is about the poor-quality care children are
subjected to, the media has recently focused on charges of sexual abuse
at child care centers. A well-known example is the story of Kelly Michaels,
who was accused of sexually abusing children under her care in New Jersey. The heinous allegations turned out to be unfounded, and Michaels
was exonerated of all charges. The situation was so out of control that
the American Psychological Association took an unprecedented step and
intervened. But what is the lasting effect of this media coverage? More
than six in ten parents (63 percent) say that they are very concerned that
"children could suffer physical or sexual abuse" in a typical day care center. One New Jersey mother added, "I guess I've been a little afraid; that
McMartin case scared me. You hear stories about things that happen."[66]
The McMartin case involved false allegations of sexual abuse in a California child care center. Still, parents are scared. Why? Glassner might tell
us that this is another case of fearing a nonexistent boogeyman instead
of our collective ineptitude in addressing the child care crisis.

Looking to the Future
A 2003 article in the *Christian Science Monitor* entitled "A Voice for Children and Families Will Soon Fall Silent" announced that the Child Care
Action Campaign, the only advocacy organization devoted strictly to child
care, would close its doors that May. According to president Faith Wohl,
with lingering questions about financial sustainability, the board had
made the "sad but sensible" decision to close. Contextualizing the loss
of this child care advocacy, she noted, "It's coming at a time when we're
closing some doors nationally for the improvement of child care and the
benefit of kids."[67]

A 2005 *New York Times* article entitled "Goals Reached, Donor on the
Right Closes Shop" announced that the Olin Foundation was closing. It
seems that this great benefactor of the far right succeeded in creating the
"premier idea factories of the right," fulfilled its founder's mission, and
left a world in which "today's conservatism has no shortage of institutions, donors, or brio."[68]

The 1971 veto of CCDA closed a window of opportunity for child
care. Since then, a powerful social conservative movement has thwarted

efforts by child advocates to create a federal system of child care. Subsequent efforts to articulate child care policy have occurred within the context of welfare reform and thus have been limited in scope to the impoverished. In 1976, Gilbert Steiner noted with prescience, "No delivery system arrangement [of child care] could overcome the philosophical antipathy inherent in the veto message to further public intervention in child development for any group other than children of AFDC [welfare] mothers."[69] Short of a revolution in how we collectively frame child care, his conclusion can hold true long into the future.

I've written elsewhere that the greatest sadness is that what was lost was an opportunity to provide good-quality developmental care to all of America's children. While it wasn't the comprehensive services that many liberal-minded advocates saw as ideal, it would have been a giant step forward. Instead, we are left with a system in which it is unclear how much damage we're doing. Should we lose all hope given the rise of the right and the relative silence of the advocates? No. Should we be complacent and advocate putting more money into a system that guarantees poor quality care for children?

In his bestseller *The World Is Flat*, Thomas Friedman challenges readers to move beyond classical economic and social statistics to measure a society and instead offers as a new metric, "Does your society have more memories than dreams or more dreams than memories?"[70] Certainly, our dreams of a system of care for all children cannot be extinguished by a right wing clinging to a nostalgic model of the family.

CHAPTER FOUR

Quality and Affordability

Child care quality matters, in terms of children's everyday
experiences, of their cognitive and linguistic competencies
and school readiness, and of their later school achievement
and social interactions.

Deborah Lowe Vandell and Barbara Wolfe

CONSIDERING THE POOR QUALITY that has characterized child care
in the United States, one might think that we lack a knowledge base about
the developmental importance of care. However, research over the past
three decades has significantly advanced our understanding of what constitutes quality child care as well as of its role in children's development
and educational success.[1] Further, we now know that good-quality care
differs depending on the age of the child. We typically think differently
about infants and toddlers, about preschoolers, and about school-age children. This chapter begins with an in-depth examination of the elements
of good-quality child care and its importance to children's development.
Next, I examine the important relationship between quality and affordability and why the inherent tension between the two requires public-
sector investment. Finally, I conclude with a discussion of promising
policy initiatives in this area and how the lessons learned from them
can be used in moving toward comprehensive large-scale policy reform.

WHAT CONSTITUTES GOOD-QUALITY CHILD CARE?

Distinguishing between good and very poor care is easy and oversim-
plifies the quality issue. Any observant person can identify care that is
clearly neglectful of or dangerous to children's physical well-being. In the
extreme, children in such environments may be subjected to abuse or ne-

glect. In less severe instances, their physical needs for nutrition, hygiene, comfort, and activity may not be met in an adequate or a timely manner. However, good-quality care involves much more than the absence of neglect or abuse, and defining it has been the focus of much research and debate. For the purposes of this discussion, it is useful to return to the distinctions made in chapter 2 among custodial, comprehensive, and developmental child care. As we noted, custodial care is essentially a container that keeps children safe while parents work but fails to address children's developmental needs. Custodial care thus does not constitute good-quality care. On the other end of the spectrum is comprehensive care, based on highly enriched early intervention models, such as Head Start, Early Head Start, and Abecedarian, and providing a range of services for children's physical, social, emotional, and mental health needs that extend beyond standard child care.[2] These programs provide services to parents as well. In the middle of the continuum is a pragmatic compromise—care that we refer to as "developmental." Such care is age appropriate, meeting at least the minimum threshold that allows for healthy all-around development of children and including important early educational opportunities. Thus, developmental care is more than custodial care in that it provides for children's physical needs and safety *and* their developmental needs; yet it is less intensive than comprehensive care in that it does not provide social services (for example, health, mental health, and family support) that are generally outside the scope of child care.

As Mary Lang and I have noted, developmental care "may not enrich but it will not compromise a child's development. It is not a luxury, but an essential."[3] Numerous small- and large-scale studies of the relationship between child care quality and children's outcomes have demonstrated that such care is characterized by "safe and healthful care, developmentally appropriate stimulation, positive interactions with adults, encouragement of the child's individual emotional growth, and promotion of positive relationships with other children."[4] Developmental care meets children's social, cognitive, physical, and emotional needs.

A growing literature has shown that children of all ages in good-quality programs perform better on measures of social, emotional, linguistic, and cognitive development than other children. For example, the National Child Care Staffing Study, the Cost, Quality and Outcomes study, and the National Institute of Child Health and Human Development Study of Early Child Care all found that children attending programs where caregivers had more training and where child-staff ratios were smaller performed better across a range of social and cognitive measures.[5] Further, there is convincing evidence that sensitive and positive caregiving is positively associated with better developmental outcomes.[6]

Thus, after almost three generations of research, the general consensus is that developmental care does not harm preschool and school-age children. However, there is less of a consensus regarding the effects of such care on infants and toddlers (see chapter 5).

Features of Developmental Care: Structure and Process
Child development experts and child care professionals have long agreed about the basic aspects of good caregiving. They know that the physical setting, group size, and staff-child ratio all relate to the quality of care. They also know that the social environment of child care is equally important: for children to thrive, caregivers must be attuned to their physical, social, emotional, and cognitive needs. Children and caregivers must have the opportunity to establish and maintain relationships that foster these domains of development. To that end, caregivers must be adequately trained and willing to stay with their jobs long enough for children to develop relationships with them. For this to happen, caregivers must have sufficient compensation.

Studies have shown that children's experiences are influenced both by process and structural features of child care settings.[7] Process features center on the actual character of the relationships between caregiver and child, such as the caregivers' interactional style (for example, frequency of smiling and holding) and responsiveness to the children's verbal and nonverbal social bids. Structural features are factors that can be regulated, such as caregiver-to-child ratios and group sizes, caregiver training, and caregiver compensation.[8] Whereas process features refer to the intangibles of the setting (such as the tone of the environment and the quality of interactions between caregivers and children), the structural features refer to the aspects of the environment that allow good process to occur. Thus, process and structural features are distinct yet interrelated, with structure facilitating the processes that enhance development.[9] Together, process and structural features create the total environment that the child experiences. Research has underscored the important relation between these two features in terms of establishing and maintaining developmental care. A thought experiment will clarify the important distinctions between process and structural features.

First, envision a preschool classroom in which there are eighteen children and two experienced, well-trained, and relatively well-compensated providers (with BAs in child development, competitive wages, and health, vacation, and retirement benefits). The building is new and well maintained. The classroom is well lit, spacious, and stocked with a wide array of developmentally appropriate, state-of-the-art, stimulating toys and equipment. The cubby area is well organized and tidy. The daily schedule posted on the "parent board" provides for a variety of large- and small-group activities as well as adequate downtime during which the children nap or have quiet time. However, when you walk into the classroom you note that the caregivers do not smile very often and that their interactions with the children tend to be perfunctory, focusing more on discipline and group management issues than on play. In fact, the caregivers do not seem to enjoy the children. Then, you notice that the children, though busy, do not seem to be truly happy; they aren't really having fun. They bicker frequently and seem to engage in attention-seeking behavior that necessitates caregiver intervention. Three children huddle around a computer, squabbling over control of the mouse. Four are at the water table, where they have splashed water onto the floor and are being reprimanded by one of the teachers. Several move aimlessly from one activity center to another, seemingly in search of something to do. One child cries in frustration when her block tower falls down. She kicks another child's tower over and is sent to "time out." Another child stands at the window, sucking her thumb, her forehead pressed against the glass, staring out at the street scene below; you wonder what she is thinking about. In short, the overall tone or mood of the room is fairly negative.

In contrast, imagine a classroom in a center that is located in an older house that could use both exterior and interior repair. The front gate does not latch properly. The classroom has adequate lighting, space, and materials, but the equipment is obviously worn—chairs and tables are mismatched, toys have lost their luster and some are broken, the wall paint is faded, and the windows should be cleaned. The children's cubbies are overflowing with clothes, artwork, and other belongings. You feel the urge to tidy up. However, the eighteen children and two caregivers are clearly having a great time. They are working in two subgroups. In the larger section of the room, the lead caregiver, who has ten years of experience but only an associate's degree in child development, is reading the story of the Tortoise and the Hare to the children, who are listening raptly. The children take turns acting out parts of the story in pairs. They are laughing; they are asking questions; they are having fun; and they are learning how to work together in a group, how to listen, and how to take turns. On the other side of the room, the other caregiver, who has one year of experience and is working on her associate's degree, is supervising "independent work time." The children are busy in various "centers." Two children are playing house in the play kitchen, where they are dressed in aprons and are preparing meals for their "babies." Two others are building a city out of blocks. Two are working on collages with materials they collected during a nature walk that morning. Two more are playing with musical instruments in the music center. One child is reading a book to a doll in the loft. The caregiver circulates among the centers, asking questions, providing assistance where needed, and commenting positively on the children's work. Although the room is noisy and cluttered, the overall feeling is energetic and joyful. Clearly, both the adults and children are engaged with and are enjoying one another.

Which classroom offers better quality? Which would you choose for your child? To answer these questions, we need to examine the structural and process features of the two settings. While the first classroom would score high on measures of structure, it would score relatively low on measures of process. Conversely, the second classroom would score relatively low on measures of structure but higher on measures of process than the first classroom. Although the ratio of caregivers to children in both rooms was good (1:9), the overall tone of the caregiver-child interactions in the second classroom was more positive than that of the first. Consequently, despite its structural deficits, the overall environment of the second classroom was of higher quality. Notably, this comparison highlights the importance of examining both types of features rather than relying on one or the other in isolation, which is all too often the case in parents' selection of settings and state oversight of child care quality.

Studies have demonstrated that structural features establish the framework that supports the provision of the process features that promote children's development and early education. Most recently, this relationship between structure and process was confirmed in analyses reported by the National Institute for Child Health and Human Development Study of Early Child Care.[10] This study also showed that process features mediate the relation between structural indicators and children's social and cognitive outcomes. As the thought exercise illustrates, structural indicators do not guarantee good process. Although the structural aspects of the second setting were poorer than those in the first setting, they were still sufficient to support good process, creating a better-quality total environment. This scenario illustrates another important point: there is a *minimal* level of structure adequate as a scaffold for good process. However, the precise level and combination of structural features necessary for good process at various ages and in various settings is not yet entirely clear, and research is only now beginning to examine the interplay among these important variables.[11] For example, if caregivers had associate's degrees, ongoing professional training, and compensation equivalent to that of kindergarten teachers, then would it be possible to reduce staff-to-child ratios for preschoolers to 1:15 and achieve equally or more favorable outcomes for children than with 1:8 or 1:10 staffing ratios and less well-trained personnel? How would these various program tradeoffs affect cost? Given the deplorable staff-to-child ratios still allowed by many states for infant and toddler care and the poor educational qualifications for most child care providers serving preschool children, child advocates have been reluctant to raise this issue. But this may be, ironically, one of the keys to breaking the deadlock on quality. For instance, the French system has a much larger number of children per caregiver, and supporters of this system have argued that well-qualified and -compensated caregivers make these higher ratios possible without compromising program quality.

Measurement of Quality

Aspects of the structural environment that are most easily measured (and therefore most easily observed and regulated) include the amount of usable space per child, safety features, sanitary conditions and facilities, the number of toys and educational materials in relation to the number of children, the caregiver-child ratio, and caregiver education and training. Everyone agrees that the physical environment must be sanitary and free of hazards, must be large enough to support children's active play and physical development, must have adequate light and ventilation, and must

include toys, games, and other materials that are in good repair and in sufficient supply to prevent undue competition among children. In addition,
there are measurable but nonregulable dimensions of structure that are
equally important to quality. Key among these is caregiver compensation,
which we will examine later in this chapter.

Because they are less tangible, process features are more difficult to
measure and regulate. Certainly such features as caregiver personality and
the prevailing mood of a child care setting could be noticed by a trained
observer as much as an exposed electrical outlet could be, but quanti-
fying these features is challenging, and they would be extraordinarily
difficult, costly, and time-consuming to assess in all licensed child care
settings.

To help address these challenges, experts at the Frank Porter Graham Child Development Center have developed a set of measures that
are now widely used to assess the overall quality of child care programs.
These measures, which include the Early Childhood Environment Rating Scale (ECERS) for child care centers, the Family Day Care Rating
Scale (FDCRS) for family child care homes, the Infant/Toddler Environment Rating Scale, Revised Edition (ITERS-R), and the School-Age Care
Environment Rating Scale (SACERS) for school-age child care settings,
provide an overall picture of the surroundings of a child care setting.[12]
For example, the ECERS rates aspects of the settings such as personal
care routines, program structure, frequency and quality of caregiver-child
interactions, space and furnishings, and parental involvement on a set of
scales ranging from 1 (inadequate) to 7 (excellent).

Measuring the quality of less formal settings is more complex. While
researchers can readily assess specific common features of each type
of child care, it is more difficult to compare the overall quality of care
provided by a loving relative who is a permanent figure in a child's life
with care provided in a regulated family child care home with a strong
preschool curriculum.[13] For this reason, the NICHD Study of Early Child
Care developed a quality measure, the Observational Record of the Caregiving Environment (ORCE), which was designed to assess quality across
a variety of possible settings, including kith and kin care, family child
care, and center-based care.[14] The ORCE includes both frequency counts
of specific caregiver and child behaviors and qualitative ratings of caregivers' interactions with children. Because it assesses a core set of com-

mon features using setting-specific criteria, it can be used across a wide variety of settings and with children of various ages.

In summary, process measures provide more information about the quality of a given setting than do structural measures. However, they are more time-consuming and expensive to administer than checklists of structural indicators, which can be completed more rapidly and without extensive training. Consequently, quality is most often measured and monitored by focusing on structural features of the environment that are more readily ascertained and more easily regulable.

HOW IS QUALITY MONITORED?

State Licensing and Regulation
In the absence of federal oversight, the establishment and enforcement of child care quality requirements is left to the states. Today, all fifty states and the District of Columbia license center-based child care, and most also license family child care providers.[15] States have established monitoring programs for the enforcement of health and fire codes, as well as, in many cases, supplemental standards to address children's development.[16] However, state licensing and regulation historically have been cursory and have tended to focus almost exclusively on structural features with relatively little attention to process features. As Gallagher and colleagues and, more recently, LeMoine and Morgan have concluded, state regulatory requirements focus on protecting children from physical harm, rather than on the features that promote high-quality adult-child and child-child interactions, which are so central to the child's development and school readiness.[17] Unfortunately, when selecting care for their children parents generally operate under the assumption that they are getting good quality if a child care setting is licensed by the state. This assumption seems reasonable given that we rely on the state to affirm everything from the potability of water from our taps to the qualification of a hairdresser. However, in the case of child care licensing this assumption is wrong, as many states fail to adequately regulate child care at even a minimally acceptable level.

For example, while forty-one states require criminal background checks on caregivers, not all do; and an even smaller number of states (twenty-four) require child abuse and neglect registry checks for caregivers.[18] On the issues most salient to the quality of care—staff-child ratios, group size requirements, and staff qualifications—two thirds of the states failed to require even minimal standards for infants and toddlers in center-based care as recently as 1999.[19] Further, preservice education and training requirements for caregivers are extremely weak. Although most states require unsupervised caregivers to have at least a high school diploma or GED, only twenty states require that caregivers have any background in early care or education in order to be employed as a caregiver in a licensed center.[20] This means that roughly half of the states permit young children to be cared for in large groups by inadequately trained providers with no assurance that those providers do not have a history of child abuse or neglect.

While these figures are alarming, some aspects of state regulation have shown measurable improvement in recent years. For instance, staff-child ratio requirements for infant classrooms in centers have improved substantially. Although only model centers have adopted the 1:3 ratio for infants and toddlers recommended in the FIDCRs and endorsed by the American Academy of Pediatrics, the most common ratio is now 1:4, which at least ensures that a caregiver can rescue the infants in her care from a burning building (one conventional litmus test for the number of infants one adult can care for safely). Further, no state currently permits one adult to care for more than six infants, and the highest permitted ratio for toddlers is 1:9. Similarly, requirements governing group sizes have also improved, with more states limiting group sizes for infants, toddlers, and preschoolers—even though limits still tend to exceed recommended group sizes, particularly for children between eighteen and thirty-six months. Ongoing professional development and training requirements for caregivers and directors have also improved. For example, more states require that caregivers participate in annual training, with ongoing training requirement ranging from three to thirty hours.[21]

Regulation of child care is seriously limited in three additional respects. First, the scope of regulation is incomplete and uneven. Regulation of family child care, for example, is much less stringent than that of center care. Only thirteen states license all family child care homes that care for any unrelated child.[22] Further, informal care, such as kith and kin care, is almost completely exempt from oversight of any kind.[23] This issue is exacerbated by the trend of states encouraging recipients of child care subsidy funds to select these less expensive settings. And as much as 50 percent of the formal child care supply, including religiously affiliated care, is legally exempt from licensure.[24] Second, even when standards are protective, they are not necessarily enforced with sufficient rigor to ensure compliance. Only twenty-two states require annual license renewal, and a majority of states do not conduct unannounced visits.[25] Moreover, not only are there insufficient numbers of licensing staff to provide regular inspections, but licensing staff often lack both the authority and the appropriate training to distinguish between major violations and offenses that can easily be corrected.[26] Finally, potential side effects of increased regulatory stringency have been identified by those investigating the economic aspects of child care.[27] More exacting licensing standards, particularly with respect to grouping and caregiver qualification requirements, can significantly increase providers' operating costs. Because parents make child care choices primarily based on cost and convenience, the child care market does not afford providers much room to pass increased costs along to consumers.[28] Consequently, it is possible for more stringent regulations to have the unintended and ironic effect of giving providers an incentive to "go underground" or of prompting parents to switch to unregulated care.

Accreditation

Along with mandatory licensing requirements, a parallel system of accreditation has developed for child care programs that voluntarily adopt higher standards in order to receive endorsement from a professional body. Although numerous national accrediting organizations exist, the National Association for the Education of Young Children is widely considered the gold standard. NAEYC established its accreditation system in 1985, and the first nineteen programs were accredited in 1986. Currently, nearly ten thousand programs are accredited in all fifty states, Canada, and Puerto Rico, and more than nine thousand are engaged in self-study in preparation for seeking accreditation.[29]

Despite the rapid increase in the number of NAEYC-accredited child care programs, only 7 percent of facilities are accredited.[30] An even smaller percentage of family child care homes is accredited by the National Association for Family Child Care (NAFCC). Although an increasing number of providers are initiating the self-study process that leads to accreditation, the rate of successful completion of the entire NAEYC accreditation process, 52 percent, is fairly low.[31]

Accredited centers have been found to provide better care as measured by objective ratings.[32] However, the low proportion of accredited providers and the relatively low success rate in achieving accreditation suggest several limitations of accreditation as a quality enhancement strategy. The primary issue is simply that many programs cannot, based on the current fees that parents pay, afford the more stringent staff-child ratios and higher levels of staff training required for accreditation. For example, NAEYC standards require a ratio of no more than ten preschoolers to one caregiver, yet licensing requirements in a majority of states exceed this, with several states permitting as many as twenty preschoolers to be supervised by one caregiver. In the highly price-sensitive child care market, it is difficult for providers to cover the costs associated with staffing standards that exceed the minimums set in state licensing requirements. In addition, procedural issues, such as agreement among validators about ratings and the difficulty in maintaining a cadre of validators sufficient to keep up with the demand for initial and follow-up accreditation visits, make the accreditation process a time- and personnel-intensive endeavor. Finally, there is preliminary evidence that the very effort to promote rapid expansion of accredited facilities may have inadvertently contributed to a relaxing of accreditation standards. Findings from several studies that included observational ratings of classroom quality, such as the ECERS, indicate that NAEYC accreditation does not necessarily ensure the achievement of quality. Although accredited providers tended to score significantly higher than nonaccredited providers, a discouraging percentage of accredited classrooms (ranging from 10 to 50 percent in different studies) received a rating of "minimal." In fact, as Whitebook and colleagues found, accreditation combined with higher caregiver compensation and retention of highly skilled caregivers predicts observed quality better than accreditation alone.[33]

To address some of these limitations, NAEYC is currently engaged in an effort to revamp its accreditation system, revising its standards and performance criteria. Assessment instruments and decision-making guidelines will support more effective self-assessment and more efficient validation and help to ensure that accredited centers actually provide high-quality care. States are increasingly promoting accreditation as well by partially offsetting the increased costs of higher-quality care by providing higher reimbursement rates for subsidized care.

HOW BAD IS CHILD CARE IN AMERICA?

Despite advances in our understanding of what constitutes good-quality care and why it is important, the quality of child care in America is distressingly poor. The NCJW reported in 1972 in *Windows on Day Care* that more than 50 percent of child care settings provided worse than mediocre care, with almost all settings providing custodial care.[34] As the NCJW discussed in its 1999 follow-up report, *Opening a New Window on Child Care,* field studies continued to paint an unflattering portrait of the safety—not to mention the quality—of both center and family child care and underscored the importance of improving the structural features that foster optimal early care environments.[35] A comparison of center and family child care quality ratings between the 1970s and the 1990s illustrates the lack of progress in improving the quality of care in these two types of settings (table 2).

Table 2

Changes in Child Care Quality from the 1970s to the 1990s

QUALITY	FAMILY CHILD CARE		CENTER CARE	
	1970s	1990s	1970s	1990s
Poor	14%	13%	30%	12–21%
Fair/Minimally Adequate	48%	75%	43%	67–74%
Good or Excellent	38%	12%	26%	12–14%

Source: Clarke-Stewart & Allhusen (2005), 61.

These data reveal two trends that merit discussion. First, note that the proportion of poor-quality family child care homes has remained relatively stable over time, whereas the proportion of poor-quality child care centers has decreased. This pattern may reflect the less rigorous regulatory oversight that family child care homes receive from state licensing agencies. Second, while the proportion of fair or minimally acceptable care in both types of settings has increased, the proportion of good-quality settings of both types has decreased over time. One plausible interpretation of this pattern is that increased attention to licensing requirements has unfortunately focused regulatory efforts on ensuring minimum quality thresholds rather than encouraging providers to strive for excellence. Indeed, states are beginning to address this drawback by expanding their licensing systems to include both minimum quality thresholds and benchmarks for higher levels of licensing. Such "tiered" systems have shown great promise.

Nevertheless, a discouraging disconnect between knowledge and application persists, and the quality of early care that many or even most children experience is worse than what is considered minimally acceptable. According to the 1995 Cost, Quality and Outcomes (CQ&O) study, only 12 percent of infant or toddler classrooms were rated as "good," with 40 percent being rated as "poor" based on observations of process variables in the classrooms. In 2000, the NICHD Early Child Care Research Network reported that positive caregiving experiences were characteristic for only 28 percent of infants and 22 percent of toddlers in center-based care.[36]

Such findings are distressing, but not surprising, given assessments of the status of specific structural variables. According to the National Child Care Staffing Study (NCCSS) and the National Day Care Study, between 1977 and 1988 the average group size decreased from 17.60 to 14.17, yet the average staff-child ratio in preschool classrooms decreased from one adult per seven children to one adult per eight children.[37] Only 36.2 percent of the child care settings in the NCCSS met FIDCR recommendations for adult-to-child ratio for infant care (1:3), and only 46 percent met the recommended ratio for toddlers (1:5).[38] More recently, the NICHD Early Child Care Research Network found that only 10 percent of infant classrooms met recommended standards for group size, caregiver-to-child ratios, and caregiver training and education. The status of informal care is no less disturbing. Galinsky and colleagues reported in 1994 that 35 percent of family child care settings were found to pose harm to children, and only 9 percent were rated as promoting healthy development. In 2002, Fuller and Kagan rated 71 percent of both kith and kin providers and licensed family child care providers at the minimal level of quality or worse.[39]

Findings such as these have prompted experts and laymen alike to wonder just what percent of child care in America is actually damaging to children's development. In answer to this question, Deborah Vandell and Kim Pierce reviewed the extant literature and determined that approximately 12 percent of care across ages and settings is of poor enough quality to potentially thwart children's development and educational success.[40] Given the information presented above, this appears to be a conservative estimate. Although 12 percent may not sound like much, when multiplied by the number of children in care you have a huge figure and a major reason why 30 to 40 percent of children appear at kindergarten unready to profit from the educational program.

HOW THE CHILD CARE MARKET UNDERMINES QUALITY

Despite a variety of initiatives over the past thirty years to make quality child care more affordable, including a quadrupling of public spending on early care and education in the past decade, it has hardly become accessible to most families. Even for care that is not of high quality, the cost is too great for many parents. In fact, the average cost of full-time care for one child has been found to be almost 20 percent of the average take-home pay for middle-income families, and infant care can consume as much as 30 percent of the average income of low-income families.[41] Indeed, the average annual cost of child care for a four-year-old in an urban child care center is higher than the average annual cost of public college tuition in all but one state, and the cost of infant care is even greater.[42] Thus, the cost of child care during the first four years of life can easily equal the total cost of college tuition at a public institution.

Given the expenses involved, parents unfortunately but understandably tend to focus on cost and factors of convenience (for example, location) when selecting child care rather than on nonprice aspects of care such as quality.[43] For example, Sharon Lynn Kagan, one of the lead authors of the Cost, Quality and Outcomes study, notes that parents spend more time shopping for cars than for child care and are "more likely to look under the hood" of a car than to examine a child care setting.[44] Parents tend to weigh factors such as cost, proximity of the provider to home or work, and hours of operation more heavily than quality of care when selecting child care settings. Moreover, when they do consider quality, they tend to focus almost exclusively on structural indicators—especially licensing—rather than on process indicators.[45] However, depending upon the state, licensing is generally a very poor indicator of the actual quality of a child care setting.

Due to lack of nonprice competition and poorly informed consumers, most economists and political scientists who study child care agree that there is failure in the child care market.[46] Consequently, there is little pressure in the market to improve the quality of available care. For example, in his discussion of market asymmetry, Mocan notes that although it costs only $243 to $324 per child per year (in 1993 dollars) to increase the quality of child care services from mediocre to good, the dynamics of the market provide disincentives for this investment. Given that it costs more to produce higher quality, providers would not have an incentive to increase the quality of their services if they cannot charge higher fees. But, because parents are unable to distinguish between high-quality and low-quality centers, they would not be prepared to pay the higher fees. Thus, "under this scenario, high quality centers would exit the market, average quality falls, and eventually the market is filled primarily with 'lemons' that provide mediocre quality."[47]

What makes good-quality care more expensive? One of the key input costs in child care is labor—the wages and other compensation provided to caregivers. However, child care workers are notoriously undercompensated. In 2002, the average wage for child care workers nationally was $8.32 per hour, or only $17,310 annually. This is not much above the 2002 poverty guidelines of $15,020 for a mother with two children. Moreover, employer-sponsored benefits are minimal for most child care workers, and even among child care centers, the availability of health care coverage for workers is inconsistent. Consequently, the child care labor force is characterized by alarmingly high turnover rates, which diminish the quality of care children receive by reducing the continuity of their caregiving experiences. Indeed, 76 percent of the caregivers employed in California child care centers studied in 1996 and 82 percent of those working in California programs in 1994 were no longer working in those child care centers in 2000.[48] Where do these caregivers go when they leave the child care workforce? While some move out of the child care workforce altogether, the more qualified providers tend to move into the public early education system, where they are better compensated and receive more attractive benefit packages. Thus, the child care workforce is characterized not only by high rates of attrition, but also high rates of selective attrition. This drain of better-qualified and experienced caregivers further erodes the quality of care in the market as better-qualified providers are replaced by less experienced and less well-trained caregivers.

PROMISING INITIATIVES

Despite the appallingly poor quality of care, there are glimmers of hope on the horizon. For example, many states are experimenting with tiered or graduated licensing systems that establish incentives for providers to exceed basic regulatory requirements. In addition, a growing number of states are offering financial incentives for caregivers who seek ongoing training and who stay in the early childhood field. At the federal level, the Department of Defense and the General Services Administration have each established commendable systems of high-quality care for children of their employees. In fact, virtually all DoD child care centers are now accredited by the NAEYC, demonstrating that a high-quality system can be built with sufficient resources and support. Further, a federally sponsored initiative funded by the Bureau of Maternal and Child Health now provides online resources designed to improve consumers' ability to assess quality. We will return to these and other quality-improvement efforts in chapter 8.

In conclusion, over three decades of research have repeatedly underscored the importance of good-quality child care to children's health, safety, development, and educational success. Yet the quality of child care in America is mediocre at best. Consequently, the development and educational potential of an unacceptably large proportion of American children is in jeopardy. To a large extent, this is due to market failures that provide disincentives for parents to select good-quality care and for providers of good-quality care to stay in the business. Although promising initiatives have demonstrated our ability to realize quality improvement, we are still far from an adequate solution to the quality and affordability issue. In the chapters that follow we will return to this dilemma as it pertains to care for children of different age groups.

CHAPTER FIVE

Infant and Toddler Child Care

THE CRITICAL CONUNDRUM

The irreducible core of the environment of early development
is people.

Ross Thompson

HOW DO WE, AS A SOCIETY, best care for children of working parents
during their first three years of life? This is perhaps the most controversial and vexing challenge of child care, and its importance cannot be
overemphasized, as it affects millions of children daily. Among mothers
of infants under age one, 59 percent are in the labor force or are actively
looking for work.[1] Consequently, a large proportion of very young children
are now placed in supplemental child care, sometimes as early as at three
weeks of age.[2] Indeed, according to a 2002 U.S. Census Bureau report,
half of all children born in 2001 were receiving nonparental care by nine
months of age. While roughly one quarter of these children were cared
for by relatives, an almost equal proportion (approximately 24 percent)
were cared for in nonrelative settings, such as family child care and child
care centers. Moreover, more than one third of infants and toddlers spent
thirty-five or more hours per week in some form of nonparental care. As
Larner and colleagues note, this constitutes a "revolution in caregiving,
and it leaves Americans uneasy."[3] This unease is manifest at both the individual and societal levels. At the individual level, new parents anguish
over decisions about whether, when, where, and how much to entrust their
children to a specific caregiving setting. On a societal level, America is
immersed in a heated and value-laden debate over the appropriate role—if
any—of public policy in assisting working parents to address the care-

82

giving needs of their very young children. I assert that while the responsibility for children's early care ultimately rests with parents, there is
an essential role for public policy in enabling working parents to make
real choices about the care their children receive in the first three, most
formative early years.

In this chapter, I begin by examining how the most recent research
on the effects of early child care on children's development informs the
historic debate over the use of nonparental care during the first years
of life—particularly for infants in their first year, the period which has
been the focus of most concern. Next, I describe the conundrum faced
by millions of parents as they struggle with decisions about how best to
care for their infants and toddlers in the absence of adequate resources
to help them do so. Finally, I conclude with recommendations for policy
to ameliorate the sorry state of infant and toddler child care in America
and to better inform parents who must rely on child care for their very
young children.

WHAT WE KNOW AND DON'T KNOW

Over the past five decades, research on the nature of early development
has prompted a major shift in our understanding of infants.[4] Whereas
infants were once viewed as passive and inactive, they are now seen as
complex, capable organisms who play an active role in their own development. We now understand that infants enter the world both vulnerable and capable. They are vulnerable to the extent that they are entirely
dependent upon caregivers for physical protection, sustenance, and the
provision of the cognitively and stimulating environment necessary for
future development. Yet, as evidenced by their innate power to capitalize
on environmental affordances and become, in essence, junior partners in
their own development, they are also miraculously capable. Thus, the first
three years constitute a "sensitive" developmental period and, depending
upon the nature of the dyadic interplay between caregiver and infant,
establish what Shonkoff and Phillips have described as "either a sturdy
or a fragile stage" on which the child later builds competencies across
multiple domains and contexts.[5]

Cross-disciplinary research, aided by neuroscientists' attention to
early brain development, has shown that the four core domains of development—physical, cognitive, social, and emotional—are interrelated

from birth.[6] Infants enter the world needy and dependent, and it is their interaction with the environment—both animate and inanimate—that establishes the foundation for development. In fact, without adequate early environmental input of both types, development can be seriously compromised. Although this process unfolds naturally, it requires that infants' physical, cognitive, social, and emotional needs are adequately addressed within the context of early caregiving relationships.

At the most basic level, infants rely on adult caregivers to meet their physical needs for adequate rest and nutrition, as well as to protect them from physical harm (such as environmental toxins and infectious disease). In addition, infants rely on caregivers for the emotional warmth and physical contact that promote healthy immune system development and for the social and cognitive stimulation that promotes healthy brain development.[7] Thus, early social and emotional interaction with warm, nurturing, and responsive caregivers is essential to healthy development.

All aspects of development occur in a social context. Infants need caregivers who are tuned in to their needs—caregivers who are able to read infants' signals and respond appropriately. Stern has referred to this as "attunement."[8] However, parents do not automatically know what their children's needs are in the first few months; they learn over time. Therefore, one of the first tasks for a new family is for all members—parent and infant alike—to adjust to their new life together. And this takes time: time for the parent and infant to get to know one another, and time to establish the rhythm of the important interactions that will nourish the child's physical, cognitive, social, and emotional growth.

Parents and infants begin to develop a rhythm as they become familiar with one another and establish mutual expectations. These interactions establish the underpinnings of attachment, the emotional bond or sense of security and love that a child develops with the people who care for and love him or her. Research on the development of early attachment has shown that by the beginning of the second year, infants form one of several types of attachment to their primary caregiver, usually but not always the mother. Infants who experience predictable, reliable, and soothing interactions with their caregiver form what are referred to as secure attachments.[9] These securely attached one-year-olds often seek contact with their mothers, cry or fuss when she disappears from sight, and tend to shun strangers. These infants use their caregiver as a secure base from which to explore the environment and exercise autonomy and competency. When stressed by unfamiliar situations or after separation from their caregivers, these infants use their caregiver as an emotional battery charger, enabling them to resume exploratory behavior and play as they did prior to the stressful event. In contrast, infants who do not experience early caregiving interactions as reliable, consistently responsive, and warm are at risk of developing insecure attachments and are less likely to use the caregiver as a secure base for exploration and as a regulatory resource in response to stress.

The importance of secure attachment is that it gives the child a sense of trust, a feeling that the world is a good place. From this foundation the child will be able to explore the world and learn about it, knowing that someone is always there to give protection and guidance. Infants who do not develop secure attachments may not feel safe enough to negotiate their environment. Their learning will suffer, they may have difficulties developing relationships with others in both childhood and adulthood, and they are more likely to develop emotional or behavioral problems.[10]

Although the primary attachment figure is usually the mother, research has shown that babies can form attachments to other significant people in their lives as well, including fathers, grandparents, and siblings.[11] However, just as with the mother, the nature of these attachments —whether secure or insecure—is a function of the history of interactions between caregivers and infants. This relation has important implications for the nonparental care of infants and toddlers, particularly during the first year of life.

In sum, we now have an unprecedented understanding of the dynamic nature of development during the formative first three years—and a profound appreciation of the importance of adult-child relationships for all aspects of development. However, this increased awareness has added to our collective unease about placing infants and toddlers in nonparental child care, even as we rely more heavily on it. As Phillips and Adams noted in a review of child care research for *The Future of Children*, "The juxtaposition of early and extensive exposure to child care with evidence of the importance of early experiences raises compelling questions about the developmental effects of child care as it is now experienced by infants and toddlers in the United States."[12] I now turn to the developmental science that has endeavored to answer these important questions.

Early Opposition to Nonmaternal Care of Infants

For more than three decades, international experts on child development have engaged in an often heated debate over the question of whether child care is bad for babies. Some, such as Mary Ainsworth, Barry Brazelton, Stanley Greenspan, Penelope Leach, and Selma Frieberg, have argued strongly against the use of nonparental care during the first year of life. Others, including Bettye Caldwell, Alison Clarke-Stewart, Jerome Kagan, and Henry Ricciuti, have argued just as strongly that nonparental care is benign or that its effects depend upon the quality of care and the individual characteristics (such as temperament) of the infant. While this often publicly contentious debate has informed our understanding of the issue, it has also inadvertently compounded the guilt already experienced by working parents who must rely on infant child care.

Opposition to nonmaternal care for infants (at least in middle-class families) actually predates the influx of women into the out-of-home workforce in the 1970s. Prior to this dramatic shift in normative patterns of infant caregiving, "evidence" of the harmful effects of nonmaternal care was cited from studies of environmental deprivation.[13] This early literature, however, confused institutional care (with its total absence of parental contact) with supplemental use of nonparental childcare during parents' working hours. Such research on environmental deprivation was, in fact, cited erroneously by conservatives who opposed the 1971 Comprehensive Child Development Act. Indeed, negative perceptions of infant and toddler child care were so deeply ingrained that the Child Welfare League of America's official position was that children should not be exposed to any form of nonmaternal care during their first year.[14] Reflecting on the establishment of the Children's Center at Syracuse University, one of the first early intervention programs to serve infants under one year of age, Alice Honig, professor of human development at Syracuse, recalled how entrenched the opposition to nonparental care for infants was at the time: "In those days . . . we had to get a special waiver from New York state to have infants in group care!"[15]

Nevertheless, early intervention research, such as the Family Development Research Program, which assessed the child outcomes of the Syracuse center, demonstrated that high-quality early child care can buffer infants from the detrimental effects of maternal depression, prematurity and low birth weight, and poverty.[16] This research indicates that rather

than having a negative impact, high-quality early care can have real benefits for children, particularly high-risk children.

The Great Infant Child Care Debate
Despite the reassuring findings about early intervention efforts in the
late 1960s, opposition to nonmaternal care of infants continued to grow
as an increasing number of American women entered the out-of-home
workforce in the 1970s. Fueled by the emergence of research on the child's
attachment to the mother and other adults, this concern focused on the
potentially damaging influences of extended mother-infant separation
during the first year. In an effort to resolve the debate empirically, several
experts conducted extensive reviews of the literature on the effects of
supplemental child care for infants. For example, Thomas Gamble and
I conducted an exhaustive and balanced review of the relevant research,
concluding that while "blanket statements about the benign effects of
infant day care on social competence, especially in males, may be premature," more research was needed and that public policy—particularly
improved regulation of child care quality and paid leave for parental infant
care—was clearly warranted.[17] In 1986, Jay Belsky, a leading developmental psychologist, also reviewed the existing studies and concluded that
out-of-home care had no adverse effects on infants. However, revisiting
the question only one year later, he changed his mind, concluding that
infants exposed to extensive nonmaternal care were at risk of developing
insecure attachments to their mothers and of experiencing poor social
adjustment later in childhood.[18] Belsky's dramatic public reversal reverber-
ated through the field, fueling general concern about the growing number of infants being placed in out-of-home care and prompting vigorous
debate within the scientific community. Perhaps the harshest criticism of
Belsky came from Phillips, McCartney, Scarr, and Howes, who criticized
his selective use of studies and his method of interpreting results. These
authors argued that the existing literature was simply not sophisticated
enough to warrant firm conclusions about the effects of infant care. More
telling was Michael Lamb's 1992 reanalysis of all studies, which concluded
that there was no convincing evidence that nonparental child care negatively impacts typical attachment behavior.[19]

Confusing matters further, another set of findings also started to
emerge suggesting that infants who were placed in child care early in the

first year were more likely than other children to behave aggressively after they transitioned to school.[20] These findings prompted some experts, such as Sir Michael Rutter, to conclude that "group day care may well incline children to be somewhat more assertive."[21] However, others were more circumspect. For instance, Haskins argued that infants who were exposed to child care settings characterized by individualized and child-centered activities might not necessarily be more aggressive—rather they might experience more difficulty adjusting to the context of the traditionally teacher-directed school classroom.[22] This question is still unresolved and has recently received renewed attention.

In response to calls for more rigorous study (along the lines of Phillips and colleagues' work) and to the confusion that experts were sowing among parents, a panel of sixteen child care researchers and experts in early development was convened in 1987. This body of experts was to develop a clear statement on the effects of child care for infants, working under the aegis of the National Center for Clinical Infant Programs (NCCIP, which is now Zero to Three) and with the Institute of Medicine of the National Academy of Sciences. The experts, including Clarke-Stewart and Belsky, disagreed about child care for infants but were charged with formulating a statement of broad consensus about the issue, which was dividing the field. The meeting, which I cochaired with Katherine Barnard, generated a consensus statement underscoring that the impact of an environment—whether in or outside the home—depended on the nature and quality of the setting. The statement also declared that "when parents have choices about the selection and utilization of supplementary care for their infants and toddlers and have access to stable arrangements featuring skilled, sensitive and motivated caregivers, there is every reason to believe that both children and families can thrive . . . [However,] inadequate care poses risks to the current well-being and future development of infants, toddlers, and their families, on whose productivity the country depends."[23]

In addition, the panel called for an investment in research to resolve a set of empirical questions regarding the impact of infant and toddler child care on children's development. This call was met shortly thereafter, when the National Institute of Child Health and Human Development, under the leadership of director Duane Alexander (who had been in attendance at the meeting of experts), committed itself to a national study on infant and toddler child care, chaired by Henry Ricciuti, a leading expert in the field. The resulting study, the NICHD Study of Early Child Care (SECC), is the most comprehensive longitudinal study of child care conducted to date in the United States.

The NICHD Study of Early Child Care

Initiated by NICHD in 1989, the SECC was designed to answer the many questions about the relationship between child care experiences and characteristics and children's developmental outcomes. After a thorough scientific review, the NICHD selected a research team drawn from universities across the United States. This Early Child Care Research Network worked cooperatively to design and implement the study and, in 1991, enrolled a highly diverse sample of children and their families at ten research sites across the country. However, although at least 10 percent of the sample was made up of low-income families, it was not nationally representative and probably did not include a representative distribution of child care settings. Thus, lower-quality child care settings may have been undersampled.

The NICHD SECC utilizes a complex and detailed study design that takes into account many variables, including characteristics of child care settings and family environments. Researchers have assessed children's development using multiple methods (observations, interviews, questionnaires, and tests) and have measured many facets of children's development (social, emotional, intellectual, linguistic, behavioral, and physical). The study has been following over one thousand children, measuring their development at frequent intervals from birth through adolescence. Data from the study are available to researchers outside of the Early Child Care Research Network and have been analyzed by numerous social scientists—including economists and political scientists.

What the Current Research Tells Us

Findings from the NICHD SECC as well as other recent studies have allayed some concerns about infant and toddler child care but have raised others. Many of these findings have been reviewed and discussed in depth in the exceptional publication *Child Care and Child Development: Results from the NICHD Study of Early Child Care and Youth Development*.[24] This emerging literature has produced several salient findings.

- Concerns regarding negative effects of infant care on attachment have been put to rest. The NCHD SECC found no evidence that nonparental care is associated with insecure mother-child attachment. Further, the study found no associations between attachment security and any of the following five child care parameters: age of entry into child care, continuity of care, type of care, quality of care, and cumulative amount of care. Across all outcome measures, parental influences have been shown to be stronger than that of child care.

- As McCartney notes, "the importance of child care quality is one of the most robust findings" to emerge from the child care literature.[25] Good-quality child care has been associated with a range of outcomes, including better cognitive, linguistic, and social development. Moreover, good-quality care can promote the school readiness and success of children from at-risk families.[26]

- Group size is particularly important with respect to health outcomes. Although the long-term implications are unclear, there is consistent evidence that more formal arrangements characterized by larger group sizes, such as child care centers, are associated with greater health risks (for example, respiratory illnesses, middle ear infections, and gastrointestinal illnesses).[27]

- The research findings regarding age of entry and time spent in child care are more complex and troublesome. In addition to the increased risk of health problems, a more controversial set of findings has shown that a greater number of hours spent in care has been associated with the development of later behavior problems. Specifically, the NICHD findings indicated that more time in nonmaternal care arrangements during the first 4.5 years of life was associated with aggression, disobedience, and conflict with adults at 54 months of age and in kindergarten.[28] However, a follow-up study has indicated that this effect of extensive care is no longer evident at third grade and seems to be restricted to center-based care.[29] Further, although children's levels of behavioral problems were elevated, they were within the normal range.

Nevertheless, these findings have prompted vigorous debate over their appropriate interpretation. The controversy is reminiscent of the attachment debates that prompted the NICHD study itself. Researchers point out that the reported effects are relatively modest, that most children with extensive early child care experience do not have behavior problems, and that the direction of effects is not clear—in other words, parents with more difficult children may enroll their children in child care for more hours. Further, Newcombe has criticized the statistical analysis employed by the NICHD researchers.[30] She questions whether their finding would exist if a better form of analysis was conducted. She also points out that the NICHD analysis obscures two factors concerning mothers' out-of-home employment—family income and maternal mental health—that have been associated with more favorable outcomes in children. Though requiring more child care, mothers' longer working hours are associated with more income and less maternal depression. Newcombe argues that any negative effects of longer stays in child care may be offset by these positive influences on child outcomes.

- Research has raised concern about children's stress levels related to nonmaternal care, looking beyond the first year of life, where concern had been centered for thirty-five years. Gunnar and colleagues found elevated cortisol levels in children who experience out-of-home early care in both centers and family child care settings during the second year of life.[31] Cortisol level is a commonly used measure of the amount of stress an individual is experiencing. Under normal circumstances, cortisol levels fluctuate throughout the day, showing a gradual decrease from the morning to afternoon hours. However, under stress, this circadian pattern is reversed. Studies examining such variations are important because exposure to elevated levels of cortisol can affect early brain development, and some studies suggest that dysregulated cortisol reactivity may be associated with compromised social adjustment, such as the externalization of behavior problems.[32]

Gunnar and colleagues have reported that elevated cortisol levels are not found among children in high-quality family child care settings.[33] As for centers, the jury is still out. Gunnar believes that the culprit in the elevated cortisol phenomenon is the toddler's novice attempts to establish early peer relations, efforts that often prove unsuccessful. She recommends as a possible remedy smaller toddler group sizes and a smaller number of children per caregiver.[34] Gunnar's views echo the Zero to Three–Institute of Medicine conference conclusion that it is the quality of the child care site that is critical.

These physiological findings, however, are so new that we have no way of determining their significance—if any—for later development. Gunnar has conceptualized a continuum of stress extending from the many daily unpleasant experiences that are inherent to the human condition to what she calls "toxic stress," which impedes optimal human development. Abuse and neglect would create toxic stress. This definition is reminiscent of the distinction between normative and non-normative stress proposed by Rebecca DelCarmen-Wiggins and Alice Carter.[35] At this time, we have no way of knowing where on Gunnar's stress continuum to place the elevated cortisol level found among infants in out-of-home toddler child care. However, the stress-producing situation that Gunnar describes strikes me as closer to normative than to non-normative or toxic stress.

What Can We Conclude about Infant and Toddler Child Care?

These recent research findings underscore the importance of high-quality infant and toddler child care—both parental and nonparental—to contemporaneous and later development. The preponderance of evidence indicates that exposure to good-quality child care—characterized by warmth, nurturance, and the provision of developmentally appropriate stimulation—promotes both cognitive and linguistic development and may serve a valuable protective function for infants and toddlers whose family environments place them at risk of poor educational outcomes. Given the newness and uncertainty surrounding the elevated cortisol findings, I feel that undue concern about negative physiological effects of early out-of-home child care is not warranted. The findings regarding socioemotional outcomes of infant and toddler child care, particularly with respect to the potential risk of increased aggressive behavior, are more mixed and must be interpreted with caution, though not dismissed, as they generate more questions than answers at this time. We still do not know enough about the extent to which the associations found thus far may persist as children grow older, may be attenuated by as-yet-unexamined moderators, or may be outweighed by offsetting benefits of extensive exposure to multiple caregiving and group socializing contexts. These questions will be addressed by future research, much of which is already under way as part of the NICHD SECC. In the meantime, we echo the conclusion that Phillips and colleagues formulated in the earliest stages of the debate over infant and toddler child care, that responsible scientists still need to say, "We don't know—the evidence is inconclusive."[36] And, because we don't know, as Mary Lang and I argued in 1991, "We must proceed with utmost caution."[37]

The current debate over possible negative socioemotional effects of early entry into many hours of nonparental child care is reminiscent of the earlier debate over attachment and infant child care. Indeed, many of the same investigators are involved, and once again, special issues of scientific journals have been devoted to examining the issue in depth. As before, some experts have made strong recommendations against the use of nonparental care for infants during the first year.[38] However, such calls, while well intended, ignore the anguishing conundrum faced by the many parents who *must* work out of economic necessity, and who must therefore place their infants and toddlers in some form of nonparental care.

In sum, I concur with Ron Lally, who notes that "the answer to 'Should a child under twelve months of age be in care outside the home?' is 'It depends.' It depends on the interaction of the quality of the child care into which the child is placed, the quality of the home care where the child resides, and the impact on family life of the economic, societal, and personal pressure that family members feel to place their young child in care . . . We would love family members to have the choice to stay home, and also the option of high quality care available to them if they need or desire it."[39]

THE CONUNDRUM

In light of the knowledge we now have regarding infant and toddler child care, it is clear that parents who need nonparental care for their young children should invest in good-quality settings. However, it is not that simple. First, there is a paucity of infant and toddler child care. Second, what care exists is often of questionable quality. Finally, few parents can afford high-quality infant and toddler child care.

Availability of Care

The availability of child care has certainly increased in recent years. As of 2002, there were more than 113,000 licensed centers and 300,000 regulated family child care homes across the nation, reflecting a roughly 500 percent increase in licensed centers and a 200 percent increase in regulated family homes since 1979.[40] There is also an extensive underground child care market composed of uncounted and unregulated family child care homes that are not reflected in these numbers. However, access to this child care—both formal and informal—is uneven. Pockets of unavailability of licensed care exist, particularly for infants and toddlers, children with special needs, and children whose families work nontraditional hours. Further, formal child care is less available in low-income neighborhoods, and informal care may be less prevalent than previously thought. Moreover, part-time care is particularly scarce, presenting a crucial problem to parents who seek to minimize their use of nonparental care for financial reasons or out of concern about potential negative effects on their babies' development.[41]

Quality of Care

The tragic reality is that the majority of available care falls short of what experts consider optimal for children's early development. For instance, one study of family child care—the setting most frequently selected for infants and toddlers—found high-quality care in only 12 percent of the family child care settings surveyed. Moreover, the same study found high-quality care in only 1 percent of relative care and inadequate care in 69 percent of these settings.[42] The status of quality in formal center-based arrangements is no more encouraging. In a landmark study of child care in four states, Helburn and colleagues found that only 8 percent of infant and toddler classrooms provided developmentally appropriate quality, whereas 40 percent were found to provide such poor-quality care that children's health and safety were put at risk.[43]

Affordability of Care

Although public spending on early care and education has quadrupled over the past decade, quality child care has hardly become affordable for most families. Affordability is often the major obstacle for families seeking good-quality infant and toddler child care. The average annual cost of child care for a four-year-old in an urban child care center is higher than the average annual cost of public college tuition in all but one state, and the cost of infant care is even greater. According to the 2006 study on child care expenses *Breaking the Piggy Bank: Parents and the High Cost of Child Care,* the average child care fees for one infant can range from

$3,803 to $13,480 per year, depending upon the setting and whether it is accredited.[44] Even for care that is not of high quality, the cost is too great for many parents, approaching the same proportion of income as rent or mortgage payments.

At the same time, in the absence of paid parental leave, most parents can ill afford to stay home to care for their infants and toddlers. Consequently, parents are left with essentially one option: select the most affordable care available, regardless of the quality of that care and its potentially detrimental effects.

MOVING FORWARD: RECOMMENDATIONS FOR POLICY AND RESEARCH

These issues have received much public attention. Books and articles abound on the "mommy wars" between working and stay-at-home mothers and on the guilt experienced by working parents who must rely on less-than-optimal child care. This topic has caused heated debate among researchers, practitioners, policy makers, and political pundits. Nevertheless, we have made pitifully little progress toward putting the knowledge at hand into action or toward the creation of meaningful child care policy for infants and toddlers. Moreover, the ongoing debates regarding potentially adverse effects on later development continue to exacerbate working parents' confusion and guilt.

To address these problems, I make the following recommendations:

1. *Strengthen efforts to improve the quality of child care for infants and toddlers, with particular emphasis on better addressing the unique needs of infants during the first year of life.* Increased attention should be paid to both the health issues around group care of infants (for example, protection from infectious diseases such as upper respiratory infections) and the importance of individualized, stable, nurturing, and stimulating caregiving environments. One large step toward this goal would be to strengthen regulatory requirements, monitoring, and enforcement.

2. *Increase consumer information so that parents are able to make better-informed decisions as consumers of child care.* Despite the controversies regarding the potential adverse effects of infant care, there is general consensus about what constitutes good-quality care and how such care

can be identified. Consumer education regarding these important indicators is vital in that it would empower parents to make better-informed child care choices based on quality as well as price. Such a change in consumer behavior could infuse the child care market with increased nonprice competition by increasing demand for higher quality care—a market dynamic that is sorely lacking now.[45] While this alone is not sufficient to remedy the market failure, it is a necessary ingredient of any meaningful solution.

3. *Provide parents with more resources to access good-quality care.* Parents need both better information about possible caregiving options (improved resource and referral networks) and the financial means to purchase good-quality care for their infants and toddlers. As I will discuss in chapters 7 and 8, this proposition is complex and expensive and will require both private- and public-sector investment (for example, paid parental leave).

4. *Increase parental choice.* Parents are the most important agents in their children's development and must have realistic options to help them make child care decisions that are in the best interest of their child and family. In addition to better access to good-quality care, parents need improved access to part-time care options and an improved ability to consider parental care if they so desire. These changes will require paying attention to the market dynamics that conspire to make part-time infant care so scarce, as well as strengthening the Family and Medical Leave Act so that all parents are covered by at least partial wage replacement should they decide to stay home with their infants (see chapter 7).

5. *Study the concurrent and long-term effects of child care on infants.* Although our knowledge has greatly improved since the Zero to Three–Institute of Medicine panel convened in 1987, the research to date has raised new questions. Specifically, research must continue to help us understand:

- whether the elevated cortisol among toddlers in full-time child care predicts later adjustment problems or is an adaptive, normative stress response to the demands of a group-caregiving environment;
- how to interpret the association of extended early care and higher levels of behavioral problems, and whether these findings persist through adolescence;

- whether there is an optimal age at which to transition infants into nonparental care, and whether infants benefit more from gradually increased hours over the first year rather than abrupt entry into full-time care;
- how to identify the most cost-effective and pragmatic investments in quality improvement and parental choice.

The available literature underscores the need for good-quality early care in a variety of settings flexible enough to meet the wide range of family needs and preferences. Further, it points to the pressing need for parents to have better access to affordable, good-quality care during their children's first three years of life, and to the critical importance of enabling parents to have choices, particularly regarding whether to care for infants at home during the first year. Despite more than three decades of effort, we are woefully short of meeting these goals. However, as I discuss in chapter 8, there has been some promising progress which might be the first step toward a more satisfactory long-term solution.

CHAPTER SIX

Preschool-Age Child Care

I fear that if arguments for preschool continue to rest so much
on the alleged promises of early academic training, the result
may be that we trade one set of stressors for another . . . One
can only hope that, as increasing numbers of public preschool
programs become a reality, some measure of common sense
will prevail.

Judith Warner

TODAY, THERE ARE MORE THAN 4.5 million three- and four-year-old
children with a working single parent or two working parents.[1] How these
children spend the day while their parents are at work has consequences
for their development, and the current system has implications for future
policy. I will consider four types of arrangements for preschoolers: full-day
child care settings (including centers, family child care providers, relatives, and babysitters); private preschools; state-funded preschools, operating in forty states; and Head Start. For each type of arrangement I will
examine how well positioned it is to meet the often competing demands
of being a service for working parents and being a developmental context
for young children. I conclude this chapter with recommendations for
policy to resolve the child care challenges of preschoolers, with specific
attention to the potential of the School of the 21st Century.

While the term "preschool" refers to any child under the typical
school age of five years, my focus in this chapter is on three- and four-
year-old children. There are roughly 7.6 million three- and four-year-olds
in the United States, and over 80 percent of them participate in nonparental child care arrangements on a regular basis.[2] The additional fact that
43 percent of preschool-age children experience two or more child care
arrangements during the week complicates our ability to neatly catego-
rize their experiences.[3] Further, the lines between arrangements blur,

98

and types of child care can overlap. For example, high-quality child care settings can provide a preschool experience. The difficulty of classifying types of arrangements is further evidence of the need for a workable system. We draw data from multiple sources to estimate the percentage of children in each type of arrangement.

Typically, data are collected on a child's primary arrangement, neglecting the fact that more than 40 percent of children are regularly experiencing more than one arrangement. For example, when employed mothers are asked to identify the child care arrangement their preschool-age child spends the most time in, they respond as follows: 45 percent center-based care, 18 percent parent care, 17 percent relative care, 14 percent family child care, and 6 percent nanny or babysitter care.[4] It is unclear what proportion of the children in center-based care also attends preschool.

More than 40 percent of three-year-olds and 65 percent of four-year-olds were enrolled in a preschool education program in 2002. Within this group, approximately 980,000 children were served by just over fifty unique state-funded prekindergarten systems operating in forty states. In 2005, 906,000 children were served by Head Start. Others still were served by private preschools supported by parent fees.[5]

Just over half of three- and four-year-old children with full-time employed mothers attended preschool, compared to 44 percent of children whose mothers did not work outside the home.[6] This statistic underscores two important points. First, only half of employed mothers chose to place their children in preschool, suggesting that preschool is not a universally viable child care solution. In fact, evidence suggests that preschool and Head Start programs may serve as barriers to employment if they fail to provide child care services during the gap between preschool operating hours and the typical workday. Indeed, most working parents use arrangements that wrap child care around part-day preschool programs or programs that provide services that more closely align with the work day (for example, full-day child care centers or family child care centers). Second, almost half of stay-at-home mothers enrolled their children in preschool, further distinguishing it from child care as a service for working parents. Why did these mothers decide to enroll their children if they had no child care needs to be met? Research has yet to empirically address this question, although I suspect that parents who are not in the paid labor force do in fact have a need for child care and perhaps also recognize the value of preschool as a developmental context.

CHILD CARE, PREKINDERGARTEN, AND HEAD START: WHAT'S THE DIFFERENCE?

In the first chapter, I identified child care, in its most basic form, as a service for working parents, a container to keep children safe while parents work. More specifically, child care is the act of "physically caring for a child and meeting his or her basic health and safety needs."[7] Early education settings inherently provide child care for the children in attendance, but not all child care settings provide early education. High-quality child care is indistinguishable from early education, apart from hours of operation, as it meets a child's developmental and educational needs while guaranteeing basic health and safety. But there is massive variability in the quality of child care, and significant numbers of children experience care that does not meet this standard.

The "early education" label applies to child care settings that are of high quality (typically center-based) and that "use developmentally appropriate curricula to foster a child's cognitive, social, and emotional development."[8] Historically, the exemplars of this arrangement have been private preschools, typically operating on a half-day schedule a few times a week and paid for with parent fees. At the wealthy end of the income spectrum, families pay highly for private preschools. (Consider the lengths that one wealthy and powerful banker took to secure high-quality preschool for his children. In 2002, Jack Grubman, respected stock analyst at Citigroup in New York, bragged in an email that he upgraded his rating of AT&T stock to do his boss Sandy Weill a favor. What did Grubman want in return? Grubman wanted Weill to use his influence to help him gain admission for his preschool-age twins into the prestigious 92nd Street Y preschool center.) While private preschools have historically focused on socialization, the recent public and media focus on school readiness has led many to integrate an educational component.

For families at the other end of the income spectrum, state-funded preschools and prekindergartens have rapidly expanded. Between 1989 and 2005 the number of states offering pre-K programs grew from twenty-seven to forty.[9] Of the states that have public pre-K classrooms, the majority focus on children who live in poor families and are considered the most "at risk."[10] The general purpose of these pre-Ks is to help children get ready for the learning opportunities that will be presented when they begin formal schooling. The specific definition and concept of what "school readiness" entails varies across states.[11]

Head Start is another early education program, launched by the federal government during the War on Poverty to help impoverished preschool-age children begin school on equal footing with their more affluent peers. Head Start has grown from an eight-week summer program to one that spans the academic year. Since its inception in 1965, it has served over 23 million children and families.[12] Congress has paid careful attention to ensuring Head Start's effectiveness in working toward its legislated goal of improving school readiness. All Head Start centers are required to participate in a monitoring system that involves performance standards and annual self-assessment. The Head Start Impact Study provides evidence that Head Start classrooms are of high quality: their mean ECERS rating is 5.2, corresponding to "good" quality.[13]

Head Start eligibility is generally restricted to children living below the federal poverty line, an income of $20,000 for a family of four in 2006. Currently, Head Start serves only 50 to 60 percent of the target population. Although Head Start is legislated to serve three- and four-year-olds, in 2002, 71 percent of Head Start attendees were enrolled for only a single year prior to kindergarten.[14]

For parents, the most important practical differences between private preschools, public pre-Ks, and child care may be hours of operation and cost. Preschool settings generally do not offer wraparound child care and thus do not accommodate parent's work schedules. Preschools, pre-K programs, and Head Start centers typically are closed during the summer, on weekends and holidays, and after 2:30 PM. Notable exceptions to this pattern include efforts in Connecticut and Ohio to integrate early education and child care into full-day, full-year programs. Additionally, more than half of Head Start centers now operate for a full day.[15] Still, for the vast majority of working parents, Head Start is not a solution to their child care needs. Many middle-class Americans have incomes neither low enough to qualify for targeted programs nor high enough to pay for private preschool programs and high-quality child care.[16] The federal government specifies that only families with incomes up to 85 percent of their state median income (SMI) are eligible to qualify for a subsidy through their state's Child Care and Development Fund (see chapter 3). Of the 15 million families that qualify under this federal definition, however, only 14 percent receive any assistance.[17] States have the freedom to move the eligibility limit down (such that, for example, families earning up to 70 percent of the SMI qualify), adjust copayment levels, adjust provider reimbursement levels, change the timing of payments to providers, and make a host of other decisions that affect who qualifies for CCDF and who chooses to participate.

Despite the overlap in purpose of child care and early education programs, the terms used to describe them reflect different underlying values and thus carry implications for public and political support. Early education, including pre-K and Head Start, enjoys broad public support. An opinion poll of voters and leaders from business, organized labor, government, religion, media, education, and child care in Massachusetts found that 100 percent believed that education should begin before kindergarten. A national survey by Opinion Research Corporation reported that four out of five respondents favored expanding Head Start programs to serve additional eligible children.[18] Public expenditures on child care, on the other hand, invoke controversy. In fact, recent polls reveal that respondents see education as benefiting all children, and thus constituting a sound and fair public investment, but see child care the financial responsibility of the family.[19] Lakoff and Grady succinctly highlight the distinction: "Education is about kids' needs; day care is about parents' needs."[20]

QUALITY OF PRESCHOOL-AGE CHILD CARE

A solid base of research tells us that the quality of an early child care environment "can pose benefits or risks to early development . . . and holds the potential to redirect developmental trajectories."[21] Children in poor-quality care are more likely to show delays in language, reading, and other cognitive skills and are more likely to display aggressive behaviors.[22] The cost isn't borne by these children alone—all of society suffers when low-quality care compromises the development of our youngest citizens. An estimated 30 to 40 percent of children arrive at kindergarten unprepared.[23] This startlingly high rate stems from children lacking access to preschool programs or experiencing poor-quality care.[24]

Nearly every policy, program, or piece of legislation includes a quality requirement. Nonetheless, there is significant variation in quality across the typology of early care and education arrangements. One trend emerges, though: highly regulated early education programs tend to operate in a narrower and higher range of quality than either unregulated child care centers or family child care arrangements. Head Start centers, for example, are highly regulated and of good quality according to the ECERS rating. However, even within public pre-K classrooms, there is wide variability in how children spend their time and thus in the educational benefit they receive. Among the state-funded pre-K classrooms in the National Center for Early Development and Learning (NCEDL) Multi-State Pre-K Study, only about 25 percent of classrooms serving four-year-olds provided students with appropriately high levels of emotional and instructional support.[25]

Full-day center-based child care is typically rated a little better than halfway between "minimal" and "good" on the ECERS (averaging a score of 4.26 out of 7).[26] Child care of this quality provides a setting where children's basic needs are met but where there are limited opportunities for learning, individual attention, or language stimulation. There is significant variation, though, with 24 percent of centers scoring within the "good" to "excellent" range (5 to 7).[27] One study found that only 34 percent of observed center-based classrooms for three-year-old children met quality standards (including child-adult ratio, group size, teacher training and education).[28]

Family child care providers typically are less well regulated and provide lower-quality care than centers. According to the Study of Children in Family Child Care and Relative Care published by the Families and Work Institute, only about 13 percent of unregulated family child care providers are of good quality, and one third of family child care programs are of such poor quality that they endanger children's development.[29] This study examined 226 family child care homes and found that a mere 8 percent were "good," while 58 percent were "adequate/custodial" and 36 percent were "inadequate."[30]

Overall, an alarming amount of child care fails to meet basic health and safety requirements.[31] A recent study by the Government Accountability Office found that thirty-eight states exempt family child care providers from regulation and only one fourth of states maintained the recommended caseload for inspectors.[32] The failure at the state level to assure basic health and safety in child care has been noted in multiple national studies. And even when they are achieved, these minimal requirements emphasize the belief that child care providers are responsible for keeping a child from harm rather than providing an environment that enhances development.[33]

There are three conclusions to draw from this literature. First, we have a growing knowledge base of what features a system needs to have to provide high-quality, affordable child care. Second, the current system fails to meet the needs of working parents. Third, and most alarming, the current system fails to meet the developmental needs of our youngest citizens.

ADDRESSING THE CHILD CARE NEEDS OF PRESCHOOLERS

The course of policy making for preschool-age child care depends again on the three necessary circumstances for changing or creating policy: a pervasive sense that a real problem exists, an effective lobby that advocates for a solution, and receptive decision makers in the legislative and executive branch (see chapter 2). Available evidence indicates that a problem is perceived in the realm of early education but not in child care for preschoolers (see chapter 3).[34] A nationwide poll conducted by the National Institute for Early Education Research (NIEER) in 2001 found that nearly 90 percent of respondents agreed that there should be state-funded, universally available preschool.[35] Likewise, as noted earlier, in a poll of leaders from business, labor, government, media, and education communities in Massachusetts, Blood reported that 100 percent believed that education should begin before kindergarten.[36] Child care, on the other hand, has been and continues to be viewed as a private family responsibility.

Friends in the Right Places
Highly organized and effective advocacy groups have been lobbying for preschool programs but not for child care. Advocates for preschool include Hollywood figures, educators, and Fortune 500 CEOs.[37] Much of the momentum for this group comes from the generalization (sometimes inappropriate) of the effects of some excellent remedial programs for economically disadvantaged children.

Perhaps the most famous and oft-cited early intervention program is the High/Scope Perry Preschool. From 1962 to 1967, the High/Scope Perry Preschool Program in Ypsilanti, Michigan, identified a sample of

123 low-income African American children who were identified as at high risk of school failure because of low intelligence test scores and family situations. Half of these children were randomly assigned to attend a two-year preschool program that operated for about two and a half hours a day, and their parents received home visits from a teacher once a week. The other children received no such services. Programs were of unusually high quality: all teachers had a bachelor's or master's degree, child to staff ratios of 8 to 1 were maintained, and the weekly home visits fostered parent involvement. Researchers have followed the two groups of children for the past four decades and found that by the time participants were nineteen years old, those who had received services were more likely to have graduated from high school, less likely to be on welfare, and less likely to be arrested, and, among females, those who had received services had fewer pregnancies than did nonparticipants. At age forty, effects persisted: former program preschoolers had higher earnings and had committed fewer crimes than had nonpreschoolers.[38]

Support from the Business Community
The real excitement about the High/Scope Perry Preschool came from cost-benefit analyses conducted by economists. They concluded that based on savings to society in the form of lower rates of special education placement, grade retention, lower crime costs, lower welfare costs, and higher earnings and tax contribution, the High/Scope Perry Preschool returned an estimated $17 savings for each $1 invested.[39] The Committee for Economic Development (CED), an independent research and policy organization of 250 business leaders, seized on these findings and published an influential report, "Preschool for All: Investing in a Productive and Just Society." The authors called for a partnership among business, parents, and the public sector to deliver free, high-quality preschool for all children ages three and over at an estimated price of $25 billion to $35 billion. This group used the early intervention research to make a business case for federal and state policy makers "to undertake a new national compact to make early education available to all children age three and over." Rolnick and Grunewald calculated the internal rate of return of the Perry Preschool Program to be 16 percent (adjusted for inflation). Further, 80 percent of the return went to the public, rather than to individuals in the program. Compared with other public investments, even those in the

private sector, an early childhood development program seemed like a good buy. The authors concluded, "We have argued that in the future, any proposed economic development list should have early childhood development at the top. The return on investment from early childhood development is extraordinary, resulting in better working public schools, more educated workers, and less crime."[40] Rob Dugger, the chairman of the CED's Invest in Kids Working Group and managing director of the Tudor Investment Corporation, warned, "We are condemning ourselves to a future of slow economic growth and high crime by not attending to what has been well known. There are huge fiscal implications to not having enough ready-for-school children."[41]

It is unrealistic to expect public early care and education systems to achieve the level of quality observed in model programs such as Perry Preschool. Public preschool programs have lower funding, less attention from program designers, and more universal admission criteria. Moreover, typical preschool programs differ from high-quality intervention programs in critical ways. It is unlikely that a preschool program mounted in the public schools could be of comparable quality and intensity. For example, in the Perry Preschool all teachers had at least bachelor's degrees; in state-funded preschools only half of head teachers have bachelor's degrees. It is critical that the level of program quality provided is commensurate with desired program results. Many advocates and policy makers have come to expect that a preschool program implemented with any level of quality and funding will achieve the same results. This belief is not realistic.[42] While the movement for universal pre-K (or UPK) has been accelerating, it is critical that it is seen in context. Preschool is just one piece of the solution to the child care needs of parents of three- and four-year-olds. Parents still need care for their children before and after school and during vacations and summer breaks.

Receptive Policy Makers

Again, state and federal policy makers are receptive to early education programs but less so to child care. UPK hit the national agenda during the course of the 2000 presidential election. In a September 2000 appearance on *The Oprah Winfrey Show,* then-candidate Al Gore asserted, "My number-one proposal is to have high-quality universal preschool for every child in every family, in every community." The female-dominated

Chicago audience applauded wildly. Within Gore's presidential platform was a ten-year, $50 billion proposal for a "universal preschool initiative that will make high-quality preschool available to every four-year-old in America and expand coverage to three-year-olds." Gore argued, "Most learning takes place in the first few years of life, and if kids get off to a good start before they ever get to kindergarten, the chance for them to succeed in life, to have good jobs, to lead fulfilling lives, is greatly enhanced."[43] Gore proposed distributing matching grants to states, which would be responsible for implementing preschools for four-year-olds.

Targeted or Universal

A debate that is currently raging is whether preschool programs funded by the government should be targeted or universal. Proponents of a targeted approach cite the literature to argue that the greatest benefits accrue to the most disadvantaged children. They ask, "Why should society provide pre-K to middle-class children who do not appear to have as much to gain and whose parents are likely already paying for early education?"[44]

Targeted programs may yield the greatest economic efficiency but may risk equity in comparison with universal programs. Proponents of a universal approach argue that: (1) evidence indicates that all children, poor and nonpoor alike, can benefit from quality preschool experiences;[45] (2) integration of children from diverse socioeconomic, racial, and ethnic backgrounds is beneficial for all children; (3) a universal program would engender a broad-based constituency, more politically powerful than the poor; and (4) a universal approach is the only equitable option. Supporters of universal programs point out that requiring parents to pay a fee calibrated to family income could lessen some of the opposition.[46]

The way I see it, publicly supported preschool available to all children is the best strategy to ensure that everyone has the chance at a strong start in elementary school. The biggest problems among targeted programs are inequitable distribution of resources and failure to address the needs of middle-class Americans. Eligible children are moving targets as families move into and out of poverty. How can a child living a few dollars a year above 85 percent of the state median income be any better off than his neighbor living a few dollars below? Perhaps the most serious problem is that if the goal is to improve early development in order to address gaps in school readiness, there is no clear line separating needy from nonneedy children.[47] On that point, Steve Barnett, director of the NIEER, argued at the 2004 Conference of the MIT Workplace Center, "If we want to deal with the high school dropout problem, if we want to deal with the school failure problem, we can't just deal with poor kids. If you solved those problems for poor kids, most of the problem would still be there, because most of the problem is with kids above the poverty line."[48] Although they cost more than targeted programs, universal programs can be sound economic policy and maximize the well-being of society as a whole.[49] Barnett went on to argue, "The truth is that programs for the poor are too often poor programs. However, the point is not simply that public support for such programs is so weak that they are politically threatened. Rather it is that such programs are so incompletely and inadequately implemented that they forgo much of their benefit, and thus universal programs are better purely on grounds of economic efficiency."[50]

The debate between universal and targeted approaches to pre-K is predicated on the assumption that government-provided pre-K is on the horizon. The debate is no longer whether there should be a government role in the daily lives of preschoolers, but rather what shape that role should take.[51] Pre-K is only part of the solution, though. The reality is that all parents, especially low-income parents, need child care services so they can support their families. At the same time, children need high-quality early education opportunities.

Ten years ago, before the wave of support for pre-K, I wrote, "Educators in several states point to parental pressure for all-day kindergarten as evidence of the value parents place on early education, but I believe that they have misread this demand. What many parents are expressing is less a burning desire for preschool education than their desperate need for quality day care."[52] We now know that preschools and even all-day kindergarten programs are not sufficient to meet the child care needs of today's working families. What is needed is a feasible solution that adjusts societal institutions to meet the dual needs of parents' work schedules and children's development.

The School of the 21st Century

Today, the most promising solution is to create a hybrid infrastructure that integrates child care and education, leveraging public and private resources, and that positions public schools as a hub. The School of the

21st Century (21C) is an example of a comprehensive program that successfully brings child care into the educational sphere. I developed the concept of 21C schools, and Matia Finn-Stevenson, also at Yale, led the national implementation in 1988. To date, 21C schools have been implemented in more than 1,300 schools around the country.

The 21C program endeavors to provide quality child care and preschool experiences for all children, while embracing a whole-child approach that nurtures not only cognitive development but also physical and mental health and social-emotional behaviors that are important to successful schooling. More than a program, though, 21C encompasses an approach to providing programs and services in the public schools to the families of children in their first twelve years of life. It was established in 1987 to create a system of child care and education by taking advantage of the natural synergies between early education and child care. Specific features of 21C include full-day, year-round preschool education with wraparound child care for three- and four-year-old children; care before and after school for children through age twelve; care during school vacations through sixth grade; outreach to family child care providers and other community-based providers; referrals for any services families may need; and mental, physical, and nutritional health and education.[53] The preschool component of a 21C-based approach would provide full-day, full-year preschool for two years, located in or administered by the public schools.[54]

The 21C program has been implemented in over 1,400 schools in twenty states. Each school develops a set of services to best meet the needs of the community. On the effectiveness of 21C, Lisbeth Schorr, the director of the Harvard University Project on Effective Interventions, says, "One of the key attributes of effective programs is that they don't clone; rather they replicate the essence of a successful intervention while allowing each new setting to adapt many of its components to that locale's particular needs and strengths. I can think of no better example of this attribute in action than the Schools of the 21st Century."[55]

Along with Matia Finn-Stevenson, director of the School of the 21st Century, I have identified six guiding principles, derived from research on effective interventions, that underscore the 21C approach.[56]

1. Child care is an important environment where young children grow and learn. The current nonsystem of care does not promote the optimal

development and school readiness of all children. A child care system must therefore become a national priority and part of the structure of our society, as is the case with education.

2. Good-quality care should be accessible to every child regardless of their racial, ethnic, or socioeconomic group. We should not accept the present two-tier system, in which some children receive good-quality care and others do not.

3. Child care practices must be based on a whole-child approach that attends to all developmental pathways: social, emotional, physical, and cognitive.[57] All aspects of growth and development are interdependent and occur simultaneously, so it is imperative to nurture all of these areas. This principle highlights the contributions of the child care setting to a child's developmental course.

4. To ensure developmental continuity, parents and caregivers must cooperate. Parental involvement is important not only in preschool, but also when children are in elementary school.[58]

5. Child care providers must be recognized, supported, and paid appropriate wages, as they are responsible for the quality of care that children receive.

6. A national child care system must be flexible and adaptable. Because family dynamics and needs are diverse, a universal system must provide a range of choices for child care. Inherent in this principle is the recognition that there are differences not only among families and children, but also among communities.

These guiding principles not only shape the theoretical framework of Schools of the 21st Century, but also provide a context for state and local implementation. Existing data indicate that 21C has been successful in providing schools with an opportunity to share a vision for high-quality child care and education while simultaneously providing them with the support and flexibility to implement a program that is responsive to their community's needs. In a national study of 21C schools, which included school districts in five states, researchers found that 21C preschool programs had a mean score of 5.7 on the ECERS, above the threshold for good-quality care (5). The study also revealed highly child-centered programs, with teachers reporting an average of more than two hours a day on child-initiated activities. Preschool teachers' median teaching experience was 8.5 years, 80 percent of teachers held a bachelor's or master's degree, and staff turnover was low, with teachers reporting a median of seven years working in the 21C program.[59]

There is extensive variation in the ways schools and districts choose to finance their 21C programs. Some schools are able to fund preschool-age and school-age child care components entirely through fees paid by parents on a sliding scale calibrated to family income. In less affluent communities, some 21C services are paid for through local, state, and federal funds. Existing sources of funds used to finance 21C programs include 21st Century Community Learning Centers, the Child Care and Development Fund, Head Start, and Title I of the Elementary and Secondary Education Act. Partnerships with local foundations, businesses, and community organizations are also critical.

Combining care and education within public schools is attractive for multiple reasons: it provides universal access to early care and education, regardless of family income or background; it offers continuity across the early years of school; it facilitates an earlier relationship between parents and school; it fosters improved public attitudes towards child care as a component of the education system and thus frames child care as deserving of high standards; and it leverages underutilized physical assets (such as school buildings) in providing care and education.

Public Schools and Child Care

Careful consideration of the role of public schools in the provision of care and education first arose in the aftermath of the failed 1971 CCDA bill. In August 1974, Mondale and Brademas introduced the Child and Family Services Act to an initially lukewarm reception. In the course of hearings on the bill, Al Shanker, then president of the American Federation of Teachers (AFT), testified before Congress that public schools should be the sponsor of any national child care program. He wrote in his weekly *New York Times* column on September 8, 1974, "The responsibility for the enlarged program [of early care and education] should be borne by the public schools."[60] Shanker's logic was that expansion of early care and education services was inevitable, and that the unorganized expansion of early care and education centers would be an inefficient use of taxpayer dollars that would result in highly duplicative and variable services. Public schools already enjoyed a place in American society and could administer a large program.[61] In 1976, the AFT articulated this sentiment in a 123-page manual for teachers titled *Putting Early Childhood and Day Care Services into the Public School: The Position of the American Federation of Teachers and an Action Plan for Promoting It.*

Prior to the launch of Schools of the 21st Century, the question of whether schools could actually implement child care programs was an empirical one. In 1978, James A. Levine took up this topic, profiling five communities in order to highlight different dimensions of the debate about child care and public schools. Although Levine ultimately opposed exclusive sponsorship by schools, he saw the potential of their involvement in child care and regarded it as unwise to ignore the possible role of schools. While the needs and resources of communities have changed since then, Levine offered four reasons why the "public school question" is likely to persist.[62] First, schools and teacher unions are a powerful political lobby for child care. Gilbert Steiner, an economist at the Brookings Institution, wrote in his book *The Children's Cause* that "renewal of the child development issue and a national program [will only occur] if self-interest specifically joins social altruism as a driving force" and that "anxiety of public school teachers to protect their job opportunities by reaching for younger clients to keep the pool full" fits the bill. Reminding child advocacy groups of their limited power relative to the powerful teachers' unions, he noted, "While not all members of the [child advocacy] coalition understand the choice as limited to a public school bill or no bill, that really is the choice." Second, schools are a major institution for all children in our society, regardless of family income or ethnicity. Public schools are not perceived as carrying the stigma of welfare or family pathology.[63] Third, even in 1978, schools were increasingly offering part-day preschool programs to children and their families. Fourth, schools represent a major resource and a major financial investment in most communities.

While putting child care in the schools is feasible and pragmatic, it is not without risk. Can schools address the failures (asymmetric information and externalities) characteristic of the private child care market? More simply, what assurance do we have that schools can reliably produce high-quality preschool and wraparound child care programs? Noted economists Suzanne Helburn and Barbara Bergmann argue against reliance on public schools in their book, *America's Child Care Program: The Way*

Out. They voice the major concern that the elementary school environment poses "a danger that there would be a drift toward a much more regimented, scholarly curriculum than [is] appropriate" for preschoolers.[64] The issue Helburn and Bergman raise is an empirical one, and the findings from 21C reported above are directly relevant to this concern. The recent data from 21C indicate that it is possible to create a high-quality, developmentally appropriate system of preschool and wraparound child care. Further, schools are already the location of much school-age child care (see chapter 7). In fact, Gerald Tirrozzi, assistant secretary for education in the Clinton administration, reflected, "As we look at successful initiatives around the nation, none has had more success than the School of the 21st Century in being replicated in multiple settings. This program truly works for today's children and families—in all their diverse shapes and forms."[65]

CONCLUSION

The demographics of working parents of preschool-age children reveal two phenomena. First, an ever-growing proportion of parents are working outside the home, leaving lower- and middle-income families in need of affordable, high-quality child care environments. Second, the child care commonly available, whether center-based or informal, is not of high enough quality to promote children's healthy development and school readiness.

While cost-benefit figures of early interventions have captured the attention of policy makers, we must remember that any enduring solution, by necessity, will have to be grounded in the needs of today's working families. Judith Warner, author of *Perfect Madness: Motherhood in the Age of Anxiety,* shared in a *New York Times* article that "I am finding the rhetoric in the debate over UPK disheartening. It's all the usual stuff about cost-benefit and outcomes . . . these points, I suppose, help convince a tax-averse electorate that funding public schooling for preschoolers will bring them back some bang for the buck . . . The argument I would rather hear is: UPK is good for today's families right now. Here's why: Families need access to child care."[66] The days when half-day pre-K programs met the needs of children and families are over. We must carefully consider what working families need, how to best serve those needs, and how institutions in our society can be adjusted most efficiently. The 21C program offers a promising solution for using schools to address the child care and early education needs of children ages three through twelve and their families.

Finally, to the extent that public and political interest in preschool is driven by recent cost-benefit analyses emerging from economic data, we must ensure that policy makers bear in mind that high-quality care for preschoolers is at the core of any solution. Conservative *New York Times* columnist David Brooks captured this in the evolution of his own thinking. Brooks wrote, "If we want young people to develop the social and self-regulating skills they need to thrive, we need to establish stable long-term relationships between love-hungry children and love-providing adults. That's why I'm grappling with these books on psychology and brain function. I started out on this wonk odyssey in the company of economic data, but the closer you get to the core issue, the further you venture into the primitive realm of love."[67] This point is true of preschool-age children but becomes particularly relevant for infant and toddler care. Love is the necessary product of warm and caring relationships. Relationships are the central moving force in human development and the central feature of good-quality child care. Good-quality child care prior to school entry is central to children's school readiness and educational success.

CHAPTER SEVEN

School-Age Child Care

Ninety-four percent of American voters agree: "There should
be some type of organized activity or place for children and teens
to go after school every day that provides opportunities for them
to learn."

Afterschool Alliance

TODAY, THERE ARE MORE THAN 28 million school-age children between the ages of five and thirteen with either one single working parent
or two working parents.[1] The gap between the end of a child's school day
and his or her parents' workday in many cases can amount to twenty to
thirty-five hours per week. According to the best estimates, 6 million
children in the United States under age thirteen spend these afternoon
hours at home alone, caring for themselves each day.[2]

Increases in maternal employment, along with research findings on
the developmental consequences of how children spend the after-school
hours, have catapulted after-school child care onto the political agenda.[3]
Research findings indicate that school-aged children who are unsupervised after school are more likely to develop social, emotional, and academic problems, and to suffer from accidents and injuries.[4] Adolescents
with high amounts of unstructured and unmonitored leisure time outside
the home are more likely to develop antisocial and criminal behaviors.[5]
A growing body of research indicates that specific organized activities
and after-school programs (ASPs) can prevent behavioral problems and
promote positive development.[6]

The purpose of this chapter is threefold: to explore how parents man-
age the gap between the end of the school day and the end of the typical
workday; to discuss the consequences of those child care choices for a

child's health, safety, and development; and to consider historical and recent efforts to address the child care needs of school-age children. A solution to the crisis of providing care for school-age children is attainable in the near future and may constitute a first step toward a universal system of care for children of all ages.

AFTER-SCHOOL CARE ARRANGEMENTS

Many parents are surprised to learn that the child care crisis does not end with a child's first day of elementary school. Rather than enjoying a respite from child care woes, parents are met with a myriad of new challenges: scheduling child care around part-day kindergarten, driving children to and from school and after-school care, coordinating and paying for a child's participation in organized activities, juggling the incongruent locations and hours of operation of child care facilities, and managing a limited availability of ASPs that include activities that attract and sustain a child's interest.

Among the most taxing of these problems is the coordination of after-school care arrangements. Poll data indicate that 87 percent of working mothers say they are most concerned about their child's safety during the hours after school. Further compounding this stress is the fact that most children move from one type of care to another over the course of a single afternoon or across the week.[7] It is estimated that 40 percent of school-age children with employed mothers do not have a primary care arrangement, but rather experience a patchwork of arrangements across an afternoon or week.[8] By all accounts what is most typical about school-age child care arrangements is that there is no typical arrangement.

When parents of children between the ages of six and fourteen are asked to identify their primary care arrangement, they respond as follows: 37 percent with parents; 14 percent with grandparents; 12 percent in organized activities; 12 percent with other relatives; 12 percent in self-care; 9 percent in nonrelative care; and 5 percent in center-based care.[9] Although estimates vary widely across different studies, school- and community-based ASPs are conspicuously absent from parent reports. This result comes in spite of a dramatic increase in the proportion of children in ASPs over the past two decades. Between 1991 and 1997, the number of children enrolled in before- and after-school programs increased from 1.7 to 6.7 million. Even so, the average attendance of an elementary-school-age ASP participant ranges from 1.9 to 2.4 days per week.[10] Since this activity does not constitute the majority of weekly after-school hours, parents may not identify ASPs as a primary arrangement even if their child regularly attends. This possibility highlights the difficulties in estimating the true prevalence of different types of child care arrangements.

The child care arrangements that a school-age child experiences vary by socioeconomic, demographic, and contextual factors. Specifically, children from more advantaged families are more likely to be in organized activities. Likewise, children of more highly educated mothers are more likely to be in nonrelative care and less likely to be in parental care. African American children are more likely to be in ASPs than are Hispanic and Caucasian children. Among ten- to twelve-year-olds, Caucasian children are twice as likely as Hispanic children, and nearly three times as likely as African American children, to use self-care as the primary form of care (30 percent of Caucasian, 15 percent of Hispanic, and 11 percent of African American children).[11] Parents' decisions about child care arrangements for school age children appear to be determined by many factors including affordability, availability, transportation, and perceptions of neighborhood safety, as well as the child's age, gender, and interests.[12]

CONSEQUENCES OF AFTER-SCHOOL HOURS FOR DEVELOPMENT

Depending on how the time is spent, the hours between the end of the school day and the end of the typical workday can either support or undermine a child's development. From kindergarten through sixth grade, this time amounts to sixteen thousand hours of a child's life. Researchers have taken a particular interest in the consequences of after-school activities because of the sheer number of hours children spend in this context, as well as the inherent risks and opportunities.[13]

Researchers and policy makers are particularly concerned with children who are left to care for themselves after school. In the past, these children were called latchkey children, owing to the keys they wore around their necks. These children often spend afternoons home alone or hanging out inside or outside the home with peers.[14] Researchers use the term "self-care" to describe these types of unsupervised arrangements. It is difficult to estimate the true prevalence of self-care because rates vary across reports depending on whether the question is asked while school is in session, how parents define self-care, whether parents consider self-care as a primary or "filler" arrangement, and parents' willingness to admit their leaving children home alone. Nationally, the best estimates suggest that approximately 10 percent of six- to nine-year-olds (1.7 million out of 16.6 million children) and 35 percent of ten- to twelve-year-olds (4.4 million out of 12.5 million children) spend some time in self-care each week.[15]

The notion of self-care elicits mixed reactions. After all, American norms exalt independence and self-reliance. Toward that end, it is normal for children to experience a gradual and age-appropriate transition from constant formal supervision to caring for themselves after school. An important area of research has been studying this transition in order to better understand the conditions under which self-care is detrimental to a child's development.

Evidence indicates that the links between self-care and children's development vary according to several factors: the child's age and previous functioning, family characteristics, neighborhood characteristics, and the amount and type of self-care. Specifically, self-care appears more problematic when it involves younger children and when it occurs alongside other factors, including prior behavioral problems, family poverty, limited monitoring by parents, unsafe neighborhoods, and unsupervised time with peers outside of the home.[16]

Self-care can limit children's access to normal activities occurring during the after-school hours and thereby compromise opportunities for optimal development. Parents, in an effort to keep children safe, may expect them to stay at home behind locked doors, isolated from playing with friends or engaging in extracurricular activities. What happens behind locked doors can be problematic too, though. Among unsupervised early adolescents, the hours immediately after school pose increased risks for sexually transmitted diseases and teen pregnancy as well as substance use and other risky behaviors.[17]

Although children left in self-care may initially feel competent and grown up, indications are that these attitudes soon give way to loneliness and fear. Numerous studies find that children who experience high amounts of self-care are more likely to be bored, lonely, frightened, and depressed. Children in self-care do not learn to organize their own time, become independent, or explore the world from the safe base of consistent, caring adult supervision. Instead, adult responsibility is thrust upon them before they are prepared for such a role.[18]

School-age children without supervision are at greater risk of physical harm, both intentional and unintentional. The crime and victimization rates among school-age children are at their highest in the hours immediately following the end of the school day.[19] Data compiled by the Federal Bureau of Investigation indicate that on school days, violent juvenile crimes and gang violence peak between 3 PM and 4 PM, immediately after school dismissal.[20]

ADDRESSING THE SCHOOL-AGE CHILD CARE CRISIS

It is easy to become desensitized to the plight of these 6 million children and their families when the discussion is based solely on the language of numbers and statistical associations. For that reason it is critical to listen to the powerful words that school-age children use to describe their experiences in self-care. This is exactly the approach taken in one of the earliest and most valiant efforts to address the problem.

The Children's Caucus—A Voice for Children

On June 9, 1983, Senator Christopher Dodd (D-CT), one of the nation's key advocates for children, teamed up with Arlen Specter (R-PA) to create the thirty-member, bipartisan Children's Caucus in the U.S. Senate.[21] With Republicans in control of the Senate, Dodd knew he needed to create a podium for the discussion of problems facing America's children, and he found a strong ally in Specter. In an interview with a New York Times columnist, Dodd noted that one of the things that alarmed him when he was first elected to the Senate was that "one out of three Americans are under eighteen, and there was no one speaking for them—there was a Senate caucus for shoes, one for ports, one for steel, but nothing for children."[22] Nearly two decades later, Dodd reflected, "It is difficult to imagine that in 1983, when Senator Arlen Specter and I established the first Senate Children's Caucus, children's needs were more typically an afterthought in federal policy."[23] The Children's Caucus had a mandate to examine issues affecting children and held the authority to convene hearings like any regular Senate committee. Perhaps what it did best, though, was act as a microphone for the voices of America's children, allowing their concerns to be heard by Congress and the nation.

When Dodd and Specter were ready to hold their first hearings, in June 1983, before the Select Committee on Children, Youth, and Families of the House of Representatives, they asked me to identify the most pressing needs of America's families. This initial hearing needed to be dramatic in order to grab public attention. I immediately identified school-age child care. School-age child care did not ignite the ideological debates over the relationship between women and society that plagued efforts for younger children. Further, the school-age child care crisis could be addressed at a fraction of the cost of care for younger children. Marsha Renwanz, then staff director of the Children's Caucus, organized two panels of witnesses for the hearings.

The first panel included the typical collection of experts who testified to the nature, scope, and consequences of the latchkey problem and identified possible remedies. I described the physical and psychological costs of self-care and testified, "There almost seems to be an assumption that when a child enters kindergarten, he no longer needs day care—he vanishes or becomes an adult . . . Two-thirds of the child care of our nation involves school-age children." I added, "But does this situation constitute a problem? Some of my colleagues disagree, but I think that latchkey arrangements represent a serious abdication of responsibility toward our nation's children . . . Unattended children in this age group are vulnerable to many kinds of harm; over six thousand children aged five to fourteen die from unintentional injuries each year, including over one thousand in fires."[24] I went on to describe heightened vulnerabilities to physical risk, sexual abuse, and psychological damage among latchkey children. Thomas and Lynette Long, coauthors of *The Handbook for Latchkey Children and Their Parents*, described findings garnered from interviews of 850 latchkey children and shared stories of children who huddled in closets while they waited for their parents to return home from work.[25]

The most powerful testimony came from the second panel, composed of a half dozen school-age children who told their own stories about how a lack of after-school care affected their lives. The Children's Caucus gave these children a platform to share their stories and generated a flood of media attention.

One young boy testified, "When I'm alone, I do what I have to do first; then I watch TV, talk on the phone, or listen to the radio or records. Sometimes I get lonely when there is nothing to do or it is raining. I get scared when our neighbor's [burglar] alarm goes off because I'm afraid that there is a robber nearby . . . One day my friend and I were making something to eat and he cut his finger . . . If a grown-up had been around it would have been okay."[26]

A ten-year-old girl described her feelings to the Select Committee this way: "Some things scare me when I'm alone, like the wind, the doors creaking, and the sky getting dark fast. This may not seem scary to you, but it is to young people who are alone."[27]

Although these hearings were highly effective in thrusting the problem of self-care onto the agenda, an expansion of the government's role in addressing child care needs was not going to be realized under the conservatism that characterized Washington in the 1980s.[28] As discussed in chapter 3, conservatives from the far right, then and now, believe that there would be no child care problems if working mothers simply resigned from the out-of-home workforce.

Babbitt's Election Campaign

In 1988 Bruce Babbitt, a candidate seeking the Democratic Party nomination for president, set out to break the relative silence in Washington on the child care crisis. Babbitt was a longtime child advocate with the battle scars to show for it. While serving as governor of Arizona, he devoted his entire 1985 State of the State address to children and was consequently mocked by Arizona's leading newspaper for serving "quiche" while evading the "meat and potatoes" of Arizona's politics.[29]

In 1988, Babbitt was determined to do something about child care, so he called a meeting of about a dozen influential child care scholars, including Sheila Kamerman, Al Kahn, and me. Babbitt wanted to know one clear course of action he could take that would be politically popular and achievable. He essentially told us that the child care problem, as he saw it, was immense. But he wanted to be pragmatic and realistic. He told us that he needed the group to identify a circumscribed effort in child care that could become a plank in his platform. Within ten minutes the group of experts had agreed that if Babbitt wanted to be opportunistic, school-age child care fit the bill. Its growing public and political popularity had made it a can't-miss issue. Although he didn't win the nomination, Babbitt went on to serve as President Clinton's Secretary of the Interior. During his candidacy, school-age child care had once again surfaced as a policy problem.

Where Are We Now?

An estimated 6 million children were unsupervised or alone this afternoon, the time of biggest concern for parents worried about their child's
safety.[30] This problem is the crisis faced by school-age children and their
families. That the nation is aware of the problem, and that after two decades of effort has not arrived at a solution—that's a national crisis.

I concluded at the 1983 Senate hearings that "unlike many of our
nation's problems, the latchkey problem is a problem with affordable solutions."[31] My optimism that a solution is on the horizon stems from
how close we are to meeting the three conditions necessary for changing
policy: a pervasive sense that a real problem exists, an effective group of
advocates, and receptive decision makers in the legislative and executive
branches (see chapter 2).

Available evidence indicates that the public perceives a real problem.
Poll data reveal that 94 percent of voters believe that there should be organized activities or places for children and teens to go every day, 74 percent
of voters favor the federal government putting aside specific funds to be
used for ASPs, and 52 percent of voters were willing to increase their own
state taxes by $100 annually to pay for every child to attend an ASP. One
third of voters identify being alone and unsupervised after school as the
biggest problem facing American children today.[32]

Moreover, highly organized and effective advocacy groups have been
pushing for after-school programs. Fight Crime: Invest in Kids, one of
the leading groups promoting organized after-school care, was founded
in 1996 by attorney Sanford A. Newman. Newman became interested in
preventing crime after he and his wife were awakened one night by an
intruder crouched between their bed and their newborn infant. Newman
consulted with Elliot Richardson (the former secretary of HEW and hero
of the 1971 Comprehensive Child Development Act discussed in chapter
2) and me about creating an organization devoted to preventing crime
and violence. In 1996, with grants from individuals and foundations and
an advisory committee that read like a Who's Who of child care experts,
Newman launched Fight Crime: Invest in Kids.[33] In their own words, their
mission was "to take a hard-nosed, skeptical look at the research about
what really works—and what doesn't work—to keep kids from becoming criminals" and to "then put that information in the hands of policy
makers and the public."[34] Today, this organization, involving more than

one thousand police chiefs, sheriffs, and prosecutors, has brought to the table the notion that child care and ASPs are invaluable tools in the fight against juvenile delinquency and criminality. One of their great successes has been keeping ASPs on the policy agenda in Washington.

The Afterschool Alliance, another leading advocacy group, describes its mission as "to ensure that all youth have access to affordable, quality after-school programs by the year 2010."[35] This group has effectively raised awareness about the need for, benefits of, and public support for ASPs. Among their most successful efforts is the annual Poll on Voters' Attitudes on Afterschool, which has consistently uncovered the massive public support for ASPs. The alliance emerged from an unprecedented public-private partnership between the Mott Foundation and the U.S. Department of Education to expand public awareness of ASPs and 21CCLCs. The federal government provided grants to local communities for ASPs, and the Mott Foundation provided technical assistance on training, evaluation, and increasing public awareness. In September 1999 several private foundations, including the J.C. Penney Company, Inc., the Open Society Institute/The After-School Corporation, the Entertainment Industry Foundation, and the Creative Artists Agency Foundation expressed a shared interest in achieving "after-school for all." The Afterschool Alliance was created.

The third circumstance for policy change, the receptiveness of legislative and executive decision makers, frames two very different stories about after-school care. The first begins in 1998, when Fight Crime's message found its way to a friendly executive branch. During his State of the Union Address that year, President Clinton affirmed his support for ASPs to Congress and the nation: "I ask you to dramatically expand our support for after-school programs . . . I think every American should know that most juvenile crime is committed between the hours of three in the afternoon and eight at night. We can keep so many of our children out of trouble in the first place if we give them someplace to go other than the streets, and we ought to do it."[36]

Congress proved to be a receptive audience and dramatically expanded support for ASPs. In 1998, the first substantive federal support began in the form of 21CCLCs—$40 million to ninety-nine grantees in thirty-four states. The programs were mandated to "offer academic, artistic, and cultural enrichment opportunities to students and their families during non-school hours." Despite increases in funding during subsequent years, by 2000 available funding was still able to meet only an estimated 24 percent of demand for ASPs.[37] That year, 2,252 communities sought new 21CCLC funding, but funding was available for only 13.7 percent of these applicants. The gap in supply and demand for 21CCLC grants was equivalent to the amount of funding needed to serve 848,000 school-age children.[38] In 2001, the grant grew to $1 billion, making it one of the fastest-growing grants in history.

The Evaluation of 21CCLCs

Our second story about 21CCLC funding begins with the 2000 election and a new administration. In 2002, funding for 21CCLCs was reauthorized under the No Child Left Behind Act, and the grant was targeted at improving academic performance among impoverished children in low-performing schools.[39] A year later, in 2003, President Bush requested that Congress reduce funding for 21CCLCs by 40 percent, to $600 million. The fiscal year 2004 Education Budget Summary and Background Information, published on February 3, 2003, explained the reduction: "The decrease in the request acknowledges that the program needs some time to address disappointing initial findings from a rigorous evaluation of the 21st Century Community Learning Centers program. The evaluation indicates that the centers funded in the program's first three years are not providing substantial academic content and do not appear to have a positive impact on student behavior."

In 1999, Mathematica Policy Research, Inc., was chosen by the Department of Education to conduct the national evaluation of 21CCLCs at a cost of $12.7 million. This was to be a two-year longitudinal study of the federal program. The authors of the evaluation themselves stated, "A major goal of the national evaluation is to learn how 21CCLC programs are implemented and how they can be made more effective."[40] The study itself, however, was plagued with too many methodological problems to be the basis for drawing conclusions about the effectiveness of 21CCLCs.[41] Even though the authors clearly did not intend for the study to be used as a justification for changes in funding, and the quality of the study itself disallowed this application, the Bush administration based its proposed cut on these preliminary results.

The 40 percent funding cut to a popular program and the flawed study upon which the cut was based precipitated a huge controversy related to the No Child Left Behind Act's emphasis on scientifically based research to guide policy. The Mathematica evaluation of 21CCLCs was criticized widely by experts in the field as inadequate and misleading. In fact, members of the study's own scientific advisory board released a statement on May 10, 2003, in which they declared, "We believe that the first-year report, issued February 3, 2003, has serious methodological problems that call into question its findings and that violate basic principles governing how evaluation should be used to guide policy and affect program budgets."[42] A flurry of rebuttals by the primary investigators and more criticisms ensued. Heather Weiss's Harvard Family Research Project newsletter published criticisms of the study by leading experts in the field, including Kathleen McCartney, the current dean of the Harvard School of Education. Joseph Mahoney and I prepared a detailed scientific critique of the report. We concluded, "In light of the criticisms described in this report, as well as concerns raised by other critics, we conclude that the first-year findings from the national evaluation fail to provide a scientific basis for drawing conclusions about the 21CCLCs. As such, the findings—based on a single evaluation over the course of one school year that is fraught with methodological problems—are inadequate as a basis for policy decisions."[43]

The premier evaluation expert in the United States, Donald Campbell, argued years ago that no program should be evaluated unless that program is "proud."[44] It takes several years of implementation before a program is finally running smoothly. Thus, the Bush administration evaluation was premature. An appropriate evaluation at that stage would have been one identifying, discussing, and troubleshooting problems in implementation. The results of such a study would have been useful for improving programs at other sites. Just such an evaluation was proposed by the Clinton administration. However, the Bush administration ignored this evaluation plan and immediately contracted for a rigorous evaluation.[45]

On May 13, 2003, the Senate Subcommittee on Labor, Health, and Human Services and Education held hearings to discuss the reduced funding request contained in the president's budget. Specter was chairman. For Specter, it had been nearly two decades to the day since he had listened to the impassioned pleas of latchkey children during the

Children's Caucus hearing. He hit the ground running as he questioned officials from the Department of Education as to why they proposed a reduction in funding of ASPs based on the highly criticized report. He began: "Well, the question, the initial question, which comes to my mind is why such a drastic reduction, when these are only preliminary findings and you have a second survey which is in process which you have not analyzed? To take it from $900 million plus and reduce it to $600 million really is an enormous reduction. It may really gut the program in many respects. Why is it sound to do that before your studies are complete?"[46] A representative from the Department of Education attempted to respond by discussing the challenges inherent in program evaluation. Specter immediately turned those words against him: "Your last answer identifies the difficulties of evaluation. And that is why, frankly, I am surprised that, when your studies are incomplete, you come in and want to reduce it from $933 million to $600 million. Your last answer articulates the difficulty of making an evaluation. And the evaluation is incomplete."[47]

Advocates testified, including California Governor Arnold Schwarzenegger and representatives of Fight Crime: Invest in Kids. Chief Harvey Sprafka of the Knoxville (Iowa) Police Department appeared on behalf of Fight Crime: Invest in Kids and testified, "When the school day ends, turning millions of kids out onto the streets with neither constructive activities nor adult supervision, juvenile violent crime soars . . . Our choice is quite simple. We can either send our children to after-school programs that will teach them good values and skills, or we can entrust them to the after-school teachings of someone like Jerry Springer, violent video games, or, worse yet, the streets."[48]

Schwarzenegger testified, "I and others in the after-school community would agree with some of those findings. But it would be a big mistake —and let me reiterate, a big mistake—to use that study as a justification to reduce current funding levels for ASPs."[49] He concluded, perhaps not surprisingly, "Remember, when it is time for the committee to consider funding for after-school programs in the next budget cycle, you can count on one thing: I'll be back."[50]

Schwarzenegger's presence had drawn a huge crowd of media and spectators, including many children, to the hearing. Specter noticed that the children were standing because all the chairs in the gallery were filled. Because some senators on the committee did not attend the hearing, there were some empty seats on the podium. Specter promptly invited some of the standing children to come up and sit in the vacant chairs, thus making them "senators for a day."

Two months later, on July 10, 2003, the Brookings Institution hosted a debate between me and Mark Dynarski, the lead author on the Mathematica 21CCLC evaluation. I was asked to place the 21CCLC evaluation in context. I began by reiterating the role of evaluation and said, "The field of behavioral science has long given up the dream of earlier years that we could mount a single perfect experiment to resolve an important scientific issue."[51] I went on to stress that the importance of the controversy is to improve thinking in the field: "The Mathematica evaluation will have considerable value if it stimulates the field to think more thoroughly about the nature of after-school programs, that is, to develop a much better conceptualization of these programs, which would lead us in turn to what would constitute sound evaluations of these programs." After the outcry from academics and advocates, Congress rebuffed the Bush proposal and restored funding to $1 billion, where it remains today.

After-school programs resurfaced again during the 2004 presidential election campaign. John Edwards, before joining the John Kerry ticket, had a plank to increase 21CCLC funding to $4 billion. Later, the Kerry-Edwards ticket presented a proposal to increase funding to $2.5 billion in 2007 and change the name of 21CCLCs to "School's Open 'til 6." The revamped program would lengthen its program hours, provide bus transportation for participants, and offer academic activities, but it would also emphasize values and decision-making skills that would encourage children to avoid drugs, crime, and risky behaviors. Kerry's plan would have provided programs for an additional 1.8 million children in 2006 and 2.2 million in 2007, though at an increased cost for states. If the state contribution of $300 per child remained constant, this increase in federal funding would have raised state contributions from $300 million to $1 billion.[52] The federal grant would continue to provide $700 per child. Of course, Bush was reelected and Kerry's plan was not implemented. The Bush administration continues to focus on improving academic achievement of low-performing students in low-income schools and has kept its 21CCLC funding request from Congress at $1 billion, apparently having learned from the debacle following the proposed cut in 2004. Some continue to worry, though, that $1,000 per child—an average of $1.85 per hour per child—is insufficient to provide high-quality programs and that annual budgets as high as $6,000 per child are needed.[53]

Program Quality: Not Just Any Program Will Do
Just as low-quality child care can put younger children in harm's way, unstructured and unsupervised ASPs can be hotbeds of deviant activity for school-age youth. For example, participation in programs at unstructured community youth centers in Sweden was linked to increases in antisocial behavior for girls and boys.[54] A director of Swedish youth centers described the priorities and goals of the programs by saying, "What's important is that there are people with life experiences that supervise the youth centers. They don't need much of a pedagogy." Another described the program's goal as establishing a place where "one can meet and be with peers, and maybe even fall in love."[55] Evaluations of these programs found, however, that those youth centers that aggregated the most antisocial peers and offered activities that lacked structure and skill-building opportunities created an environment promoting antisocial behavior that persisted well into adulthood.[56]

Researchers in the United States have found that aggregating groups of high-risk adolescents into intervention programs can actually have the effect of increasing problematic behaviors. Researchers use the term "deviancy training" to capture the process by which peers react positively to deviant behavior and endorse rule-breaking activities. This deviancy training has been associated with increased use of addictive substances, self-reported delinquency, and police-reported violent behaviors.[57] This result has two obvious implications: that programs must be structured, challenging, and engaging, and that there must be a socioeconomic mix of youth.[58]

An Ideal After-School Program?
Experts have yet to agree on what an absolute model program for after-school programs would entail. Nevertheless, it is important to rely on the most recent research on the features of ASPs that have demonstrated the greatest success in reaching the goals for out-of-school-time care. Determining what features after-school care arrangements should include can be mind-boggling at first. Consider three recent comments on the direction of after-school care arrangements given by experts in the field:

It's got to be a lot more than just baby-sitting.
—Herbert Sturz, chairman of the After-School Corporation,
an initiative funded in large part by George Soros[59]

We have to be very careful not to over-program . . . [it's]
very important just to kind of have downtime where kids
can be together.
—Dr. Gil Noam, professor of medicine and education at
Harvard University[60]

While there is general consensus that after school shouldn't
look like "more school," there is far less clarity about what
should occur during the many hours young children are not
in school.
—Dr. Beth Miller in a review of after-school programs
commissioned by the Nellie Mae Foundation[61]

One way to clarify and unify the diverse opinions on programming is
to create logic models. A logic model summarizes the key elements of
a program, identifies the rationale behind its approach, and articulates
the intended outcomes for children and how those outcomes will be measured.[62] It states the specific goals of a program and specifies which activities are necessary in order to achieve these goals. In the case of ASPs,
a logic model would essentially be an overview of the ASP's theory of
change. Articulating a logic model is critical to creating, implementing,
and evaluating theoretically grounded after-school programs.

At the Brookings Institution debate I identified four goals of ASPs:
(1) the facilitation of parents' employment and their peace of mind while
working; (2) academic improvement; (3) general positive youth development; and (4) recreational activities allowing children to have fun and
develop more positive attitudes toward school. During the debate I asserted, "Many see conflict among these goals, and champion one and
belittle the others. On the contrary, I feel these goals are interrelated and
synergistic."[63]

Although considerable evaluation research has been conducted on
community-sponsored programs, developmental research, which compares
different types of activities is relatively new.[64] Currently, the field is trying
to move beyond the question of whether ASPs can affect development,

to attempt to identify what features of organized activities promote positive development. The National Research Council and the Institute of Medicine identified the features of developmental contexts that are particularly well suited for promoting positive development. These features include physical and psychological safety, appropriate structure, supportive relationships, opportunities for belonging, positive social norms, support for self-efficacy, opportunities for skill building, and integration of family, school, and community efforts. The researchers cautioned, however, that when considering features of a context, one should realize that no single feature is sufficient to ensure positive adjustment and that few contexts provide optimal experiences in all of these areas.[65]

One clear finding from this area of research is that the extent to which a program confers benefits to participating children varies as a function of the children, the contexts, and the type of activities.[66] At the most basic level, children need to participate in activities to benefit from them. Participation in programs is affected by factors including availability, accessibility, and affordability. The content of the program is also critical for engaging students, which in turn is related to whether program participation is associated with beneficial outcomes for children. For example, researchers found that all ASP participants had better academic results, but only those children who were rated by program staff as engaged in program activities showed increased motivation for schoolwork.[67] Moreover, children who regularly attended the program but were not engaged in activities showed markedly lower motivation for school. Interestingly, programs that offered extracurricular activities and did not focus exclusively on homework engendered the greatest program engagement and were associated with the largest increases in academic performance. I will revisit these findings in chapter 8 when we consider possible policy solutions to the school-age child care crisis.

While researchers are working to understand the processes by which ASPs influence children's development, practitioners are striving to apply the latest findings to improve the delivery of services. The Promising Practices in Afterschool Systems (PPAS) was created by the Academy for Educational Development Center for Youth Development and Policy Research to identify and disseminate effective practices of existing ASPs. An advisory group composed of advocates, researchers, practitioners, and volunteers identified seven key areas of ASP components: community and family involvement, program content, management and administration, staffing and training, financing, research and evaluation, and policy and advocacy. Practitioners are encouraged to submit descriptions of practices in each of these key areas. Trained volunteers then review them according to standards created by the advisory group and publicize the most promising practices through the PPAS email list, website, and newsletter and at conferences.[68]

Another critical question is where ASP programs should be located. The 21CCLC grant takes the pragmatic approach of using school buildings. For school-age children, the school is already the center of much of their daily lives. Further, schools have the facilities that support educational and recreational activities for children: gymnasiums and athletic equipment, playgrounds, libraries, bathrooms, cafeterias, child-sized furniture, and health and safety features and practices, such as fire drills.[69] These facilities and familiar activities combine to make schools safe, comfortable, and welcoming places for children.

Using school buildings to house ASPs is not a new idea. In fact, Al Shanker, then president of the American Federation of Teachers (affiliated with the AFL-CIO), testified before the Senate in 1975 that public schools should serve as sponsors of school-age child care programs. Reflecting the unanimous conclusion of the AFL-CIO executive council, Shanker testified, "We feel that prime sponsorship should rest with the public schools because we have within the public schools a national system of governance . . . It would certainly be wasteful to pay for either constructions or renting other facilities."[70] School-based before- and after-school care programs constitute one of the six components of the School of the 21st Century. Indeed, the proportion of public schools offering extended-day programs, which include before- and after-school activities, tripled between 1987 and 1999, from 16 to 47 percent.[71]

While school-based programs are clearly popular, it is important not to overlook the disadvantages of relying on a school-based child care solution. Critics worry that schools are already overburdened and that there are many effective community programs which would essentially be squeezed out of the market (for example, Boys and Girls Clubs). Further, school-based programs may focus on academics and remedial tutoring to the exclusion of extracurricular activities.[72]

Perhaps what is most exhilarating, though, about the discussions surrounding after-school care are the issues being debated. The question is not whether there should be a government role in after-school child care, but rather what shape that role should take. This is a completely different debate than we have historically witnessed for the provision of child care for infants, toddlers, and preschoolers. Child care for school-age children does not ignite the ideological debates over the role of women within society that have plagued efforts for younger children. It is because of massive political and public popularity, effective advocacy, and valiant efforts within Congress, especially from Dodd and Specter in the Senate, that after-school care for all American children may be an achievable first step in a larger effort to create a system of universally available voluntary child care.

The overall child care problem in America is an extremely complex one, and any overall solution would cost tens of billions of dollars if it were attempted as a single federal government effort. This approach is what was attempted in the 1971 Comprehensive Child Development Act, and it will probably never be attempted again. The culture wars are still with us, and powerful social forces continue to argue that child care is a private family issue and not a governmental one. Disregarding the large percentage of women working outside the home, several think tanks continue to argue that government should not promote family lifestyles in conflict with the 1950s model of the working father and stay-at-home mother. As the child care crisis has grown ever larger and more complex, the hope for a single comprehensive solution has become more illusory. Currently the child care issue is best viewed as a panoply of circumscribed problems related to the age of the child (infant, preschool, school age) or setting (center-based child care, school-based ASP).

Child care experts have long felt that providing school-age child care was a target of opportunity readily open to solution (unlike the thorny issue of infant and toddler care). The foundations for a solution are today firmly in place. Parents, policy makers, and educators are all concerned about what children do during out-of-school time, and all agree that children age five to approximately age fourteen should not be on their own but rather receive care and supervision by sympathetic and knowledgeable adults. Today there exist several effective national organizations that have made solutions to the school-age child care problem a high priority. Decision makers have already expressed considerable interest in a government solution to this problem. The Clinton administration expanded the 21CCLC program from $44 million to $1 billion. While the Bush administration wanted to cut the program, no one proposed ending it. Further, the administration restored its request for funding to $1 billion in the years following the attempt to cut the program. The Child Care Bureau funds the Afterschool Investments Project, which supports the Finance Project to offer technical assistance to CCDF and other state and local leaders working to provide after-school child care. This resource provides examples of states' program developments, identifies possible funding streams, creates tools and materials to support the development and sustainability of ASPs, and shares relevant and timely research findings with providers.

My optimistic assessment of our progress in dealing with the afterschool child care problem does not mean we are even close to a viable solution. Even with parent fees, the funds currently committed to ASPs do not begin to meet the great recognized need. Remember that most available funds are directed to the poor, ignoring the needs of the near-poor, the working class, and the lower middle class. Further, no consensus has been reached on what would constitute the ideal ASP. Relevant here is the still unanswered question of how these programs should vary as a function of the age of the participants. Obviously an ideal program for children ages five to eight would be far different than a program for children ages eleven to fourteen. Further, we must still determine the appropriate training and credentialing of a large cadre of caregivers in ASPs. Finally, considerable controversy remains concerning the goals by which the efficacy of these programs can be assessed.

While much thinking and research remains to be done, there is no question that solving the school-age child care problem is much further along than solutions to the other problems discussed within this book. Not only has this issue been included as a plank in the platforms of presidential candidates, but solving this problem also has considerable bipartisan support in Congress and in state legislatures.

CHAPTER EIGHT

Moving Forward

PROMISING DEVELOPMENTS

If our American way of life fails the child, it fails us all.

Pearl S. Buck

IN THE PRECEDING CHAPTERS, I examined the dynamics of America's child care tragedy in depth. As bleak as the situation is, there has been some progress—albeit fragmented and confined—since the failure of the Comprehensive Child Development Act. In this chapter, I discuss the most important of these developments and examine both their promise and limitations. Perhaps the most serious lesson of these years is that the solution to America's child care problem does not lie at the federal level. Rather, the most significant progress has evolved at the state level. Therefore, I close this chapter with a description of how three states have developed innovative models of child care policy.

TAKING STOCK: WHAT PIECES DO WE HAVE?

Despite the distressingly slow pace toward addressing America's child care needs, some important steps have been made at the national level. In this section, I describe the most salient of these developments.

The Establishment of the Child Care Bureau

The Child Care Bureau was created in early 1995 under the Clinton administration, with Joan Lombardi as its first head. The founding of the bureau was among the most significant accomplishments in recent years, signifying that child care was now an issue of importance for the federal government and that it deserved a voice in the executive branch. Further, the existence of a dedicated bureau elevated child care from a workforce issue to one focusing on the needs of children, thus acknowledging the essential duality of child care.

Over the years, the Child Care Bureau has served multiple functions: as an increasingly valuable coordinator of research initiatives via its Child Care Research Consortium; as the hub for distribution of funding and information on child care research and consumer information via its National Child Care Information and Technical Assistance Center (NCCIC); and as the coordinator of technical assistance through the Child Care Technical Assistance Network. In addition, it has spearheaded the coordination of interagency collaboration to improve child care quality, including cooperation with the Bureau of Maternal and Child Health in support of the National Resource Center for Health and Safety in Child Care. The Child Care Bureau has coordinated research on child care, and it has also regularly convened valuable conferences for state officials and others, providing opportunities for the exchange of information regarding best practices and lessons learned at the state and local levels. Perhaps the most important contribution of the bureau over the years has been the development of a highly effective research-to-policy-to-practice triangle, which has energized state-level developments such as those I highlight later in this chapter.

Much of the credit in realizing the Child Care Bureau's promise goes to Lombardi's dynamic leadership in the early years and, more recently, the excellent stewardship of Shannon Christian. Although the bureau was given a key role during the course of the 1996 welfare reform, its charge was broader—focusing on child care for all children rather than only those whose parents were transitioning off welfare. Cohen notes, "Child care policy experts gave high praise to Joan Lombardi. They recognized her indefatigable commitment to strengthening the federal government's role in child care. Reflecting back, Lombardi said, 'It created an agency involved with child care that was not inextricably linked with welfare.'"[1] Shannon Christian adopted the same approach, emphasizing improvement of care for all children regardless of family income.

This broad focus abruptly narrowed in May 2006, when the Child Care Bureau became part of the Office of Family Assistance (OFA) within the Administration for Children and Families, U.S. Department of Health and Human Services. According to the bureau's website, "Combining the Child Care Bureau with the OFA, which administers Temporary Assistance for Needy Families, allows for greater coordination of the child care subsidy program with welfare reform efforts."[2] Advocates and policy makers expressed concern at the move because it could lead federal child care assistance to function solely as a work support for TANF families, rather than as both a work support and a key to children's educational success. Senator Dodd of Connecticut said, "Watering down the role of the Child Care Bureau diminishes the purpose of child care as both a support for working parents and an early learning experience for children."[3] Indeed, these concerns were warranted. The reorganization of the Child Care Bureau under OFA has gutted federal support for child care system-building at the state level and has limited the bureau's focus to child care as a workforce support, primarily as a welfare-to-work strategy. Given the laudable accomplishments of the bureau prior to this reorganization, this setback is truly tragic.

Family and Medical Leave Act

A major victory in the effort to address the child care needs of infants was the enactment of the Family and Medical Leave Act (FMLA). Child advocates have agreed for some time that a family leave policy, enabling parents to stay home to care for their infants, should be one element of a coherent system of early care. Indeed, I proposed a partially paid leave as one solution to the child care problem as early as 1977. Prompted to a great extent by the Infant Care Leave Project conducted by scholars at the Yale Center in Child Development and Social Policy, the FMLA was finally enacted into law in 1993.[4] Much credit for this success goes to Dodd, who championed the cause in the face of fierce opposition by national business organizations. The FMLA provides for up to twelve weeks of job-protected leave for the purpose of caring for a newborn or adopted child, tending to an ill family member, or recovering from a serious illness.

Although the FMLA represents a significant advance in the application of developmental science to policy affecting children, it is limited in three important respects. First, it applies to a limited number of working parents: only employers with more than fifty employees are required to provide a job-protected leave, and then only to workers who have been on the job for at least a year. Second, the twelve-week leave period is short.

Finally—and most significant—the leave is not paid. Not only are about half of U.S. workers ineligible for the leave because of their employment status, but far more cannot afford to take time off without pay. Only 2 percent of parents work for employers that actually provide a paid leave.[5]

These limitations did not go unacknowledged by proponents of the FMLA on the hill. Indeed, the paid leave movement gained momentum when I was asked to testify before both a Senate subcommittee and the Women's Caucus of the House of Representatives on the social policy implications of research on children's early brain development. Noting the developmental importance of the time that parents and newborns spend together, I argued that a clear implication of this research is the need for a paid leave, since so many parents work paycheck to paycheck and simply cannot afford to forgo wages for very long. Following the testimony, Representative Lynn Woolsey met with me and pledged to spend the rest of her career in Congress working for a paid leave that covers all parents. She has proved to be a congresswoman of her word. She sponsored a House breakfast at which I spoke on the medical and behavioral scientific basis of a paid leave. A large number of notables attended, including Richard Gephardt, then Speaker of the House, and Patricia Schroeder, former chairperson of the House Subcommittee on Children and Youth. Also in attendance was the leadership of the National Partnership for Women. This Washington-based organization has taken upon itself the task of coordinating the national paid leave movement, which appears to be progressing state by state.

In contrast to the United States, almost all other industrialized *and* developing nations mandate paid leaves. Among member nations of the Organization for Economic Cooperation and Development (OECD), for instance, only the United States and Australia lack a paid parental leave policy. According to Kammerman, the European Union has a mandated fourteen-week maternity leave, and the average leave in OECD member states is thirty-six weeks. Seven European countries provide 100 percent income replacement for workers who take parental leave to care for their infants.[6]

Some progress has been made toward instituting paid leave in the United States, primarily through expansion of the FMLA at the state level. In 2004, California pioneered the use of temporary disability insurance to provide at least partial wage compensation during parental leave to care for a new baby, adopted child, or foster child. The program is financed completely by employee contributions to the State Disability Insurance Program, which average $46 per worker per year. In 2006, benefits replaced approximately 55 percent of wages to a maximum of $840 per week.[7]

Twelve additional states have introduced FMLA expansions of one type or another that provide at least partial wage replacement to help working parents care for their children or other dependent family members. For example, New Jersey has modeled a program after California's use of disability insurance, and Washington state has initiated a program allowing public and private workers to use sick leave and other paid time off to care for ill family members, including sick children.

Child Care and Development Block Grant
The primary federal source of child care assistance has been the Child Care and Development Block Grant. The CCDBG was enacted in 1990 and reauthorized during the 1996 welfare reforms. With the enactment of TANF, child care assistance was consolidated under the Child Care Bureau and renamed the Child Care and Development Fund (CCDF). CCDBG is administered by the Department of Health and Human Services and provides block grants to states, according to a formula that includes mandatory entitlement funding and discretionary funding. Since 1996, states have been given the option of transferring up to 30 percent of their TANF funds into CCDBG. States could also spend TANF funds directly on child care (instead of or in addition to the transfer to CCDBG). Any TANF funds that were transferred into CCDBG had to abide by CCDBG guidelines (for example, a 4 percent set-aside for quality improvements), but TANF funds spent directly were not subject to these requirements.[8]

As welfare reform got under way, TANF caseloads dropped precipitously, especially from 1997 to 2000. With reduced caseloads, states had surplus funds to spend on child care. By 1999, aside from cash assistance, child care was the largest use of TANF funds.[9] Another major driver of the sharp increase in TANF expenditures on child care was a change in TANF regulations that essentially enforced a "use it or lose it" rule. States were encouraged to spend their surplus TANF funds accrued between 1997 and 1999 or risk forfeiting the money. In 2000, TANF funding of child care actually exceeded CCDBG.

In other words, unspent welfare money provided more funds for child care than the very grant created to subsidize child care. While in theory this method of financing freed up more money for needed child care services, there are several reasons to be concerned. First, this approach frames child care as a service necessary for moving mothers from the welfare rolls to work, thus disregarding the need for quality services for all children. Second, leftover TANF funds are an unstable and unsustainable revenue source. An examination of child care spending revealed that after the fiscal crisis of 2001, when many states depleted their TANF funds, those states that relied most heavily on TANF money for child care were forced to create waiting lists, reduce reimbursements to providers, increase parent copayments, and take other measures to reduce expenditures.[10]

Third, the mix of funding from TANF transfers, TANF direct, CCDBG, and other revenue streams greatly complicates determining how much money is being spent on child care and what that money is buying. For example, Besharov and Higney calculate that combined federal and state child care spending (including Head Start) increased between 1997 and 2001 from $11.09 billion to $18.78 billion.[11] This rapid increase was largely driven by redirected TANF funds. From 2001 to 2003, as surplus TANF funds dried up, expenditures rose only about 3 percent per year. So, while their conclusion that spending across the seven years spanning 1997 to 2003 rose by 83.6 percent is true, it disguises the underlying dynamics of those increases. Analyses from the Center for Legal and Social Policy found that in 2004, total spending on child care fell for the first time since the 1996 welfare reforms, a trend that continued in 2005. Further, CCDBG did not receive an increase from 2002 until 2006, which means that the real value of the block grant declined with inflation. Best available estimates indicate that of 15 million families eligible for CCDBG assistance, only 14 percent receive it.[12]

A major challenge to advocates of quality child care is that CCDBG contains only minimal regulations. States have considerable flexibility in determining family as well as caregiver eligibility, provider reimbursement rates, and parent copayments. This has created huge variations across states in access, availability, and quality of care. The federal statute does require states to spend a minimum of 4 percent of the grant on quality improvements, but it does not stipulate how to invest the set-aside. In 2004, the proportion of CCDBG grants spent on quality varied across states from 4 percent to 18 percent, with an average of 7 percent. States also differ significantly in their monitoring practices. For example, a 2004 report from the Government Accountability Office found that thirty-eight states exempted all family child care providers from being regulated. Many states also exempt relatives and religiously affiliated providers. Monitoring is likewise abandoned in the widespread use of vouchers, which permit recipients to purchase care from anyone regardless of their qualifications or potential risks to a child.

In sum, CCDBG constitutes the largest source of federal money for child care. That this dedicated funding stream exists at all represents significant progress. However, CCDBG is sorely limited, particularly with respect to quality assurance, coverage of eligible recipients, and account-ability. Although CCDBG was created with the intention of maximizing flexibility and parental choice, the low level of regulation combined with underfunding has failed to empower parents to make real choices.

Child Care Tax Credit

The child and dependent care tax credit, commonly referred to as the de-pendent care credit, was enacted in 1976 and is the second-largest source of federal child care assistance.[13] Taxpayers may claim employment-related child care expenses of up to $3,000 annually for one child and up to $6,000 for two or more children. The credit itself is calculated on a slid-ing scale, decreasing as the taxpayer's income rises. Taxpayers with an adjusted gross income (AGI) of $15,000 or less get credit for 35 percent of allowed expenses, while those with an AGI above $43,000 may claim 20 percent. Thus, the credit is designed to target the greatest amount of assistance to lower-income families.

The credit has several desirable features. First, it covers both in- and out-of-home care in a variety of child care settings, thus accommodating individual preferences. Second, it provides benefits to families across the income spectrum, giving it a more universal application than traditional direct-spending programs that target the poor. Third, because it involves money not coming into the treasury rather than money being paid out, it is not stigmatized as a government spending program and is less vul-nerable to changes in the political and economic climate than are direct expenditures, which are typically dependent on annual legislative appro-priations. Finally, the credit has the potential to serve as an incentive for parents to choose quality child care programs. To claim the benefit taxpayers must list the provider's tax identification number, which encourages parents to avoid caregivers who operate underground to avoid licensing requirements. Some states have a similar credit that applies against state income taxes, and Arkansas and Maine allow a higher credit for payments to programs that have achieved certain quality benchmarks.

Despite these benefits, the dependent care tax credit does not go very far in making child care more affordable to working parents. One reason is that the credit is not refundable, meaning that low-income families who have a small or nonexistent tax liability can take little or none of their calculated credit. A major weakness is that the credit is paltry considering actual child care expenditures for a typical family. In 2006, the maximum credit for a family with an adjusted gross income of less than $15,000 was only $1,050 for one child and $2,100 for two or more. For a family with an AGI above $43,000, the maximum credit was $600 for one child and $1,200 for two or more. These amounts are woefully insufficient in the face of the child care expenses incurred by most working parents, particularly those with infants and toddlers, whose fees may exceed $1,000 per month.

Another major flaw with the dependent care credit is that, unlike the personal exemption and the earned income tax credit, income levels and allowed expenses are not automatically indexed to inflation. For example, for the eighteen years between 1982 and 2000, the maximum child care expenses eligible for the credit were $2,400 for one child and $4,800 for two or more. Adjusting for inflation, these expenses would have been $4,500 and $9,000 in 2000 dollars.[14] The amounts were finally raised in 2003, but only to $3,000 and $6,000—an increase dwarfed by rising costs.

The Universal Preschool Movement

As I discussed in chapter 6, there is a fast-growing movement in the states to make preschool programs universally available. Buoyed by media fascination with early brain development and a growing awareness of the value of early education, state policy makers are rapidly expanding the number of pre-K slots available to four-year-olds and, in some places, three-year-olds. Today there are at least fifty-two unique early education programs operating in forty states. Thirty-five percent of elementary schools had preschoolers in their building in 2002, and that number has surely grown.[15] In 2005, twenty state governors proposed increased funding for their state pre-K programs, nearly twice the number who did so just a year before.[16] Noting the activity in the states, Washington concluded, "The field of early care and education is at a crossroads, where the hoped-for remedy is not a national framework of care but the evolution of fifty unique state solutions."[17]

Despite its aggressive growth, the preschool movement still faces serious challenges. Experts debate whether programs should be universal or targeted; conservatives contend that publicly funded pre-Ks amount to the actions of a "nanny state";[18] "school readiness," the most commonly stated goal of pre-K programs, has multiple definitions, some of which favor strictly academic versus whole-child approaches to learning; and the evidence fails to offer clear guidance on the most cost-effective and efficient training levels for teachers and staff.

Of course, the most imposing barrier to universal pre-K is a financial one. The federal government funds programs targeted to high-risk groups through Head Start, Early Head Start, and Title I of the No Child Left Behind Act, as well as the CCDF. States rely on a creative mix of taxes, sales levies, lottery proceeds, and other targeted funding streams. Together with my colleagues Stephanie Jones and Walter Gilliam, I have proposed a plan that includes a fee calibrated to family income to support the cost of preschool and extended-day programming.[19] Relying on parent fees has two key advantages. First, it deflates the argument that public preschool will yield greater economic savings to wealthy families (who would have sent their children to preschool anyway) than to low-income families; and second, it attracts a broader constituency of parents who will fight for continued funding and quality improvements.

21st Century Community Learning Centers

21CCLC is the only source of federal support directed exclusively at after-school programming for school-age children. Originally funded in 1997 with an annual budget of $1 million, it grew into a $1 billion program with more than 8,000 centers nationwide. In 2001, 21CCLC was reauthorized under NCLB, changing the emphasis from after-school care to academic enrichment for children living in high-poverty, low-performing schools. At the same time, administration of the program was devolved from the federal Department of Education to state education agencies.[20] Many schools that had operated 21CCLC programs but were not in high-poverty districts were thus forced to secure other funding sources. A review by the Finance Project revealed that after their 21CCLC grants expired, many schools were not able to sustain their programs and had to reduce enrollment or take other measures to reduce costs. The authors of the review, Szekely and Padgette, noted, "Many grantees regret making sacrifices . . . but lack the resources to offer programming of the same richness and quality as they did with 21CCLC funding."[21]

State administrators reported that the narrow focus of the program on at-risk children living in low-performing districts "creates a stigma around the program, making it less appealing to the community and a broad range of potential funders."[22] Funding partners are more difficult to find when programs are restricted in their target audience. Administrators also reported mixed feelings on the strengthened academic focus under NCLB. Some found it too limited and unrealistic given the length of the program, while others reported that it was easier to "sell" the program to school officials. Many students appear to have voted with their feet and dropped out once the program became an extension of the academic day.

As I noted in chapter 7, the expansion of 21CCLC to meet demand for school-age programs was a promising development toward the child care solution. With the changes imposed on the program, the challenge now is to balance the four purposes of school-age care (to facilitate parents' employment, improve academic performance, encourage positive development, and provide recreational activities). This effort will be an uphill battle in a policy climate that emphasizes academic remediation.

QUALITY IMPROVEMENT

Although the overall quality of care remains woefully inadequate, there has been increasing attention paid to strategies that provide incentives for quality improvement. The most promising of these combine incentives for providers with consumer information designed to introduce competition into the market via parental demand for better care.

Tiered Licensing and Reimbursement
According to the NCCIC, at least thirty states have enacted some form of a tiered licensing system that links increased funding to the achievement

of higher quality standards.[23] Of these states, at least four require centers to be accredited by the NAEYC to receive higher levels of funding. Three states require programs to meet standards based on observations of the caregiving environment using established tools such as the Early Childhood Environment Rating Scale, the Infant/Toddler Environment Rating Scale, and the School-Age Care Environment Rating Scale. Two states have voluntary county-driven systems.

The incentive structure represented by accreditation and tiered licensing, combined with tiered reimbursement, shows promise but needs time to have a broader impact on quality. In North Carolina, for example, despite a reimbursement structure that provides as much as a 45 percent increase to providers who achieve the highest licensing level, only 3.5 percent of centers and 2.8 percent of family day care homes are licensed at the five-star highest level. While the majority of centers are licensed at the three-star level, most family child care providers have only one star. Further, the lowest licensing level in most tiered systems tends to be set too low.[24] As Gormley points out, differential payment rates do not significantly increase accreditation rates unless the financial incentive is at least a 15 percent increase.[25] Finally, tiered reimbursement structures only serve as an incentive to programs that receive public funding.

Professional Development and Compensation
The most important determinant of child care quality is the quality of caregiving, which in turn is linked to caregiver training. To address the need for qualified workers, the child development associate (CDA) credential was initiated in 1972. The CDA is competency based and is earned through both classroom time and in-service training. In the past thirty years, the CDA program has expanded greatly; more than 115,549 teachers nationwide now have a CDA, and forty-six states incorporate the CDA into their licensing regulations. As the program has expanded, it has also matured. Training standards and assessment have grown more stringent, and requirements have been increased from 120 hours of informal training to 480 hours of formal training and work experience. Moreover, there is a greater focus on professional development after caregivers have received their CDA. They must join a professional organization in the field of early child development and education and must take college-level courses to maintain their CDA credential.[26]

Another way to improve the quality of the child care workforce is to strengthen the link between professional development and compensation. The T.E.A.C.H. model, for example, is a scholarship program that helps providers receive college degrees and certification in early childhood education. To address the problem of turnover, participating caregivers receive higher pay if they commit to working in their child care program for a specific period of time. The program was founded in North Carolina and is rapidly being adopted elsewhere. Currently, twenty-two states operate T.E.A.C.H. projects, and this number is expected to increase to twenty-six in the next five years. According to the Administration for Children and Families, nearly twice as many states reported spending CCDF funds for T.E.A.C.H. in 2002 than in their previous survey.[27] The T.E.A.C.H. Early Childhood Technical Assistance Center provides networking and technical assistance to states implementing the T.E.A.C.H. program.

A companion initiative, the Child Care WAGE$ Project, provides education-based salary supplements to low-paid teachers, directors, and family child care providers who work with children up to age five. Once providers attain degrees and certification, they often leave for better-paying jobs in elementary education. The Child Care WAGE$ Project gives caregivers a financial incentive to stay in their child care programs after they complete their training. The ultimate goal is to increase the quality of care not only by keeping well-qualified providers but also by providing children with greater continuity of care and thus more stable relationships. Offered statewide in North Carolina, the Child Care WAGE$ Project is also found in Florida, Kansas, and South Carolina.

The National Association of Child Care Resource and Referral Agencies
The National Association of Child Care Resource and Referral Agencies (NACCRRA) supports more than eight hundred Child Care Resource and Referral agencies (CCR&Rs) located in communities across the country. These agencies work to increase the capacity of their communities to provide affordable, high-quality child care and education for all children. Efforts include helping parents find and pay for child care, increasing the supply of quality care by training providers, and leveraging public and private funds.

NACCRRA provides national leadership to advance the future of child care. The group was created in 1987 with a mission to "provide vision, leadership, and support to community CCR&Rs and to promote national policies and partnerships committed to the development and learning of all children." The strategic plan is to make "child care—specifically high-quality, affordable, and universally accessible child care—a national priority."[28] This effort involves four key strategic imperatives: building systems of care, promoting quality in all settings, engaging families, and building excellence in CCR&Rs.

To inform this strategy, Linda Smith, executive director of NACCRRA, applies her experience as the former director of child development programs for the Secretary of Defense during the implementation of the remarkably successful Military Child Care Act of 1989. For example, in an effort to professionalize the workforce, NACCRRA borrowed from the military model to create a system that tracks training at the level of the provider rather than employer. Currently being pilot tested, this effort will ultimately enable parents to look up the training levels of staff caring for their child.

The second critical piece of NACCRRA's policy agenda is to "develop an effective strategy to engage and educate parents so that public demand for improvements will move the agenda."[29] Over 58,000 parents have already signed up through NACCRRA's Parent Central website. The reasoning is that parents can be educated on the importance of quality child care and mobilized to exert pressure on the child care market for improved quality.

Employer-Sponsored Care

Another promising development has been an increase in the number of employer-sponsored child care programs. Although such efforts have not lived up to former president Reagan's hope that the private sector would solve the child care problem, the most successful of these programs demonstrate the powerful contribution that employers can make when they recognize that child care is a workforce issue and that parents are more productive when they are not worrying about the care their children are receiving.

Bright Horizons

Bright Horizons Family Solutions (BHFS) is a for-profit company that provides child care services for more than six hundred corporate clients. Employers contract with BHFS to provide onsite or near-site child care for their workers. The company's motive is well stated on their website: "By driving down turnover, reducing absenteeism, and increasing productivity on the job, child care and work/life programs are not only an investment in employees, but an investment in the success of your company."[30]

The numbers support the argument: unscheduled absences cost employers between $650 and $1,000 per employee per year.[31] Further, employer-sponsored child care is key to recruitment, retention, job satisfaction, and performance of employees. A survey by BHFS, which is obviously not a neutral party, emphasizes trends that have been apparent in the field for some time: among employees who did not plan to return to work after the birth or adoption of a child, 86 percent indicated that they would reconsider their decision if worksite child care were available. Of the one third of employees who considered quitting because of child care issues, 50 percent indicated that an onsite child care center would significantly encourage them to stay. Support among employees for onsite centers is high: 91 percent of all respondents, including those without children, believed worksite child care would have a positive impact on the organization for which they work.[32]

One of the most promising aspects of the Bright Horizons model is the high quality of their centers. To date, over 80 percent of Bright Horizons centers have achieved NAEYC accreditation, compared with 8 percent of centers nationally. To a great extent this emphasis on quality is a function of economies of scale and of Bright Horizons' unique business model, which leverages employer in-kind contributions (such as space and furnishings) and employer subsidies for parents. This amount of support enables the company to reinvest in quality maintenance efforts (for example, caregiver training and compensation) while maintaining a minimal profit margin.

Department of Defense and General Services Administration Child Care Models

Although Congress has balked at imposing federal regulations on child care for citizens and feared that subsidizing child care for any but the poorest families smacked of socialism, policy makers have enacted two systemic child care models for federal employees: one for military families and another for employees of federal agencies.

The Military Child Care Act of 1989 set in place a military child care system that, as Lang and I noted, is still the dream of child care advocates.[33] Basic standards affecting staff-child ratios and staff training have been established in all settings, including centers, family child care homes, and school-age programs. In a study of these standards, Marsland and her colleagues gave the Army a good rating for caregiver qualifications, which require a baccalaureate degree for program directors and a CDA credential plus more than twenty-four hours of annual in-service training for teachers. In addition, the act requires that all providers become accredited. To date, 95 percent of military child care centers are NAEYC-accredited. Tuition is subsidized on a sliding scale, with families paying fees that are 25 percent lower than those paid by civilians for comparable care.[34]

In 1985, Congress enacted the Trible Amendment, which gave federal agencies the authority to establish child care centers for their employees.[35] Acting in a way as the federal government's landlord, the General Services Administration (GSA) provides space and services for child care centers in federal buildings. Providers operate the centers under a revocable license agreement, which requires that they become NAEYC-accredited within one year and that at least 50 percent of their enrollment be children of federal employees. Remaining available slots may be open to the general public.

By 2002, there were 112 centers operating in GSA-sponsored spaces, and 84 percent of eligible centers were accredited by the NAEYC.[36] Centers that do not achieve accreditation within the specified time frame receive enhanced technical assistance through the GSA Office of Child Care and more stringent oversight until they do so or until their agreement with the GSA is revoked.

In striking contrast to the field of child care generally, GSA centers pay relatively high salaries, all provide paid vacation, and 96 percent offer health insurance. Moreover, federal agencies are authorized to help lower-income employees with their child care costs by allocating appropriated funds to a tuition assistance program. Parent fees are competitive, ranging from an average of $68 per week for school-age care to $174 per week for infant care.

STATE EFFORTS TO CREATE SYSTEMS OF CARE

In the absence of a national child care system, innovative models of child care system-building are emerging at the state level, where states are experimenting with a range of initiatives to braid together existing funding streams and to leverage existing resources. Although there are numerous outstanding examples of state-level innovation, here we discuss models developed in North Carolina, Arkansas, and Ohio, each of which has initiated the process of system building differently.

North Carolina

The best-funded initiative, relative to the size of its state's population of children, is North Carolina's Smart Start, which was championed by Governor James B. Hunt and enacted in 1993 to make high-quality early care and education services available to all children under the age of six.[37] In 2001 Smart Start was supported by $260 million in state general revenue and $55 million in private contributions. The program entails comprehensive services to improve early care and education, subsidies for children from low-income families, and health and family support services.

Elements of system reform start with governance of the programs at both the state and local levels. The North Carolina Partnership for Children is a public-private corporation run by a board of directors appointed by legislative leaders and the governor. Local boards must include parents, business representatives, the local directors of social services, the superintendent of schools, the community college president, a center-based provider, and a family child care provider. There are also representatives from Head Start and from the local CCR&R or another nonprofit agency related to child care. Major achievements include the creation of 48,000 new child care spaces, upgrading the quality of care through tiered licensing and professional development initiatives such as T.E.A.C.H., and supporting child care subsidies for more than 132,000 children. Smart Start has also been strengthened by an independent accountability evaluation component conducted by the University of North Carolina.

Arkansas School of the 21st Century

Another model of child care system-building has developed in Arkansas, where the School of the 21st Century is being implemented statewide through an ambitious public-private partnership. The goal is to improve the school readiness and educational success of Arkansas children through high-quality preschool education, child care, and family support services.

The first 21C site in the state, Paragould, was established in 1992. Within a few years, other schools expressed an interest in the program, and in 1997 the Yale Center in Child Development and Social Policy started working on a statewide presence with the Arkansas Department of Education. Growth was spurred when the Ross Foundation made a substantial investment in the Arkadelphia school district to enable district-wide implementation and outreach to the wider community. Seeing 21C as a means to address the early care and education needs of all children in Arkansas, the Winthrop Rockefeller Foundation initiated a five-year partnership with the Yale Center (now the Zigler Center) to support the development of a statewide 21C network (AR21C). The Yale component of this partnership is led by Matia Finn-Stevenson.

Currently the AR21C network includes 166 schools, organized under thirty-five programs in forty school districts. Each school serves as a year-round, full-time community hub focused on providing high-quality early education and care, after-school care for school-age children, school-based health care, parent education, and resource and referral services. One of the strengths of the Arkansas model is its emphasis on quality. Results of an ongoing evaluation show that the observed quality of AR21C programs ranges from good to excellent.[38] To support the development of new 21C programs, Arkansas recently implemented a peer training system in which trainers from established sites provide consultation and technical assistance to others who are in the process of implementing the 21C components. The initiative is a model of how philanthropic organizations can team with government and program developers to support practical solutions to meet children's early care and education needs. Arkansas is well on its way to following Kentucky, which already has a statewide network of 21C sites called Family Resource Centers.

Ohio

Ohio has a long history of involvement in child care planning, but beginning in 2003 several forces coalesced to create a set of interrelated child care initiatives that have placed the state at the forefront of system building nationwide. First was President Bush's Good Start, Grow Smart initiative, which contained specific recommendations for child care as a means to promote school readiness. This initiative prompted additional reporting requirements in the CCDBG state plan regarding how funds earmarked for quality would be used to support school readiness initiatives. A second force was the governor's authorization of the use of TANF funds to create a program that combined the efforts of the Ohio Department of Education (which administered Head Start) and the Ohio Department of Job and Family Services (which administered TANF) to create a new program, the Early Learning Initiative. This action enabled child care programs to become Early Learning Initiative providers alongside Head Start and public preschools, giving child care services recognition as an important context to support children's school readiness.

Thus, a window of opportunity was created for the development of fiscal and human capital to support child care improvement efforts in alignment with the Early Learning Initiative goals. What was needed were people with the expertise and willingness necessary to seize the opportunity. Enter two champions: Jamie Gottesman, who had just arrived as the new assistant chief of the Ohio Bureau of Child Care and Development, and Alicia Leatherman, executive director of the Ohio Child Care Resource and Referral Association. The two collaborated to implement three initiatives targeting improvements in infant and toddler care, child care quality, and child care regulation. These became First Steps, Ohio's infant and toddler initiative; Step up to Quality, Ohio's voluntary ratings system; and Regulation for the 21st Century.

First Steps is designed to improve the quality of infant and toddler care by focusing on training. Caregivers receive professional development coupled with intensive, job-embedded coaching and mentoring by infant and toddler specialists. The specialists, who are placed in the twelve resource and referral agencies across the state, are certified in WestEd's Program for Infant/Toddler Care (PITC) and are trained to assess quality of care using professional environmental rating scales. Gottesman and her team assessed the impact of First Steps by randomly assigning participating programs to one of three levels of intervention: a low intervention group, which received environmental quality rating scores by mail; a medium intervention group, which received scores and was given PITC training from the specialists in their area; and a high intervention group, which received the scores, PITC training, and onsite coaching and assistance from the regional specialists. The programs were reevaluated one year later.

Results of the pilot project were illuminating. Not surprisingly, a large proportion of infant and toddler settings were categorized as inadequate. Although the effect of intervention varied depending on the individual specialist, the high level of intervention was the most effective for improving the quality of activities that promote school readiness. Subsequently, guidelines were developed to systematize the quality of assistance provided by the specialists. The program is in the process of being expanded statewide.

Step up to Quality was developed to provide an incentive for child care programs to voluntarily exceed Ohio's minimal licensing requirements and to provide parents with an easy tool to help them select quality early care and education programs. Thus, in some respects, it is analogous to North Carolina's rating system. However, Step up to Quality links early learning benchmarks with quality indicators and includes extensive oversight and enforcement. Ratings are suspended or removed for serious licensing noncompliance. The system includes three quality steps, with the third step indicating consistently high process and structural quality. Programs that participate receive financial incentives commensurate with their quality rating, such as T.E.A.C.H. accreditation grants and quality improvement grants.

Regulation for the 21st Century is in its formative stage and aims to apply the lessons learned from Step up to Quality toward the improvement of minimal licensing requirements and support for providers striving to attain higher quality ratings. Project staff are working to develop exacting enforcement requirements that will force low-performing providers to exit the system.

The three elements of the Ohio system are interrelated and work synergistically to enable parents to select good-quality care and to increase the capacity of child care providers to meet the school readiness needs of Ohio's children. A major strength is that the model leverages public support for early education by linking school readiness with child care experiences. As Gottesman points out, the work of the BUILD Initiative, a national effort currently headed by Garrit Westervelt that assists states in developing comprehensive early education and care systems, was critical in this respect. Through extensive research and public outreach,

BUILD developed the slogan for the Ohio model, "Early experiences last a lifetime," which Gottesman credits with helping to cultivate the public will that has made Ohio's success possible.[39]

In sum, although the pace of progress has been disappointing, we have made significant, albeit fragmented, steps toward addressing our nation's child care problem over the last three and a half decades. Much of this progress has occurred at the state level and has been facilitated by the Child Care Bureau. Nevertheless, these efforts have not made a sufficient impact on the hodgepodge nonsystem of care in America, which is inefficient and allows scarce public funds to be wasted on poor-quality care. In the absence of a federal child care system, we must find another way to achieve a sustainable long-term solution. As we will discuss in our final chapter, one opportunity is to leverage the momentum of the UPK and school-age child care movements, as Arkansas is doing with the School of the 21st Century. While this will address the child care needs of three- to twelve-year-old children, it will not address the plight of infants and toddlers. A true remedy to our tragedy must tackle this problem head on.

CHAPTER NINE

Envisioning a Solution

If every child is a national resource, then every child's welfare
is a national responsibility. Unless we make every effort to insure
that all children have an opportunity to grow and develop as they
should, we will be shortchanging not only the children but our
nation's future.

Zigler and Lang

IN THE FIRST THREE CHAPTERS of this book, I reviewed the growing
body of knowledge about the developmental needs of young children
and the valiant efforts of advocates and concerned policy makers to address those needs. I argued that our nation continues to experience what
has been aptly referred to as a "silent crisis" in child care.[1] The next five
chapters of the book discussed the depth of the child care problem, efforts
to relieve the crisis, and opportunities for future action. Now I return to
what I see as the weaknesses of child care policy in the United States and
what can be done to remedy the situation.

At this time I believe it would be unrealistic to expect a national policy
like the Comprehensive Child Development Act of 1971, which would
have solved the child care problem before it became enormous. The veto
of that act was the greatest failure of my professional life, and that child
care has emerged and reemerged in the policy agenda over the ensuing
decades without meaningful solutions is a tragedy for America's families.
It is shocking that we, as a nation, seem unable—or unwilling—to apply
what is known about child development to the caregiving environments
where young children spend a considerable part of their earliest years.
And it is sad that decade after decade, our nation's leaders have chosen
not to provide a remedy to help struggling parents, their employers, and
the next generation of American workers.

The price of our paralysis is high and paid by nearly everyone. The price is paid daily by those unfortunate infants, toddlers, and preschoolers who receive care that is of such poor quality that their development is compromised. The price is paid by millions of school-age children left to care for themselves after the closing school bell rings. The price is paid by parents who struggle to find and finance safe child care arrangements. The price is paid by businesses that lose millions of dollars in productivity each year as parents miss work because of child care issues or spend work time worrying about their children's well-being. Ultimately the price will be paid by our society, which by its inaction is systematically compromising its own future. We simply cannot afford to continue to do nothing.

I realize that our recommendations for a meaningful solution to the child care crisis will not please everyone and will appeal to a smaller constituency than did the Comprehensive Child Development Act. Yet we must be mindful of the words of historian Kimberly Morgan concerning the act's failure: "In sum, the passions of both the left and the right jointly defeated an attempt to form a national, unified day-care policy."[2] Indeed, the values that were central in defining the scope and content of the child care debates in the 1970s are just as pertinent today. This time it is critical that a viable solution be created and that all factions avoid the temptation of letting the perfect become the enemy of the good.

I hold the needs of the child to be primary and treat the child care environment as an important setting for cognitive, social, and emotional growth. My recommendations are based on evidence from the scientific study of child development and are grounded on four core principles. First, good-quality child care is critical to the optimal development of children, and improving the quality of care must be a national priority. Second, a viable solution must ensure that high-quality programs are universally accessible and that parents are able to choose the type of setting they prefer. Third, a solution must address the unique challenges associated with infant and toddler, preschool-age, and school-age child care. Finally, given the scope of the problem, we must define roles for all stakeholders—federal and state governments, the private sector, parents, and practitioners—who can make unique contributions to the solution.

In sum, I recognize that a national child care policy, such as that set forth in the Comprehensive Child Development Act, is now unrealistic both pragmatically and politically. Therefore, I articulate a hybrid solution that includes a national plan for infants and toddlers, a state-level plan for children ages three through twelve, and a federally coordinated effort to improve the quality of all care by addressing both the supply and demand sides of the market and supporting research to inform best practices.

CARE FOR CHILDREN FROM BIRTH TO AGE THREE

As I discussed in chapter 5, care for infants and toddlers is the most challenging piece of the child care problem. Good-quality care is essential to healthy development during this period of rapid growth and learning. Such care is expensive, whether parents select a high-quality child care setting or opt to stay home to care for their baby. Most families face this expense early in their wage-earning years, at precisely the time when they can least afford it. Those who cannot forego wages are faced with the task of finding a child care slot, armed only with their level of knowledge about quality indicators and their ability to pay. With good care often unavailable or unaffordable, many of our youngest children are placed in poor-quality care during their formative early years. This is unacceptable, and it is well past time that we recognize the need for a national investment in infant and toddler care. I propose a two-pronged solution to achieve this goal.

Paid Parental Leave

Experts in early development agree that, ideally, infants should be cared for by their parents rather than by substitute caregivers. Yet, as I noted in the previous chapter, the current provisions for parental leave under the Family and Medical Leave Act are woefully inadequate, providing neither universal coverage nor wage replacement. Therefore, our first recommendation is that the FMLA be expanded to mandate that *all* employees —regardless of the size of the employer—have access to a job-protected leave for up to three months after the birth or adoption of a new baby. In keeping with the recommendations set forth by the Yale Bush Center Advisory Committee on Infant Care Leave, the leave would provide both job protection and benefit continuance.[3] To enable more parents to benefit from the time at home, mechanisms should be put in place to provide at least partial wage replacement—at minimum, 75 percent of salary.

History teaches us that expansion of the FMLA to include paid leave is not viable at the federal level in the near term. However, as is often the case when the federal government fails to provide leadership, innovative solutions are emerging at the state level. Several states have made strides toward enacting paid leaves using mechanisms such as temporary disability insurance programs. Such efforts are more promising than anything else on the horizon and should be cultivated. Therefore, our second recommendation is that the federal government establish grants to assist states in developing paid family leave programs. Legislation to support such state efforts has been proposed by Christopher Dodd in the Senate and Lynn Woolsey in the House. Indeed, bipartisan support for paid leave has been demonstrated by the introduction of landmark legislation by Senators Dodd and Ted Stevens, which would provide up to eight weeks of paid leave. This proposal, the Family Leave Insurance Act of 2007, would establish a Family Leave Insurance Fund, through which employers, employees, and the federal government would share the cost of providing compensation to families during illness or after the birth or adoption of a new child. Full wage compensation would be offered to parents earning up to $20,000 annually and partial compensation to those earning up to $97,000 annually. Although a longer, fully paid leave would be ideal, the shorter, partially paid leave proposed here would at least afford those parents who elect to use it the time to adjust to their new roles as parents and to make informed decisions about the type of child care they plan to use as their babies grow.

Affordable, Good-Quality Care
Proposed models of care for infants and toddlers can be categorized into three general approaches. The first is a centralized and subsidized child care system like the one established in Quebec in 1997. The appeal of this model is its universality and affordability. All families in Quebec are eligible to participate, and no family, regardless of their income level, pays more than $7 per child per day. Although the system enjoys tremendous support, it has been criticized on several points. First, all subsidized care is center based and does not accommodate the preferences of families seeking different types of child care or the need for part-time or shift care.[4] Second, the quality of care provided in the centers is highly variable.[5] Because of the system's already sizable public cost, its ability to obtain funding for quality improvements is limited. Such a model would thus necessitate an enormous investment of public funds but would neither

assure quality nor support parental choice. Consequently, I do not see this as a viable model in the United States.

An alternative model has been proposed by economists Suzanne Helburn and Barbara Bergmann.[6] In their groundbreaking analysis of the child care problem, they outline three versions of a national plan, one of which might be modified to address the child care needs of infants and toddlers. This model, which they refer to as "affordable care of improved quality," would provide subsidies to all families to pay for care at a level of quality equal to the current national average. They define affordable care as not costing a family more than 20 percent of their income above the poverty line. Thus, this model would provide fully subsidized care for poor families and partially subsidized care for low- and middle-income families. Although the system would require a substantial infusion of new money, some of the costs could be offset by elimination of the child care tax credit and by redirection of funds currently spent on CCDBG. One of the most attractive aspects of the plan is that it gives providers higher reimbursement rates if they achieve higher quality standards. In theory, this means that all parents would have the ability to purchase good-quality care and that providers would have an incentive to offer it. However, a major drawback of the proposal is that it would only subsidize nonparental care. Therefore, it fails to meet one of our core principles of a viable policy—that parents be supported in selecting care that best meets their needs and preferences, particularly during the first three years, when many parents prefer to care for their children themselves.

The model I propose for infant and toddler care is a child allowance trust fund, based on a proposal by Jule Sugarman.[7] The trust fund would serve as a means of assisting parents to care for their very young children with whatever combination of parental and supplementary care best suits their circumstances. The fund would provide all families with an annual stipend generous enough to assist in the purchase of good-quality care or to supplement the income of parents who wish to remain at home. Thus, the child allowance would be a demand-side subsidy and a universal cash benefit not restricted by income. The size of the allowance would be based on estimates of the cost of good care.

As Lang and I have described, the trust fund would draw revenues from a new payroll tax added to social security deductions.[8] Money in the trust would be entirely separate from other social security accounts, and no exchange of funds between the two systems would be possible. Funds from the trust would be distributed directly to families with children aged three months to three years, although parents who opt not to take the full three-month paid leave when their babies are born could access the funds upon their return to work. With this financial support, as well as improved consumer education regarding the features of good-quality care, more parents would be able to choose environments—whether at home or in a child care setting—that support their children's growth and learning.

The child allowance would be designed to be self-supporting and would not affect the ailing social security trust at all. Rather, it would merely piggyback on the existing payroll tax mechanism to avoid the need for a new tax collection infrastructure. There is some appeal to linking the cost of caring for dependent children to social security, if only in name. Good child care is, after all, a deposit toward the security of the society. This notion is in keeping with other ideas to finance child care that have been floated over time.[9] For example, Walker proposed a mechanism to enable parents to use future social security benefits as collateral for low-interest loans to cover their child care costs.[10] However, the looming crisis in social security could make this suggestion unpalatable to policy makers. Our child allowance program would frame the costs of children's early care as a social good worthy of societal investment but would not place any financial burden on the social security system itself.

PRESCHOOL-AGE CHILD CARE

To address the child care needs of three- and four-year-old children, I envision universally accessible preschools with wraparound child care based on the School of the 21st Century model. The state preschool movement has strong momentum and a broad following. Surveys and public opinion polls repeatedly show that the majority of taxpayers approve state funding of preschool.[11] As these programs are created and expanded, they bring the possibility of a new venue for the provision of preschool child care. Wraparound care must be available to meet the needs of working parents, and, to accommodate the developmental needs of preschoolers, curricula should follow a whole-child approach as opposed to a strictly academic approach.

This prekindergarten system comes from the proposal in the recent book I wrote with Walter Gilliam and Stephanie Jones, *A Vision for Universal*

Preschool Education.[12] This model assumes universal availability of pre-school and seizes the opportunity to classify high-quality child care as an equal contributor to school readiness. The proposal is not only firmly rooted in developmental science but also politically workable. All children, not only poor children, benefit from high-quality preschool, and a universal approach attracts a broader group of supporters. Robert Lawrence noted the value of this large constituency in creating Georgia's universal preschool program: "You can't mount a sustainable program without support from the middle class that votes."[13] More voices create a stronger call for high quality and continued funding.

This state-based UPK program would be administered by the public school system. As discussed in chapter 6, placing preschools under the auspices of the public school system does not necessarily mean they will be physically located in the schools. Depending on local resources, preschool could be delivered in community facilities or other outside settings, as they are in Georgia. The critical aspect is that there would be one entity responsible for program policies and practices, quality standards, and oversight.

While the evidence is mixed on the most efficient level of teacher qualification, the final report of the National Research Council's Committee on Early Childhood Pedagogy, "Eager to Learn: Educating our Preschoolers," calls for increases in the education and training of preschool teachers.[14] Voicing the leading perspective shared among researchers, Gilliam, Jones, and I recommend that UPK teachers have bachelor's degrees and certification in early childhood education or a related field and that assistant teachers have at least associate's degrees in early childhood education or Child Development Associates (CDAs). To ensure that the learning environment is adequately structured for active learning and supports quality adult-child and peer interactions, teacher-child ratios should be capped at one to ten, which is consistent with both the Head Start Performance Standards and NAEYC's accreditation criteria for preschool programs.

Current funding streams for preschool should be maintained and expanded. At the federal level these include Head Start, Title I of NCLB, the CCDBG, and the Individuals with Disabilities Education Act. Under the proposed model, the federal government would provide funds for children and families at the highest risk, and state and local governments would support access for the rest of the population. Parents, many of whom already pay for preschool care, would be charged fees calibrated to their income. The 21C model has successfully employed a sliding-scale fee and demonstrated that programs can operate in the black.

Certainly not all working parents will choose pre-K with wraparound care as the most appropriate arrangement for their preschoolers. They may prefer family day care or less formal arrangements such as neighbor or relative care. In the 21C model, school personnel engage in outreach to and support of community child care providers. They offer training, support networks, and other services to improve the quality of care available to district residents. I envision that much of this capacity building and quality support will be accomplished in collaboration with state and local CCR&Rs and other state-level coordinating bodies, such as the State Early Learning Councils.

SCHOOL-AGE CHILD CARE

To address the child care needs of children ages five through thirteen, I envision statewide networks that build on the success of the 21st Century Community Learning Centers. Like UPK, after-school programs are quite popular. According to the Afterschool Alliance, 6.5 million children are enrolled in ASPs, and the parents of another 15.3 million say their children would participate in a program if one were available. As discussed in chapter 7, the 21CCLC initiative is the only federal funding source dedicated exclusively to after-school care. Currently 21CCLCs are authorized under NCLB to receive funding of $2.5 billion. The total federal investment in school-age child care is estimated at $3.6 billion when TANF, Title I, Food and Nutrition grants, and Social Services Block Grants are considered. In my proposal, these multiple funding streams would be aligned within a block grant to states that would expand the availability of 21CCLCs.

The challenge for state policy makers has recently shifted from increasing the availability of 21CCLCs to creating sustainable programs. When federal grants for 21CCLCs were reauthorized under NCLB, the purpose of the grants shifted to being a short-term source of funding for startup or expansion of after-school programs. Once these moneys are exhausted, operating costs must be covered by other sources.

Funding for 21CCLC programs needs to be expanded. In 2004, for example, only 38 percent of communities who applied for 21CCLC grants were awarded them.[15] To supplement federal support, states have been making commitments, but their progress has been uneven.

QUALITY IMPROVEMENT: THE KEYSTONE

We have stressed over and over again in this volume that the quality of child care primarily depends on the caregiving staff. Unfortunately, the current dynamics of the child care market do not promote the provision of high-quality care. Parents sometimes do not demand quality because of lack of information or ability to pay, and providers find it difficult to supply quality due to the high costs required, primarily that of skilled labor. As Blau has noted, a solution must address both sides of the market.[16] In this section, I describe a role for the Child Care Bureau in promoting child care quality and potential ways to implement strategies at the state level.

The Coordinating Role of the Child Care Bureau

The Child Care Bureau was created in 1995, charged with "enhancing the quality, affordability, and availability of child care for all families."[17] As discussed in chapter 8, the Bureau made great strides under its first director, Joan Lombardi, and her successor, Shannon Christian. However, despite Christian's valiant efforts, the Bureau has been starved of the resources necessary to do its job. Most recently, the Bureau's mission was redefined to focus exclusively on the child care needs of low-income families, and the Bureau itself was relocated to the Office of Family Assistance. This constitutes a monumental step backward, once again framing child care as a welfare and workforce issue instead of a child development issue. I join the call made by Senator Dodd and others to reverse this decision.

Returning the Bureau to the Administration on Children, Youth, and Families is not enough to enable it to realize its potential. A harsh lesson of the last five years is how vulnerable the Bureau was from its inception. Though not apparent when the Bureau flourished with the support of the White House, Secretary of Health and Human Services Shalala, and Director Lombardi, this vulnerability became increasingly obvious as the political and ideological tides turned over time. The Bureau needs a new and stronger base from which it can launch long-term strategies and planning. Therefore, I view the current situation as a window of opportunity for strengthening the federal government's role in supporting the child care needs of both parents and children. In essence, after the CCDA debates of the early 1970s, this constitutes a second golden moment.

Specifically, I recommend that a new Office of Child Care be created by statute. This office would function in parallel with the Office of Head

Start within the Administration on Children and Families. It would be charged with the Child Care Bureau's original mission—to enhance the quality, affordability, and availability of child care for *all* families—and also with supporting state efforts to create comprehensive systems of early care. The language of the statute should mandate that the department's budget be sufficient to adequately staff the office. In this way, a center for federal initiatives on child care would be established legislatively and elevated to a level that would enhance its ability to work across agencies (for example, with the Office of Head Start and the Bureau on Maternal and Child Health) to support state-level efforts to braid together resources and align systems.

Like the Child Care Bureau before it, the Office of Child Care would have responsibility for administering the CCDBG, with two major additions. First, the office would work with the Office of Family Assistance to track discretionary TANF spending on child care beyond the 30 percent allowable transfer to CCDBG so that all use of TANF funds for child care is transparent. Second, the office would work with the states to ensure that funds spent on child care through both CCDBG and TANF are used to purchase good-quality care.

To achieve this second objective, the CCDBG would be sufficiently funded to achieve its legislative mandates, and the minimum quality set-aside would be increased from 4 percent to 10 percent. The role of the Office of Child Care in this respect would be to monitor state plans for administration of CCDBG funds and for quality improvement efforts. In other words, rather than creating a federal child care system, the office would guide the development of state systems of care.

As the state initiatives described in chapter 8 illustrate, the driving force underlying state system building will vary from state to state. In some cases it may be driven by UPK and school-readiness initiatives, while in others it may be related to Head Start or public health initiatives. Regardless of the starting point, states will need incentives and assistance in leveraging resources, streamlining program administration, and aligning services. This suggests an important role for the federal government. Specifically, the Office of Child Care would be responsible for:

1. Administration of incentive grants to states to build strong child care systems. Currently, there is a great deal of energy in the states being

spent on the development of pieces of early care and education systems. However, this activity is often fragmented and results in mini-systems, or "silos," working inefficiently in parallel or, worse, at cross-purposes. For example, massive efforts may be undertaken to develop school readiness programs, while other parts of government may be working on child care for children with special needs or those whose parents have reached the time limit for receiving welfare benefits. What would be helpful in this situation is a way to bring together the expertise emerging in both areas of activity. Ideally, the contributions of all stake-holders in a state would be pooled in a truly aligned system.

2. Administration of workforce improvement grants to states to strengthen their capacity to train providers and retain the best workers through programs such as T.E.A.C.H. and WAGE$. As state preschool systems evolve, such programs will become increasingly important in order to attract and retain qualified infant and toddler caregivers.

3. Ongoing research to inform policy and program development at the federal and state levels. Among the many laudable accomplishments of the Child Care Bureau under the stewardship of Lombardi and Christian was the establishment of a specialized research office and a tight research-policy-practice triangle. Under the current organiza-tion, this triangle has been broken, and research responsibilities have been relocated to the Office of Planning, Evaluation, and Research. To best inform innovative policy and program development and identify effective practices, the new office must restore the research-policy-practice connection, particularly as states develop effective models of early childhood service coordination.

The Potential Contributions of Resource and Referral Agencies
Although historically weak, the child care resource and referral system has grown impressively over recent years and can assume an important role in quality improvement efforts. At the local level, CCR&Rs offer community-based expertise to three core groups: families, providers, and communities. For families, they provide information about identifying good child care. An example is the booklet entitled *Is This the Right Place for My Child? 38 Research-Based Indicators of High-Quality Child Care.* Local CCR&Rs also help families identify available financial supports. For providers, the agencies facilitate access to training and professional

development opportunities and address other challenges of improving quality. In fact, CCR&Rs currently train nearly half of our nation's 1.2 million child care providers. While most of these students are caregivers in centers and family child care settings, a small percentage of them are relatives, friends, and neighbors who care for children—a group traditionally outside the audience of skill-development programs.[18] Many of the courses offered by CCR&Rs are designed to help providers earn the CDA credential, certification, accreditation, higher state quality ratings, or college credits.

For communities, CCR&Rs conduct needs assessments, monitor the availability of care, and advise local leaders on the coordination of child care with other family services. A promising development is that thirty-four states have formed R&R networks to coordinate and provide leadership to the local CCR&Rs.[19] These networks compile information on the cost, quality, and availability of child care throughout the state and can serve as a resource to state policy makers. Strong network offices can contribute to improving accessibility and availability of quality care. Some states' networks, however, are only voluntary or remain underfunded.[20]

Fortunately, there is an umbrella organization perfectly suited to develop the potential of local CCR&Rs to bring much-needed improvements to child care services. As described in chapter 8, the National Association of Child Care Resource and Referral Agencies is a network of approximately 860 state and local member organizations. NACCRRA conducts activities that would be impractical for its constituents to undertake individually, such as strategic planning, leadership, and national advocacy. It also provides a variety of support services, including programs to help parents find licensed care and to support quality improvement. I envision a strong role for NACCRA in helping to address both the supply and demand sides of the child care market.

In the conclusion of their strategic plan for 2006–2011, NACCRRA's board of directors revealed their role in a moment of self-reflection: "Because CCR&Rs provide the most consistent source of data, and because they have nationwide coverage and routinely interact with parents, providers, and business and policy leaders, a strong, well-organized system of state and local CCR&Rs can become the catalyst for change."[21] Under the direction of Linda Smith, NACCRRA seems poised to assume a leadership role in coordinating quality improvement efforts at the state and local levels. The group has now developed a twelve-point plan for improving our nation's training of caregivers, based largely on the models of Head Start, Early Head Start, and military child care. I enthusiastically endorse this plan and strongly recommend that the Child Care Bureau support NACCRRA's efforts to deploy the knowledge base.

WHERE DO WE STAND NOW?

I have noted that a solution to the child care tragedy depends on three circumstances necessary for policy development to take place: a pervasive sense that a real problem exists, an effective lobby to advocate for action, and receptive policy makers to legislate change. I conclude with a discussion of where we stand with respect to each of these prerequisites.

Growing Awareness

Though families continue to struggle with their child care problems in isolation, there is growing public awareness of the importance of early learning environments to children's school readiness and of school-age child care to students' academic and social well-being. This awareness has been heightened by the emphasis on school readiness in the Goals 2000: Educate America Act of 1994, the well-publicized success of several early intervention programs, and media attention to the importance of development during the first three years of life. Acknowledgment of the problem is evident in calls by business leaders and economists for greater investments in early education, by law enforcement officials for greater availability of school-age child care, and by educators for greater alignment of child care with school readiness initiatives.

A proven strategy for building public awareness is to frame child care as an important contributor to children's school readiness and later academic success. This approach is taken by Educare, a multimillion-dollar public-private partnership in Colorado focused on improving both the quality of child care in the state and public awareness of why quality is so important. Spearheaded by Doug Price, the president of one of the state's largest banks and chairman of the Governor's Business Commission on Child Care Financing, Educare created, validated, and implemented a quality-rating system that is coupled with resources and technical assistance for child care providers and education and outreach efforts for parents. The initiative began in Denver, ultimately merged with the Colorado Office of Resource and Referral Agencies, and has now become a federally funded, statewide quality improvement system. The merged organization, Qualistar, uses both private and public dollars to promote child care quality through fifteen CCR&R affiliates. Most important, the Educare initiative helped to link the notion of high-quality early care and education with student achievement in the eyes of both the public and the legislature. In this way, Educare demonstrates the power of the business and philanthropic communities to help reframe child care, cultivate political support for public investment, and give the issue traction.[22]

Another example of the emerging role of the private sector in championing child care quality improvement is First Children's Finance (FCF). Led by Jerry Cutts with a board headed by Linda Smith of NACCRRA, FCF provides child care entrepreneurs with the tools they need to successfully run a small business. The reality is that many operators of child care facilities, while knowledgeable about children, lack financial expertise and often do not recognize themselves as owners of small or moderate-size businesses. With funds drawn primarily from the private sphere, FCF provides loans to caregivers and also offers technical support, consulting services, and formal business training. Their help is contingent on the operator's commitment to improving the quality of services provided to children. FCF also works to develop public and private partnerships, enabling it to expand its reach. They now provide services statewide in Minnesota and are currently expanding to six other states. Their ultimate goal is to make their services available nationwide. FCF offers a unique and valuable contribution to professionalizing the child care industry.

Similarly, the BUILD Initiative, a multistate partnership created by a consortium of national and local foundations with grant-making programs in early childhood care and education, has been instrumental in reframing child care as an investment in early learning. In Ohio, BUILD helped create the slogan for the state's Infant and Toddler Guidelines and Step up to Quality programs: "Early experiences last a lifetime." In addition, BUILD cultivated business and legislative support by emphasizing the economic rationale for investment in good-quality child care and early education.

Linked to school readiness and academic success, child care is an issue that is gaining momentum—particularly with respect to preschool and school-age child care, and increasingly with respect to the importance of quality care during the first three years of life. What is needed now is a vehicle to harness this awareness and channel this energy into an effective lobby for action.

An Effective Lobby?

The demise of the Child Care Action Campaign in 2003 silenced the only voice devoted specifically to child care on the national level. In the absence of a national umbrella organization, advocacy has become fragmented, with several organizations now addressing separate facets of the child care problem. For example, the Center for the Child Care Workforce advocates for improved compensation and training of caregivers, and the National Women's Law Center advocates for policies to improve the affordability of high-quality care. One young advocacy group that is gaining prominence is the Children's Project, which was established in 2002 and is now working in conjunction with the Center for Law and Social Policy. The group is attempting to create partnerships with local and national organizations to promote sound child care policies. The project is also enlisting new voices to speak out on issues affecting young children and families, including professionals from the business, medical, and law enforcement communities, as well as parents. Eventually this organization's reputation may grow enough for it to fill the void left by the Child Care Action Campaign.

Other efforts are also under way to form an effective lobby of women in support of universal child care and parental leaves. Increasingly, mothers have moved from voicing their frustration to organizing in an attempt to improve the situation. They are using the Internet to reach out to one another. Thus far, the leading group appears to be Moms Rising, a group whose founders are forming alliances with other advocacy groups such as Mothers and More, Mothers Movement Online, Mothers Ought to Have Equal Rights, and the National Association of Mothers' Centers. These groups are sharing information and joining together at rallies. They are also beginning to partner with labor groups and feminist groups like the National Organization for Women, voices that have been historically muted on this issue.

These relatively new advocates are concentrating their efforts on state legislatures and have already scored some small victories in Washington state and California. Moms Rising, however, has broken through to the national scene. The group produced a documentary that was shown in Washington, DC, to a crowd that included several influential senators, so they are definitely making inroads. The organizer's goal is to build a nonpartisan grassroots movement, millions strong. This goal appears to be realistic: in its first few months, Moms Rising attracted more than 80,000 members, and membership continues to grow steadily.[23]

Although these emerging voices appear to be gaining strength, I have several concerns about their potential to serve as an effective lobby for the bold policy development that will be required to address the multiple dimensions of the child care crisis. First, viable policy solutions must be bipartisan, yet organizations such as Moms Rising are viewed as highly partisan. Second, though the specific goals of these groups are admirable, they each speak to different facets of the child care problem and thus fail to address the totality of the child care dilemma. Perhaps most important, with the exception of the Children's Project, these groups tend to reinforce the view of child care as an adult issue rather than underscoring the essential duality of child care as both a support for working parents and an environment to support children's development. In sum, I applaud these groups and am optimistic that they will play an important role in driving child care policy forward; however, the absence of a clear voice dedicated exclusively to child care is resounding.

Receptive Leaders
Receptive leaders appear to be emerging at both the national and state levels. In the states, officials like the former governor of North Carolina, Jim Hunt, have taken the lead in promoting investment in child care and the development of coordinated systems of early care and education. At the national level too, child care is beginning to receive serious bipartisan attention. One sign is the recent creation of the Senate Caucus on Children, Work, and Family, cochaired by Christopher Dodd and Arlen Specter. In their letter inviting other senators to join them, Dodd and Specter wrote, "Workplace policies play an integral role in the lives of families." The establishment of this caucus, together with increased attention to children's issues as highlighted by House Speaker Nancy Pelosi at the National Summit on America's Children in May 2007, promises to give renewed momentum to child care as a social issue rather than an

individual problem, and the timing could not be better. Given the earlier success of Dodd and Specter in championing school-age child care policy and the demonstrated commitment of Representatives DeLauro, Miller, and Woolsey in the House, I am optimistic about the potential power of this nascent effort. I strongly recommend that Congress move expediently to bolster federal support for child care by sponsoring legislation to create a new Office of Child Care through statute.

In conclusion, child care in America is in crisis, and it is a tragedy that this crisis has been allowed to fester for so long and at the expense of so many children who have been subjected to poor-quality care. Although experienced individually, child care is not an individual problem. It is a societal problem, and it is long past time that it be recognized as such. Given the body of knowledge at hand, the lessons of the past thirty-five years, and the resources available, failure to act can be interpreted to mean that our nation simply does not care about young children or about its own future.

There is no easy or inexpensive solution to a problem of this magnitude and importance. We will only make real progress when child care is treated as a national issue related to the quality of our workforce development, our nation's productivity, and our ability to compete in the world market. Leading economists, including Nobel laureate James Heckman, have elevated preschool education to this level and have called for increased investment in systems of early care and education. To maximize the return on such investments, however, quality improvement is paramount. Continued spending on poor-quality care wastes money and squanders children's potential.

In addition to investment, a true solution will also require compromise. Child care is a highly value-laden issue that resonates with many deeply held personal and cultural beliefs. Therefore, viable policy solutions must allow states and communities the flexibility to craft systems that best address the needs and preferences of their citizens and that afford parents choice. Regardless of whether these solutions emerge organically from the bottom up or are driven from the top down, they will require coordination in order to optimally leverage resources and maximize value added. Failure to ensure adequate coordination will only exacerbate the fragmentation that characterizes the current nonsystem.

As a country, we have an opportunity to remedy this tragedy and put in place policies that support working families and the children who will one day assume control of our democracy. As adults, we owe it to our children to promote their well-being and enable them to optimize their potential. The time is now. The responsibility is ours.

NOTES

PREFACE

1. M. D. Keyserling (1972), *Windows on day care* (New York: National Council of Jewish Women).
2. National Council of Jewish Women (1999), *Opening a new window on child care: A report on the status of child care in the nation today* (New York: National Council of Jewish Women).
3. Cost, Quality, and Child Outcomes Study Team (1995), *Cost, quality, and child outcomes in child care centers, public report*, 2nd ed. (Denver: Economics Department, University of Colorado).
4. G. Collins (2007), "None dare call it child care," *New York Times*, October 18.
5. N. Shpancer (2003), "The effects of daycare: Persistent questions, elusive answers," *Early Childhood Research Quarterly* 21:227–237.
6. D. Kirp and D. Kong (2007), "Who cares for the children?" in *The sandbox investment*, ed. D. Kirp (Cambridge, MA: Harvard University Press), 136–152.
7. Ibid.
8. Ibid.
9. Collins, "None dare call it child care."
10. D. Ewen and H. Matthews (2007), "Title I and early childhood programs: A look at investments in the NCLB era," *CLASP Policy Paper* no. 2.
11. H. Stebbins and J. Knitzer (2007), *State early childhood policies* (New York: National Center for Children in Poverty).

CHAPTER 1. THE CHALLENGE OF CHILD CARE

1. White House Conference on Children (1970), *Report to the President* (Washington, DC: U.S. Government Printing Office).

2. S. W. Helburn, ed. (1999), "The silent crisis in U.S. child care," *Annals of the American Academy of Political and Social Science* 563.

3. E. Rose (1999), *A mother's job: The history of day care, 1890–1960* (New York: Oxford University Press).

4. U.S. Bureau of Labor Statistics (2005), *Women in the labor force: A data book*, http://www.bls.gov/cps/wlf-databook2005.htm (retrieved March 17, 2007); Employment Policy Foundation (2004), *The balancing act*, October 28, http://web.archive.org/web/20050117191207/www.workandfamily.org/newsletters/2004/ba20041028.pdf.

5. Forum on Family Statistics (2006), *America's children in brief: Key national indicators of well-being* (Washington, DC: Federal Interagency Forum on Child and Family Statistics), http://childstats.gov/americaschildren/pop6 .asp; L. M. Casper and S. M. Bianchi (2002), *Continuity and change in the American family* (Thousand Oaks, CA: Sage).

6. H. Lu and H. Koball (2003), *The changing demographics of low-income families and their children* (New York: National Center for Children in Poverty).

7. E. Smolensky and J. A. Gootman, eds. (2003), *Working families and growing kids: Caring for children and adolescents* (Washington, DC: National Academies Press).

8. H. B. Presser (1999), "Toward a 24-hour economy," *Science* 284: 1778–1779; T. M. Beers (2000), "Flexible schedules and shift work: Replacing the '9–5' workday?" *Monthly Labor Review* 123(6): 33–40, http://www.bls.gov/opub/mlr/2000/06/art3full.pdf.

9. G. M. Mulligan, D. Brimhall, J. West, and C. Chapman (2005), *Child care and early education arrangements of infants, toddlers, and preschoolers: 2001*, NCES 2006–039, U.S. Department of Education, National Center for Education Statistics (Washington, DC: U.S. Government Printing Office).

10. Smolensky and Gootman, *Working families and growing kids*.

11. B. Downs (2003), "Fertility of American women: June 2002," *Current Population Reports P20–548* (Washington, DC: U.S. Census Bureau).

12. M. Brown-Lyons, A. Robertson, and J. Layzer (2001), *Kith and kin— informal child care: Highlights from recent research* (New York: National Center for Children in Poverty).

13. C. D. Hayes, J. L. Palmer, and M. J. Zaslow, eds. (1990), *Who cares for America's children? Child care policy for the 1990s* (Washington, DC: National Academy Press).

14. E. Galinsky, C. Howes, S. Kontos, and M. Shinn (1994), *The study of children in family child care and relative care* (New York: Families and Work Institute).

15. J. Wrigley and J. Dreby (2005), "Fatalities and the organization of child care

in the United States, 1985–2003," *American Sociological Review* 70(5): 729–757.

16. Editorial, "Day care's cosmic crapshoot" (1987), *New York Times*, June 26.

17. Hayes, Palmer, and Zaslow, *Who cares for America's children?*; J. Shonkoff and D. Phillips, eds. (2000), *From neurons to neighborhoods: The science of early child development* (Washington, DC: National Academy Press).

18. Cost, Quality, and Child Outcomes Study Team (1995), *Cost, quality, and child outcomes in child care centers: Public report*, 2nd ed. (Denver: Economics Department, University of Colorado).

19. M. Whitebook, C. Howes, and D. Phillips (1998), *Worthy work, unlivable wages: The national child care staffing study, 1988–1997* (Washington, DC: Center for the Child Care Workforce).

20. D. Vandell and B. Wolfe (2000), *Child care quality: Does it matter and does it need to be improved?* (Madison: Institute for Research on Poverty, University of Wisconsin), http://www.aspe.hhs.gov/hsp/ccquality00/ccqual.htm; J. M. Love, P. Z. Schochet, and A. L. Meckstroth (1996), *Are they in any real danger? What research does—and doesn't—tell us about child care quality and children's well-being* (Princeton, NJ: Mathematica Policy Research).

21. D. Cryer (1999), "Defining and assessing early childhood program quality," *Annals of the American Academy of Political and Social Science* 563(1): 39–55.

22. D. Vandell and K. M. Pierce (2003), "Child care quality and children's success at school," in A. Reynolds, M. Wang, and H. Walberg, eds., *Early childhood programs for a new century* (Washington, DC: Child Welfare League), 115–139.

23. J. J. Heckman and D. V. Masterov (2004), *The productivity argument for investing in young children*, Working Paper 5, Invest in Kids Working Group, Committee for Economic Development.

24. S. Helburn and B. Bergmann (2002), *America's child care problem: The way out* (New York: Palgrave for St. Martin's); Love, Schochet, and Meckstroth, *Are they in any real danger?*; Vandell and Pierce, "Child care quality and children's success."

25. Vandell and Wolfe, "Child care quality: Does it matter?"

26. K. Schulman (2000), *Issue brief: The high cost of child care puts quality care out of reach for many families* (Washington, DC: Children's Defense Fund).

27. National Association of Child Care Resource and Referral Agencies (2006), *Breaking the piggy bank: Parents and the high cost of child care* (Washington, DC: NACCRRA).

28. Center for the Child Care Workforce (2004), *Current data on the salaries and benefits of the U.S. Early Childhood Education Workforce* (Washington, DC: American Federation of Teachers Educational Foundation).

29. S. Herzenberg, M. Price, and D. Bradley (2005), *Losing ground in early childhood education: Declining workforce qualifications in an expanding industry, 1979–2004* (New York: Foundation for Child Development).

30. Ibid.

31. E. E. Kisker, S. L. Hofferth, D. A. Philllips, and E. Farquhar (1991), *A profile of child care settings: Early education and care in 1990* (Washington, DC: U.S. Department of Education).

32. M. Whitebook, L. Sakai, E. Gerber, and C. Howes (2001), *Then and now: Changes in child care staffing, 1994–2000* (Washington, DC: Center for the Child Care Workforce).

33. Shonkoff and Phillips, *From neurons to neighborhoods.*

34. Whitebook et al., *Then and now.*

35. Herzenberg, Price, and Bradley, *Losing ground,* 8.

36. J. Lombardi (2003), *Time to care: Redesigning child care to promote education, support families, and build communities* (Philadelphia: Temple University Press); The Children's Foundation (2002), *The 2000 child care center licensing study* (Washington, DC: Children's Foundation).

37. Lombardi, *Time to care;* B. Fuller, S. L. Kagan, G. L. Caspary, and C. A. Gauthier (2002), "Welfare reform and child care options for low-income families," *Future of Children* 12(1): 97–120; D. Phillips, ed. (1995), *Child care for low-income families: Summary of two workshops* (Washington, DC: National Academy Press).

38. B. Holcomb (1998), *Not guilty! The good news about working mothers* (New York: Scribner), 264.

CHAPTER 2. A GOLDEN MOMENT SQUANDERED

1. W. Gormley (1995), *Everybody's children: Child care as a public problem* (Washington, DC: Brookings Institution).

2. R. Thompson (2001), "Development in the first years of life," *Future of Children* 11(1): 21–34.

3. H. L. Hodgkinson (2003), *Leaving too many children behind: A demographer's view on the neglect of America's youngest children* (Washington, DC: Institute for Educational Leadership).

4. A. Bachu and M. O'Connell (2001), "Fertility of American women: June 2000," *Current Population Reports P20–526* (Washington, DC: U.S. Census Bureau).

5. J. Brauner, B. Gordic, and E. F. Zigler (2004), "Putting the child back into child care: Combining care and education for children ages 3–5," *Social Policy Report* 18(3): 3–16; A. Leibowitz (1996), "Child care: Private cost or public responsibility?" in V. R. Fuchs, ed., *Individual and social responsibility: Child care, education, medical care and long-term care in America* (Chicago: University of Chicago Press), 33–54.

6. White House Conference on Children (1970), *Report to the President* (Washington, DC: U.S. Government Printing Office); U.S. House of Representatives, Committee on Ways and Means (2004), *Green book: Section 7* (Washington, DC: U.S. Government Printing Office).

7. K. McCartney and D. Phillips, eds. (2006), *The handbook of early child development* (Oxford: Blackwell Publishers).

8. R. Nelson (1977), *The moon and the ghetto: An essay on public policy analysis* (New York: W.W. Norton), 14.

9. G. Steiner (1981), *The futility of family policy* (Washington, DC: Brookings Institution).

10. Ibid., 462.

11. A. de Tocqueville (2000), *Democracy in America* (Chicago: University of Chicago Press).

12. M. Harrington (1999), *Care and equality: Inventing a new family politics* (New York: Knopf).

13. S. B. Kamerman and A. J. Kahn (1994), *A welcome for every child: Care, education and family support for infants and toddlers in Europe* (Arlington, VA: Zero to Three), 375.

14. R. N. Brandon (1998), "Public attitudes about early childhood care and education," *Effective language for discussing early childhood education and policy* (Washington, DC: Benton Foundation); A. E. Smith and R. Ribeiro (2004), *Changing the terms of the debate: Child care as a public concern*, http://www.daycarecouncil.org/EEP/Economic%20Impact/ Changing%20the%20Terms%20of%20the%20Debate.pdf.

15. E. Goodman (2003), "Where's the political will for help on child care?" *Boston Globe*, December 7.

16. S. Farkas, A. Duffet, and J. Johnson (2000), *Necessary compromises: How parents, employers, and children's advocates view child care today* (Washington, DC: Public Agenda), 10.

17. "Poll supports aid to child centers" (1969), *New York Times*, July 13; Early Care and Education Collaborative (2005), *Public attitudes towards early care*, http://www.earlycare.org/index.htm.

18. Harrington, *Care and equality*, 30.

19. J. W. Kingdon (2003), *Agendas, alternatives, and public policies* (New York: Longman).

20. C. Ryan (1991), *Prime time activism: Media strategies for grassroots organizing* (Boston: South End), 53.

21. K. Morgan (2001), "A child of the sixties: The great society, the new right, and the politics of child care," *Journal of Policy History* 13(2): 219.

22. R. P. Petchesky (1981), "Antiabortion, antifeminism, and the rise of the New Right," *Feminist Studies* 7(2): 206–246.

23. Morgan, "A child of the sixties," 219.

24. S. Cohen (2001), *Championing child care* (New York: Columbia University Press); S. D. Holloway and B. Fuller (1999), "Families and child care: Divergent viewpoints," *Annals of the American Academy of Political and Social Science* 563(1): 98–115; Morgan, "A child of the sixties"; E. F. Zigler and E. W. Gordon, eds. (1982), *Day care: Scientific and social policy issues* (Boston: Auburn House).

25. W. B. Hixson (1992), *Search for the American right wing: An analysis of the social science record 1955–1987* (Princeton, NJ: Princeton University Press).

26. G. Lakoff (2002), *Moral politics: What conservatives know that liberals don't* (Chicago: University of Chicago Press), 18.

27. J. DeParle (2005), "Goals reached, donor on right closes up shop," *New York Times*, May 29.

28. W. G. Gale and L. J. Kotlikoff (2004), *Effects of recent fiscal policies on today's children and future generations* (Washington, DC: Urban Institute).

29. Goodman, "Where's the political will?"

30. Morgan, "A child of the sixties"; J. B. Richmond (2005), "An early administrator's perspective," in E. Zigler and S. J. Styfco, eds., *The Head Start debates* (Baltimore: P. H. Brookes).

31. E. Zigler and S. Muenchow (1992), *Head Start: The inside story of America's most successful educational experiment* (New York: Basic Books), 134.

32. Ibid.; Morgan, "A child of the sixties."

33. D. Dinner (2003), "Transforming family and state: Women's vision for universal childcare, 1966–1971," 2004 Interdisciplinary Law and Humanities Junior Scholar Workshop Paper 5.

34. M. B. Norton, ed. (1989), *Major problems in American women's history: Documents and essays* (Lexington, MA: D.C. Heath), 397–400.

35. *Congressional Record* (1971), 92nd Congress, 15683.

36. Dinner (2003), "Transforming family and state," 21.

37. Ibid.

38. S. Michel (1999), *Children's interests/mothers' rights: The shaping of America's child care policy* (New Haven, CT: Yale University Press), 10.

39. Dinner, "Transforming family and state."

40. E. Rose (1999), *A mother's job: The history of day care, 1890–1960* (New York: Oxford University Press), 211–212.

41. Nelson, *The moon and the ghetto*; E. Zigler and N. Hall (2000), *Child development and social policy: Theory and applications* (Boston: McGraw-Hill); Zigler and Muenchow, *Head Start*.

42. Zigler and Styfco, *Head Start debates*; Zigler and Muenchow, *Head Start*.

43. J. Quadagno (1994), *The color of welfare: How racism undermined the War on Poverty* (New York: Oxford University Press).

44. Cohen, *Championing child care*, 25.

45. Ibid.

46. *Congressional Quarterly Almanac* (1969), 34.

47. Zigler and Muenchow, *Head Start*.

48. Michel, *Children's interests/mothers' rights*; J. Nelson (1982), "The politics of federal day care regulations," in Zigler and Gordon, *Day care*, 257–306; C. D. Hayes, J. L. Palmer, and M. J. Zaslow, eds. (1990), *Who cares for America's children? Child care policy for the 1990s* (Washington, DC: National Academy Press); Morgan, "A child of the sixties."

49. Cohen, *Championing child care*, 44.

50. *Family Assistance Act of 1970,* HR 16311, 91st Cong., 2nd Sess.

51. House of Representatives, Committee on Education and Labor (1972), "Report on the Comprehensive Child Development Act together with minority and additional views," Report no. 92-1570, October 11, p. 8.

52. M. D. Keyserling (1972), *Windows on day care* (New York: National Council of Jewish Women), ii.

53. Ibid., 5.

54. White House Conference on Children (1970), *Report to the President* (Washington, DC: U.S. Government Printing Office).

55. Nelson, "Politics of federal day care recommendations."

56. Cohen (2001), *Championing child care;* Michel, *Children's interests/mothers' rights.*

57. Morgan, "A child of the sixties," 235.

58. Michel, *Children's interests/mothers' rights.*

59. *Congressional Record* (1971), 92nd Congress.

60. Cohen, *Championing child care.*

61. Morgan, "A child of the sixties."

62. "Nixon must veto child control law" (1971), *Human Events* 31:1.

63. E. Zigler and M. E. Lang (1991), *Child care choices: Balancing the needs of children, families, and society* (New York: Free Press).

64. Cohen (2001), *Championing child care,* 41.

65. Ibid.; Dinner, "Transforming family and state," 51.

66. Cohen, *Championing child care,* 41.

67. Ibid., 47.

68. Morgan, "A child of the sixties," 233.

69. Dinner, "Transforming family and state," 49.

70. Cohen, *Championing child care,* 49.

71. Zigler and Muenchow, *Head Start,* 146.

72. *Congressional Record* (1971), 92nd Congress, 21129.

73. Hixson, *Search for the American right wing;* Morgan, "A child of the sixties."

74. Cohen, *Championing child care.*

75. Morgan, "A child of the sixties," 238.

CHAPTER 3. AN AMERICAN CHILD CARE POLICY

1. E. F. Zigler and E. Gilman (1996), "Not just any care: Shaping a coherent child care policy," in E. F. Zigler, S. L. Kagan, and N. W. Hall, eds., *Children, families, and government: Preparing for the twenty-first century* (New York: Cambridge University Press), 94–116.

2. National Council of Jewish Women (1999), *Opening a new window on child care: A report on the status of child care in the nation today* (New York: National Council of Jewish Women), 4, 15.

3. "Federal Interagency Day Care Requirements" (1980), *Federal Register,* Part V, 45(55): 17870–17885; C. D. Hayes, ed. (1982), *Making policies for children: A study of the federal process* (Washington, DC: National Academy Press).

4. D. Philips and E. Zigler (1987), "The checkered history of federal child care regulation," *Review of Research in Education* 14:21.

5. R. Nelson (1982), "The politics of federal day care regulations," in E. W. Gordon and E. Zigler, eds., *Day care: Scientific and social policy issues* (Boston: Auburn House).

6. E. Zigler and M. Lang (1991), *Child care choices: Balancing the needs of children, families, and society* (New York: Free Press); Zigler and Gilman (1996), "Not just any care," 94–116.

7. U.S. Senate, Subcommittee on Children of the Committee on Labor and Public Welfare, and U.S. House of Representatives, Select Subcommittee on Education of the Committee on Education and Labor (1974), *Joint hearings on the Child and Family Services Act,* 93rd Cong., 2nd sess., August 8–9.

8. S. Cohen (2001), *Championing child care* (New York: Columbia University Press).

9. *Congressional Record* (1975), 37380.

10. L. B. Francke and D. Camper (1976), "Child-care scare," *Newsweek,* April 5, 77.

11. *Congressional Record* (1975), 37380.

12. J. Colwell (1975), "Brademas victim of political 'dirty trick,'" *South Bend Tribune,* November 2.

13. Francke and Camper, "Child-care scare."

14. R. P. Petchesky (1981), "Antiabortion, antifeminism, and the rise of the New Right," *Feminist Studies* 7(2): 206–246; K. Phillips (1975), *Mediacracy: American parties and politics in the communications age* (Garden City, NY: Doubleday); J. A. Smith (1991), *The idea brokers: Think tanks and the rise of the new policy elite* (New York: Free Press).

15. J. DeParle (2005), "Goals reached, donor on right closes up shop," *New York Times,* May 29.

16. Cohen, *Championing child care.*

17. Petchesky, "Antiabortion, antifeminism, and the rise of the New Right."

18. Cohen, *Championing child care;* Phillips, *Mediacracy.*

19. T. Frank (2004), *What's the matter with Kansas? How conservatives won the heart of America* (New York: Metropolitan Books), 1.

20. Ibid., 127.

21. S. D. Levitt and S. J. Dubner (2005), *Freakonomics: A rogue economist explores the hidden side of everything* (New York: William Morrow), 148.

22. L. S. Barber (2003), "Uncovering the day care industry's deception," *Intellectualconservative.com,* http://www.intellectualconservative.com/article2685.html (accessed August 8, 2008).

23. B. Glassner (1999), *The culture of fear: Why Americans are afraid of the wrong things* (New York: Basic Books), 16–17.

24. B. Holcomb (1998), *Not guilty! The good news about working mothers* (New York: Scribner), 79.

25. P. Schlafly, ed. (1989), *Who will rock the cradle?* (Dallas: Word).

26. Cohen, *Championing child care,* 59.

27. Francke and Camper, "Child-care scare," 77.

28. Cohen, *Championing child care,* 59.

29. Ibid.

30. Ibid., 60.

31. A. S. Grossman (1982), *More than half of all children have working mothers,* Special Labor Force Report (Washington, DC: U.S. Bureau of Labor Statistics).

32. Cohen (2001), *Championing child care,* 59.

33. "Federal Interagency Day Care Requirements," 17870–17885; Phillips and Zigler, "Checkered history."

34. Kimmich (1985), *America's children, who cares? Growing needs and declining assistance in the Reagan era* (Washington, DC: Urban Institute); Zigler and Gilman, "Not just any care," 94–116.

35. Zigler and Lang, *Child care choices.*

36. S. E. Shank (1988), "Women and the labor market: The link grows stronger," *Monthly Labor Review* 111(1): 3–8; S. L. Hofferth and D. A. Phillips (1987), "Child care in the United States, 1970 to 1995," *Journal of Marriage and the Family* 49(3): 559–571.

37. Select Committee on Child, Youth, and Families (1989), *U.S. children and their families: Current conditions and recent trends* (Washington, DC: U.S. Government Printing Office).

38. C. M. Johnson, A. M. Sum, and J. D. Weill (1988), *Vanishing dreams: The growing economic plight of America's young families* (Washington, DC: Children's Defense Fund), 197.

39. U.S. Bureau of the Census (1987), "Who's minding the kids? Child care arrangements: Winter 1984–1985," *Current Population Reports,* Series P-70, No. 9; S. Stephan (1988), *Child day care: Federal policy issues and legislation,* Congressional Research Services Issue Brief No. IB 87193 (Washington, DC: Library of Congress).

40. Holcomb, *Not guilty!* 271.

41. *Act for Better Child Care* (1987), S 1885, 100th Cong., 1st sess., *Congressional Record,* S1655.

42. U.S. House of Representatives, Subcommittee on Human Resources of the Committee on Education and Labor (1988), *Hearing on Child Care,* 100th Cong., 2nd sess., 164.

43. Cohen, *Championing child care.*

44. U.S. Senate, Subcommittee on Children, Family, Drugs, and Alcoholism of the Committee on Labor and Human Resources (1987), *Act for Better Child Care Services of 1987,* 216.

45. Cohen, *Championing child care.*

46. Ibid., 116.

47. Ibid.

48. J. Gress-Wright (1992), "Liberals, conservatives, and the family," *Commentary* 93(4): 43–46.
49. Zigler and Gilman, "Not just any care," 94–116.
50. Holcomb, *Not guilty!* 270.
51. Ibid.
52. Ibid., 270.
53. E. Zigler and M. Finn-Stevenson (1995), "The child care crisis: Implications for the growth and development of the nation's children," *Journal of Social Issues* 51(3): 215–231; Zigler and Gilman, "Not just any care," 94–116.
54. K. McCartney and D. Phillips, eds. (2006), *The handbook of early child development* (Oxford: Blackwell).
55. U.S. House, Committee on Ways and Means (2004), *Green book.*
56. N. Gilbert (2005), "What do women really want?" *Public Interest,* http://findarticles.com/p/articles/mi_m0377/is_158/ai_n8680969 (accessed August 8, 2008).
57. A. Hochschild (2001), *The time bind: When work becomes home and home becomes work* (New York: Metropolitan); S. Douglas and M. Michaels (2004), *The mommy myth: The idealization of motherhood and how it has undermined women* (New York: Free Press).
58. J. C. Williams and N. Segal (2002), "Beyond the maternal wall: Relief for family care-givers who are discriminated against on the job," *Harvard Women's Law Journal* 26:77–162.
59. S. Rose and H. Hartmann (2004), *Still a man's labor market: The long-term earnings gap* (Washington, DC: Institute for Women's Policy Research).
60. Williams and Segal, "Beyond the maternal wall."
61. S. Nall Bales (1999), "Public opinion and the challenge of children's issues," in *Effective language for communicating children's issues* (Washington, DC: Benton Foundation), 2–7.
62. G. Lakoff and J. Grady (1998), "Why early ed benefits all of us," in *Effective language for discussing early childhood education and policy: Strategic communication working papers* (Washington, DC: Benton Foundation); S. Nall Bales (1998), "Early childhood education and the framing wars," in *Effective language for discussing early childhood education and policy;* J. Brauner, B. Gordic, and E. F. Zigler (2004), "Putting the child back into child care: Combining care and education for children ages 3–5," *Social Policy Report* 18(3): 3–16.
63. S. Farkas, A. Duffet, and J. Johnson (2000), *Necessary compromises: How parents, employers and children's advocates view child care today* (Washington, DC: Public Agenda).
64. E. Hawes (1993), *New York, New York: How the apartment house transformed the life of the city, 1869–1930* (New York: Knopf); M. Sarbaugh-Thompson and M. N. Zald (1995), "Child labor laws: A historical case of public policy implementation," *Administration and Society* 27(1): 25–53.

65. S. Iyengar (1991), *Is anyone responsible? How television frames political issues* (Chicago: University of Chicago Press).

66. Farkas, Duffet, and Johnson, *Necessary compromises,* 20.

67. M. Gardner (2003), "A voice for children and families will soon fall silent," *Christian Science Monitor,* April 23.

68. DeParle, "Goals reached."

69. G. Steiner (1976), *The children's cause* (Washington, DC: Brookings Institution), 5.

70. T. Friedman (2005), *The world is flat: A brief history of the twenty-first century* (New York: Farrar, Straus and Giroux), 451.

CHAPTER 4. QUALITY AND AFFORDABILITY

1. J. M. Love, P. Z. Schochet, and A. L. Meckstroth (1996), *Are they in any real danger? What research does—and doesn't—tell us about child care quality and children's well-being* (Princeton, NJ: Mathematica Policy Research); D. L. Vandell (2004), "Early child care: The known and the unknown," *Merrill-Palmer Quarterly* 50(3): 387–414; D. Vandell and K. M. Pierce (2003), "Child care quality and children's success at school," in A. Reynolds and M. Wang, eds., *Early childhood learning: Programs for a new century* (Washington, DC: Child Welfare League), 115–139; D. Vandell and B. Wolfe (2000), *Child care quality: Does it matter and does it need to be improved?* (Madison: Institute for Research on Poverty, University of Wisconsin), http://www.aspe.hhs.gov/hsp/ccquality00/ccqual.htm.

2. L. A. Karoly et al. (1998), *Investing in our children: What we know and don't know about the costs and benefits of early childhood interventions* (Santa Monica, CA: Rand); E. Zigler, W. S. Gilliam, and S. M. Jones (2006), *A vision for universal preschool education* (New York: Cambridge University Press).

3. E. Zigler and M. Lang (1991), *Child care choices: Balancing the needs of children, families, and society* (New York: Free Press).

4. D. Cryer (1999), "Defining and assessing early childhood quality," *Annals of the American Academy of Political and Social Science* 563(1): 39–55.

5. M. Whitebook, C. Howes, and D. Phillips (1998), *Worthy work, unlivable wages: The national child care staffing study, 1988–1997* (Washington, DC: Center for the Child Care Workforce); Cost, Quality and Child Outcomes Study Team (1995), *Cost, quality and child outcomes in child care centers: Public report,* 2nd ed. (Denver: Economics Department, University of Colorado); NICHD Early Child Care Research Network (2002), "Child-care structure→process→outcome: Direct and indirect effects of child-care quality on young children's development," *Psychological Science* 13(3): 199–206.

6. K. McCartney (1984), "The effect of quality of day care environment upon children's language development," *Developmental Psychology* 20:244–260; NICHD Early Child Care Research Network (1998), "Early child care and self-control, compliance, and problem behavior at twenty-four and thirty-

six months," *Child Development* 69:1145–1170; NICHD Early Child Care
Research Network (2000), "Characteristics and quality of child care for
toddlers and preschoolers," *Applied Developmental Science* 4(3): 116–135;
NICHD Early Child Care Research Network (2005), *Child care and child
development: Results from the NICHD study of early child care and youth development* (New York: Guilford); D. A. Phillips, K. McCartney, and S. Scarr
(1987), "Child care quality and children's social development," *Developmental Psychology* 23:537–543; E. Peisner-Feinberg and M. Burchinal (1997),
"Concurrent relations between child care quality and child outcomes: The
study of cost, quality and outcomes in child care centers," *Merrill-Palmer
Quarterly* 43:451–477.

7. Cryer, "Defining and assessing early childhood quality"; C. D. Hayes, J. L.
Palmer, and M. J. Zaslow, eds. (1990), "Who cares for America's children?
Child care policy for the 1990s" (Washington, DC: National Academy
Press); NICHD Early Child Care Research Network, "Child-care structure
→process→outcome."

8. D. Phillips and C. Howes (1987), "Indicators of quality in child care:
Review of research," in D. Phillips, ed., *Quality in child care: What does
research tell us?* (Washington, DC: National Association for the Education
of Young Children).

9. S. Friedman and J. Amadeo (1999), "The child-care environment: Conceptualizations, assessments, and issues," in S. Friedman and T. D. Wachs,
eds., *Measuring environment across the lifespan* (Washington, DC: American
Psychological Association), 127–165.

10. NICHD Early Child Care Research Network, "Child-care structure→
process→outcome."

11. Ibid.

12. T. Harms, R. M. Clifford, and D. Cryer (1998), "Early childhood environ-
mental rating scale, revised edition" (Carrboro: Frank Porter Graham Child
Development Institute, University of North Carolina); T. Harms and R. M.
Clifford (1989), *The family day care rating scale* (New York: Teachers College
Press); T. Harms, R. M. Clifford, and D. Cryer (2003), *Infant/toddler envi-
ronmental rating scale, revised edition* (Carrboro: Frank Porter Graham Child
Development Institute, University of North Carolina); T. Harms, E. V.
Jacobs, and D. R. White (1996), *School-age care environment rating scale*
(New York: Teachers College Press).

13. B. Fuller and S. L. Kagan, eds. (2000), *Remember the children: Mothers balance work and child care under welfare reform. Growing up in poverty project
2000; Wave 1 findings—California, Connecticut, Florida* (Berkeley: Graduate
School of Education, University of California).

14. NICHD Early Child Care Research Network (1996), "Characteristics of infant child care: Factors contributing to positive caregiving," *Early Childhood
Research Quarterly* 11:269–306; NICHD Early Child Care Research Net-

work (2000), "Characteristics and quality of child care for toddlers and preschoolers," *Applied Developmental Science* 4(3): 116–135.

15. National Association for Regulatory Administration and National Child Care Information and Technical Assistance Center (2006), *The 2005 child care licensing study, Executive Summary* (Washington, DC: NARA and NCCIC).

16. D. Phillips and E. Zigler (1987), "The checkered history of federal child care regulation," *Review of Research in Education* 14:21.

17. J. Gallagher, R. Rooney, and S. Campbell (1999), "Child care licensing regulations and child care quality in four states," *Early Childhood Research Quarterly* 14(3): 313–333; S. LeMoine and G. Morgan (2004), *Do states require child care programs to educate children? State center licensing requirements for child development and early education, report no. 1* (Urbana-Champaign: Clearinghouse on Early Education and Parenting, University of Illinois), http://ceep.crc.uiuc.edu/docs/cc-educate/report1.pdf (accessed September 2006).

18. NARA and NCCIC, *2005 child care licensing study.*

19. K. T. Young, K. W. Marsland, and E. Zigler (1997), "The regulatory status of center-based infant and toddler child care," *American Journal of Orthopsychiatry* 67(4): 535–544; K. Marsland, E. Zigler, and A. Martinez (2003), "Regulation of infant and toddler child care: Are state requirements for centers adequate?" (unpublished manuscript, Yale University).

20. S. Azer, S. LeMoine, G. Morgan, R. M. Clifford, and G. M. Crawford (2002), "Regulation of child care," *Early Childhood Research and Policy Briefs* 2(1): 1–2.

21. NARA and NCCIC, *2005 child care licensing study.*

22. G. Morgan, S. Azer, and S. LeMoine (2001), *Family child care: What's in a name?* (Boston: Wheelock College Institute for Leadership and Career Initiatives).

23. M. Brown-Lyons, A. Robertson, and J. Layzer (2001), *Kith and kin— informal child care: Highlights from recent research* (New York: National Center for Children in Poverty).

24. S. L. Kagan and N. E. Cohen (1997), *Not by chance: Creating an early care and education system for America's children* (New Haven, CT: Bush Center in Child Development and Social Policy, Yale University).

25. Children's Foundation (2002), *The 2000 Child Care Center Licensing Study* (Washington, DC: Children's Foundation).

26. Azer et al., "Regulation of child care."

27. S. Helburn and B. Bergmann (2002), *America's child care problem: The way out* (New York: Palgrave for St. Martin's).

28. S. L. Hofferth and D. Wissoker (1992), "Price, quality, and income in child care choices," *Journal of Human Resources* 27:70–111.

29. National Association for the Education of Young Children (2005), "Annual report: September 1, 2004–August 31, 2005"; M. Whitebook, L. Sakai, and

C. Howes (1997), *NAEYC accreditation as a strategy for improving child care quality* (Washington, DC: National Center for the Early Childhood Work Force).

30. Helburn and Bergmann, *America's child care problem.*

31. W. T. Gormely (2002), "Differential reimbursement policies and child care accreditation" (unpublished manuscript, George Washington University).

32. Whitebook, Sakai, and Howes, *NAEYC accreditation;* Cost, Quality and Child Outcomes Study Team, *Cost, quality and child outcomes.*

33. Cost, Quality and Child Outcomes Study Team, *Cost, quality and child outcomes;* Whitebook, Sakai, and Howes, *NAEYC Accreditation;* W. S. Gilliam (2000), *The school readiness initiative in south-central Connecticut: Classroom quality, teacher training, and service provision, final report of findings for fiscal year 1999* (New Haven, CT: Yale University Child Study Center), http://nieer.org/resources/research/CSRI1999.pdf; Whitebook, Howes, and Phillips, *Worthy work, unlivable wages.*

34. M. D. Keyserling (1972), *Windows on day care* (New York: National Council of Jewish Women).

35. National Council of Jewish Women (1999), *Opening a new window on child care: A report on the status of child care in the nation today* (New York: National Council of Jewish Women).

36. Cost, Quality and Child Outcomes Study Team, *Cost, quality and child outcomes;* NICHD Early Child Care Research Network, "Characteristics and quality of child care for toddlers and preschoolers."

37. Whitebook, Howes, and Phillips, *Worthy work, unlivable wages;* R. Ruopp, J. Travers, F. Glantz, and C. Coelen (1979), *Children at the center: Final report of the National Day Care Study* (Cambridge, MA: Abt Books).

38. U.S. Department of Health, Education, and Welfare (1980), "Day care regulations, final rule," *Federal Register* 45(55): 17870–17885; Whitebook, Howes, and Phillips, *Worthy work, unlivable wages.*

39. NICHD Early Child Care Research Network, "Child-care structure→ process→outcome"; E. Galinsky, C. Howes, S. Kontos, and M. Shinn (1994), *The study of children in family child care and relative care: Highlights of findings* (New York: Families and Work Institute); Fuller and Kagan, *Remember the children.*

40. Vandell and Pierce, "Child care quality."

41. R. Brandon and D. Smith (1996), *Access to quality early childhood care and education* (Seattle: Human Services Policy Center, University of Washington); National Association of Child Care Resource and Referral Agencies (2006), *Breaking the piggy bank: Parents and the high cost of child care* (Washington, DC: NACCRRA).

42. National Council of Jewish Women, *Opening a new window;* K. Schulman (2000), *Issue brief: The high cost of child care puts quality care out of reach for many families* (Washington, DC: Children's Defense Fund).

43. L. S. Sosinsky (2005), "Parental selection of child care quality: Income, demographic risk and beliefs about harm of maternal employment to children" (Ph.D. dissertation, Yale University).

44. S. L. Kagan (2006), personal communication, August.

45. H. N. Mocan (2001), *Can consumers detect lemons? Information asymmetry in the market for child care* (Washington, DC: National Bureau of Economic Research), http://ssrn.com/abstract=270201.

46. D. Blau (2003), "Do child care regulations affect the childcare and labor markets?" *Journal of Policy Analysis and Management* 22(3): 443–465; Gormely, *Differential reimbursement policies;* Mocan, *Can consumers detect lemons?*

47. Mocan, *Can consumers detect lemons?*

48. National Women's Law Center (2004), "Child care providers: Increasing compensation raises women's wages and improves child care quality," http://www.nwlc.org/pdf/WomenAsProvidersFactSheet2004.pdf; M. Whitebook and L. Sakai (2003), "Turnover begets turnover: An examination of job and occupational stability among child care center staff," *Early Childhood Research Quarterly* 18:273–293.

CHAPTER 5. INFANT AND TODDLER CHILD CARE

1. U.S. Census Bureau (2002), *Families and living arrangements* (Washington, DC: U.S. Labor Department, Census Bureau).

2. J. L. Kreader, D. Ferguson, and S. Lawrence (2005), "Impact of training and education for caregivers of infants and toddlers," *Child Care and Early Education Research Connections* 3.

3. M. B. Larner, R. E. Behrman, M. Young, and K. Reich (2001), "Caring for infants and toddlers: Analysis and recommendations," *Future of Children* 11(1): 7.

4. J. Kagan (1982), *Psychological research on the human infant: An evaluative summary* (New York: William T. Grant Foundation); W. Kessen, M. Haith, and P. Salapatek (1970), "Human infancy: A bibliography and guide," in P. H. Mussen, ed., *Carmichael's manual of child psychology,* vol. 1 (New York: Wiley); J. P. Shonkoff and D. A. Phillips, eds. (2000), *From neurons to neighborhoods: The science of early childhood development* (Washington, DC: National Research Council Institute of Medicine).

5. Shonkoff and Phillips, *From neurons to neighborhoods.*

6. Shonkoff and Phillips, *From neurons to neighborhoods;* E. F. Zigler, M. Finn-Stevenson, and N. W. Hall (2002), *The first three years and beyond: Brain development and social policy* (New Haven, CT: Yale University Press); R. Thompson (2000), "Early sociopersonality development," in W. Damon and N. Eisenberg, eds., *Handbook of child psychology: Vol. 3, Social, emotional, and personality development,* 5th edition (New York: Wiley).

7. National Scientific Council on the Developing Child (2005), "Excessive

stress disrupts the architecture of the brain," Working Paper 3, http://
www.developingchild.net/pubs/wp/Stress_Disrupts_Architecture
_Developing_Brain.pdf (accessed August 8, 2008); R. Shore (1997),
Rethinking the brain: New insights into early development (New York:
Families and Work Institute).

8. D. N. Stern (1977), *The first relationship: Mother and infant* (Cambridge,
MA: Harvard University Press).

9. J. Bowlby (1969/1982), *Attachment and loss: Loss, sadness and depression*
(New York: Basic Books); M. D. S. Ainsworth, M. C. Blehar, E. Waters,
and S. Wall (1978), *Patterns of attachment: A psychological study of the strange
situation* (Hillsdale, NJ: Lawrence Erlbaum).

10. J. Cassidy and P. R. Shaver, eds. (1999), *Handbook of attachment: Theory,
research, and clinical applications* (New York: Guilford); Thompson, "Early
sociopersonality development."

11. M. E. Lamb (1981), "The development of father-infant relationships," in
M. E. Lamb, ed., *The role of the father in child development*, 2nd edition
(New York: Wiley).

12. D. Phillips and G. Adams (2001), "Child care and our youngest children,"
Future of Children 11(1): 38.

13. Child Welfare League of America (1960), *Standards for day care service*
(New York: Child Welfare League of America); S. Fraiberg (1977), *Every
child's birthright: In defense of mothering* (New York: Basic Books).

14. R. A. Spitz (1945), "Hospitalism: An inquiry into the genesis of psychiatric
conditions in early childhood," *Psychoanalytic Study of the Child* 1:53–74.

15. A. S. Honig (2006), personal communication, March 9.

16. J. F. Cohn, R. Marias, and E. Z. Tronick (1986), "Face-to-face interactions of
depressed mothers and their infants," *New Directions for Child and Adolescent Development* 34:31–46; K. Lee (2005), "Effects of experimental center-
based child care on developmental outcomes of young children living in
poverty," *Social Service Review* 79:158–179; M. C. McCormick et al. (2006),
"Early intervention in low birth weight premature infants: Results at 18
years of age for the Infant Health and Development Program," *Pediatrics*
117(3): 771–780; F. A. Campbell, C. T. Ramey, E. Pungello, J. Sparling, and
S. Miller-Johnson (2002), "Early childhood education: Young adult outcomes from the Abecedarian Project," *Applied Developmental Science* 6(1):
42–57; A. S. Honig (2004), "Longitudinal outcomes from the Family Development Research Program," *Early Child Development and Care* 174(2):
125–130.

17. T. J. Gamble and E. Zigler (1986), "Effects of infant day care: Another look
at the evidence," *American Journal of Orthopsychiatry* 56(1): 39.

18. J. Belsky (1987), "Risks remain," *Zero to Three* 7(3): 22–24.

19. D. Phillips, K. McCartney, S. Scarr, and C. Howes (1987), "Selective review
of infant day care research: A cause for concern!" *Zero to Three* 7(3): 18–21;
Lamb, "Development of father-infant relationships."

20. J. Belsky and L. D. Steinberg (1978), "The effects of day care: A critical review," *Child Development* 49(4): 929–949; J. C. Schwarz, G. Krolick, and R. G. Stickland (1974), "Effects of early day care experience on adjustment to a new environment," *American Journal of Orthopsychiatry* 43(3): 340–346; A. G. Vlietstra (1981), "Full-versus half-day preschool attendance: Effects in young children as assessed by teacher ratings and behavioral observations," *Child Development* 52(2): 603–610.

21. M. Rutter (1981), "Social-emotional consequences of day care for preschool children," *American Journal of Orthopsychiatry* 51(1): 12.

22. R. Haskins (1985), "Public school aggression among children with varying day-care experiences," *Child Development* 56(3): 689–703.

23. National Center for Clinical and Infant Programs (1987), "Consensus on infant/toddler day care reached by researchers at NCCIP meeting" (press release, November 10).

24. NICHD Early Child Care Research Network (2005), *Child care and child development: Results from the NICHD study of early child care and youth development* (New York: Guilford).

25. K. McCartney (2004), "Current research on child care effects," in R. E. Tremblay et al., eds., *Encyclopedia on early childhood development: Child care 0–5* (Montreal: Centre of Excellence for Early Childhood Development), 2.

26. K. M. Pierce and D. L. Vandell (2006), "Child care," in G. G. Bear and K. M. Minke, eds., *Children's needs III: Development, prevention, and intervention* (Washington, DC: National Association of School Psychologists); D. Vandell and K. M. Pierce (2003), "Child care quality and children's success at school," in A. Reynolds, M. Wang, and H. Walberg, eds., *Early childhood learning: Programs for a new century* (Washington, DC: Child Welfare League), 115–139; D. Vandell and B. Wolfe (2000), *Child care quality: Does it matter and does it need to be improved?* (Madison: Institute for Research on Poverty, University of Wisconsin), http://www.aspe.hhs.gov/hsp/ccquality00/ccqual.htm; NICHD Early Child Care Research Network (2002), "Early child care and children's development prior to school entry: Results from the NICHD Study of Early Child Care," *American Educational Research Journal* 39(1): 133–164.

27. A. S. Johansen, A. Leibowitz, and L. J. Waite (1988), "Child care and children's illness," *American Journal of Public Health* 78(9): 1175–1177; B. Schwartz, G. S. Giebink, F. W. Henderson, M. R. Reichler, J. Jereb, and J. P. Collet (1994), "Respiratory infections in day care," *Pediatrics* 94(6): 1018–1020.

28. NICHD Early Child Care Research Network (2003), "Does amount of time spent in child care predict socioemotional adjustment during the transition to kindergarten?" *Child Development* 74(4): 976–1005; NICHD Early Child Care Research Network (2006), "Child-care effect sizes for the NICHD study of early child care and youth development," *American Psychologist* 61(2): 99–116.

29. D. L. Vandell (2004), "Early child care: The known and the unknown," *Merrill-Palmer Quarterly* 50(3): 387–414; N. S. Newcombe (2003), "Some controls control too much," *Child Development* 74(4): 1050–1052.

30. Newcombe, "Some controls control too much."

31. A. C. Dettling, M. R. Gunnar, and B. Donzella (1999), "Cortisol levels of young children in full-day child care centers: Relations with age and temperament," *Psychoneuroendocrinology* 24(5): 519–536; S. E. Watamura, B. Donzella, J. Alwin, and M. R. Gunnar (2003), "Morning-to-afternoon increases in cortisol concentrations for infants and toddlers in child care: Age differences and behavioral correlates," *Child Development* 74(4): 1006–1020.

32. National Scientific Council on the Developing Child, *Excessive stress;* M. R. Gunnar, K. Tout, M. de Haan, S. Pierce, and K. Stansbury (1997), "Temperament, social competence, and adrenocortical activity in pre-schoolers," *Developmental Psychobiology* 31(1): 65–85.

33. A. C. Dettling, S. W. Parker, S. Lane, A. Sebanc, and M. R. Gunnar (2000), "Quality of care and temperament determine changes in cortisol concentrations over the day for young children in childcare," *Psychoneuroendocrinology* 25(8): 819–836.

34. M. Gunnar (2006), personal communication.

35. R. DelCarmen-Wiggins and A. Carter, eds. (2004), *Handbook of infant, toddler and preschool mental health assessment* (New York: Oxford University Press).

36. D. Phillips et al., "Selective review."

37. E. F. Zigler and M. E. Lang (1991), *Child care choices: Balancing the needs of children, families, and society* (New York: Free Press).

38. T. B. Brazelton and S. I. Greenspan (2000), *The irreducible needs of children: What every child must have to grow, learn, and flourish* (New York: Perseus Books); P. Leach (1997), *Your baby and child: From birth to age five* (New York: Alfred A. Knopf); B. White (1993), *The first three years of life* (New York: Fireside).

39. R. Lally (2006), personal communication, October 30.

40. Children's Foundation (2002), *The 2000 child care center licensing study* (Washington, DC: Children's Foundation).

41. J. Lombardi (2003), *Time to care: Redesigning child care to promote education, support families, and build communities* (Philadelphia: Temple University Press); B. Fuller, S. L. Kagan, G. L. Caspary, and C. A. Gauthier (2002), "Welfare reform and child care options for low-income families," *Future of Children* 12(1): 97–120; D. Phillips, ed. (1995), *Child care for low-income families: Summary of two workshops* (Washington, DC: National Academy Press).

42. S. Kontos, C. Howes, M. Shinn, and E. Galinsky (1994), *The study of children in family child care and relative care* (New York: Families and Work Institute).

43. Cost, Quality and Child Outcomes Study Team (1995), *Cost, quality and*

child outcomes in child care centers: Public report, 2nd edition (Denver: Economics Department, University of Colorado).

44. K. Schulman (2000), *Issue brief: The high cost of child care puts quality care out of reach for many families* (Washington, DC: Children's Defense Fund); National Association of Child Care Resource and Referral Agencies (2006), *Breaking the piggy bank: Parents and the high price of child care* (Washington, DC: NACCRRA).

45. D. M. Blau (2001), *The child care problem: An economic analysis* (New York: Russell Sage Foundation); H. N. Mocan (2001), *Can consumers detect lemons? Information asymmetry in the market for child care* (Washington, DC: National Bureau of Economic Research), http://ssrn.com/abstract=270201.

CHAPTER 6: PRESCHOOL-AGE CHILD CARE

1. U.S. Census Bureau (1999), *Who's minding the kids? Child care arrangements* (Washington, DC: U.S. Labor Department, Census Bureau).

2. U.S. Census Bureau (2001), "Summary file 1" (October 2001); J. Capizzano, G. Adams, and F. Sonenstein (2000), *Child care arrangements for children under five: Variation across states* (Washington, DC: Urban Institute).

3. J. Capizzano and G. Adams (2000), *The hours that children under five spend in child care: Variation across states* (Washington, DC: Urban Institute), http://www.urban.org/url.cfm?ID=309439 (accessed December 27, 2006).

4. Capizzano, Adams, and Sonenstein, *Child care arrangements.*

5. W. S. Barnett and D. J. Yarosz (2004), *Who goes to preschool and why does it matter?* Preschool Policy Matters 7 (New Brunswick, NJ: National Institute for Early Education Research); E. Zigler, W. S. Gilliam, and S. M. Jones, eds. (2006), *A vision for universal preschool education* (New York: Cambridge University Press); U.S. Department of Health and Human Services, Administration for Children and Families (May 2005), *Head Start impact study: First year findings,* http://www.acf.hhs.gov/programs/opre/hs/impact _study/reports/first_yr_execsum/frst_yr_execsum.pdf (accessed December 20, 2006).

6. Barnett and Yarosz, *Who goes to preschool?*

7. J. Brauner, B. Gordic, and E. Zigler (2004), "Putting the child care back into child care: Combining care and education for children ages 3–5," *Social Policy Report* 18(3): 1–15.

8. Ibid.

9. W. S. Barnett, K. B. Robin, J. T. Hustedt, and K. L. Schulman (2003), *The state of preschool: 2003 state preschool yearbook* (New Brunswick, NJ: National Institute for Early Education Research); A. Mitchell, M. Seligson, and F. Marx (1989), *Early childhood programs and the public schools: Between promise and practice* (Dover, MA: Auburn House).

10. R. M. Clifford, O. Barbarin, F. Chang, D. Early, D. Bryant, C. Howes, M. Burchinal, and R. Pianta (2003), *What is prekindergarten? Trends in the development of a public system of prekindergarten services* (working paper draft,

National Center for Early Development and Learning, University of North Carolina at Chapel Hill).

11. W. S. Gilliam and C. H. Ripple (2004), "What can be learned from state-funded prekindergarten initiatives: A data-based approach to the Head Start devolution debate," in E. Zigler and S. J. Styfco, eds., *The Head Start debates* (Baltimore: Paul H. Brookes), 477–497.

12. U.S. Department of Health and Human Services, Administration for Children and Families, *Head Start impact study.*

13. Ibid.

14. S. Styfco (2006), "A place for Head Start in a world of universal preschool," in E. Zigler, W. S. Gilliam, and S. M. Jones, eds., *A vision for universal preschool education* (New York: Cambridge University Press), 216–240; R. Schumacher and K. Irish (2003), *What's new in 2002? A snapshot of Head Start children, families, teachers and programs* (Washington, DC: Center for Law and Social Policy).

15. K. Hamm (2006), *More than meets the eye: Head Start programs, partici-pants, families, and staff in 2005,* Policy Brief 8 (Washington, DC: Center for Law and Social Policy).

16. Barnett and Yarosz, *Who goes to preschool?*; K. Schulman (2000), *Issue brief: The high cost of child care puts quality care out of reach for many families* (Washington, DC: Children's Defense Fund).

17. H. Matthews and D. Ewen (2006), *Child care assistance in 2005: State cuts continue* (Washington, DC: Center for Law and Social Policy).

18. M. Blood (2000), *Our youngest children: Massachusetts voters and opinion leaders speak out on their care and education* (Boston: Strategies for Children); PaxWorld/NHSA Survey (2003), "More than 9 out of 10 Americans support existing Head Start program" (press release, September 4).

19. Blood, *Our youngest children.*; Brauner, Gordic, and Zigler, "Putting the child care back into child care"; S. Farkas, A. Duffet, and J. Johnson (2000), *Necessary compromises: How parents, employers, and children's advo-cates view child care today* (Washington, DC: Public Agenda).

20. Brauner, Gordic, and Zigler, "Putting the child care back into child care."

21. D. Phillips (2004), "Better child care for all: What will it take?" *Social Policy Report* 18(3): 5.

22. B. Bowman, M. S. Donovan, and M. S. Burns, eds. (2001), *Eager to learn: Educating our preschoolers* (Washington, DC: National Academy Press).

23. Zigler, Gilliam, and Jones, *Vision for universal preschool education.*

24. D. Vandell and B. Wolfe (2000), *Child care quality: Does it matter and does it need to be improved?* (Madison: Institute for Research on Poverty, University of Wisconsin), http://www.aspe.hhs.gov/hsp/ccquality00/ ccqual.htm.

25. R. C. Pianta (2007), "Preschool is school, sometimes: Making early child-hood education matter," *Education Next* 7(1): 44.

26. Cost, Quality and Child Outcomes Study Team (1995), *Cost, quality and*

child outcomes in child care centers: Public report, 2nd edition (Denver: Economics Department, University of Colorado).

27. Bowman, Donovan, and Burns, *Eager to learn;* E. S. Peisner-Feinberg, M. R. Burchinal, R. M. Clifford, M. L. Culkin, C. Howes, S. L. Kagan, and N. Yazejian (2001), "The relation of preschool child-care quality to children's cognitive and social developmental trajectories through second grade," *Child Development* 72(5): 1534–1553; E. S. Peisner-Feinberg (1999), *The children of the cost, quality, and outcomes study go to school: Technical report* (Carrboro: Frank Porter Graham Child Development Center, University of North Carolina).

28. NICHD Early Child Care Research Network (1999), "Child outcomes when child care centers meet recommended standards for quality," *American Journal of Public Health* 89(7): 1072–1077.

29. E. Galinsky, C. Howes, S. Kontos, and M. Shinn (1994), *The study of children in family child care and relative care* (New York: Families and Work Institute); S. Azer, S. LeMoine, G. Morgan, R. M. Clifford, and G. M. Crawford (2002), "Regulation of child care," *Early Childhood Research and Policy Briefs* 2(1): 1–2.

30. S. Kontos, C. Howes, M. Shinn, and E. Galinsky (1995), *Quality in family child care and relative care* (New York: Teachers College Press).

31. S. Helburn and B. Bergmann (2002), *America's child care problem: The way out* (New York: Palgrave for St. Martin's); U.S. Consumer Product Safety Commission (1999), *Consumer Product Safety Commission staff study of safety hazards in child care settings* (Washington, DC: U.S. Consumer Product Safety Commission), http://www.cpsc.gov/library/ccstudy.html (accessed December 30, 2006).

32. Government Accountability Office (2004), *Child care: State efforts to enforce safety and health requirements* (Washington, DC: U.S. Government Printing Office).

33. Zigler, Gilliam, and Jones, *Vision for universal preschool education;* Helburn and Bergmann, *America's child care problem.*

34. Zigler, Gilliam, and Jones, *Vision for universal preschool education.*

35. Barnett, Robin, Hustedt, and Schulman, *State of preschool.*

36. Blood, *Our youngest children.*

37. Zigler, Gilliam, and Jones, *Vision for universal preschool education.*

38. L. J. Schweinhart, H. V. Barnes, and D. P. Weikart (1993), *Significant benefits: The High/Scope Perry Preschool study through age 27,* Monographs of the High/Scope Educational Research Foundation 10 (Ypsilanti, MI: High/Scope); L. J. Schweinhart, J. Montie, Z. Xiang, W. S. Barnett, C. R. Belfield, and M. Nores (2005), *Lifetime effects: The High/Scope Perry Preschool study through age 40,* Monographs of the High/Scope Educational Research Foundation 14 (Ypsilanti, MI: High/Scope).

39. Schweinhart et al., *Lifetime effects.*

40. A. Rolnick and R. Grunewald (2003), "Early childhood development:

Economic development with a high public return," *The Region,* supplement (Minneapolis, MN: Federal Reserve Bank of Minneapolis), 11, http://minneapolisfed.org/research/studies/earlychild/abc-part2.pdf.

41. L. J. Calman and L. Tarr-Whelan (2005), *Early childhood education for all: A wise investment* (New York: Legal Momentum), 24.

42. J. Brooks-Gunn (2003), "Do you believe in magic? What we can expect from early childhood intervention programs," *Social Policy Report* 17(1): 3–14.

43. Y. Abraham (1999), "Gore promotes $50B free preschool for 4-year-olds," *Boston Globe,* December 22.

44. R. G. Lynch (2004), *Exceptional returns: Economic, fiscal, and social benefits of investment in early childhood development* (Washington, DC: Economic Policy Institute); Business Roundtable and Corporate Voices for Working Families (2003), "Early childhood education: A call to action from the business community," http://www.businessroundtable.org/pdf/901.pdf (accessed April 2005).

45. W. S. Barnett and C. R. Belfield (2006), "Early childhood development and social mobility," *Future of Children* 16(2): 73–98; W. T. Gormley, T. Gayer, D. Phillips, and B. Dawson (2005), "The effects of universal pre-K on cognitive development," *Developmental Psychology* 41(60): 872–884; J. M. Larsen and C. C. Robinson (1989), "Later effects of preschool on low-risk children," *Early Childhood Research Quarterly* 4(1): 133–144; K. Magnuson, M. Meyers, C. Ruhm, and J. Waldfogel (2004), "Inequality in preschool education and school readiness," *American Educational Research Journal* 41(1): 115–157.

46. Zigler, Gilliam, and Jones, *Vision for universal preschool education;* M. Malakoff (2006), "The need for universal preschool access for children not living in poverty," in Zigler, Gilliam, and Jones, *Vision for universal preschool education,* 89–106.

47. S. Barnett (2006), "Economics of early education: Benefits and costs of quality early education for all" (lecture, Wisconsin Speaker's Task Force on 4-Year-Old Kindergarten), http://nieer.org/docs/index.php?DocID=60 (accessed December 30, 2006).

48. Calman and Tarr-Whelan, *Early childhood education for all.*

49. J. Gelbach and L. Pritchett (2002), "Is more for the poor less for the poor? The politics of means-tested targeting," *Topics in Economic Analysis and Policy* 2(1), http://www.bepress.com/bejeap/topics/vol2/iss1/art6.

50. Barnett, *Economics of early education.*

51. Zigler, Gilliam, and Jones, *Vision for universal preschool education.*

52. S. L. Kagan and E. Zigler, eds. (1987), *Early schooling: The national debate* (New Haven, CT: Yale University Press).

53. M. Finn-Stevenson and E. Zigler (2006), "What the School of the 21st Century can teach us about universal preschool," in Zigler, Gilliam, and Jones, *Vision for universal preschool education.*

54. Zigler, Gilliam, and Jones, *Vision for universal preschool education.*

iv

ne thinking.

55. *School of the 21st Century Newsletter* (2005), "Responding to the needs of today's children and families" (New Haven, CT: Yale University).

56. Finn-Stevenson and Zigler, "What the School of the 21st Century can teach us."

57. E. Zigler, D. G. Singer, and S. J. Bishop-Josef, eds. (2004), *Children's play: The roots of reading* (Washington, DC: Zero to Three Press).

58. C. Henrich and R. Blackman-Jones (2006), "Parent involvement in preschool," in Zigler, Gilliam, and Jones, *Vision for universal preschool education*, 149–168.

59. C. Henrich, M. Finn-Stevenson, and E. Zigler (in progress), *Quality in 21C schools*.

60. A. Shanker (1974), "Where we stand," *New York Times*, September 8.

61. J. A. Levine (1978), *Day care and the public schools: Profiles of five communities* (Newton, MA: Educational Development Center).

62. Ibid.

63. Ibid.

64. Helburn and Bergmann, *America's child care problem*, 63.

65. *School of the 21st Century Newsletter*, "Responding to the needs of today's children and families."

66. J. Warner (2006), "The real value of public preschool," *New York Times*, December 7.

67. D. Brooks (2006), "Of love and money," *New York Times*, May 25.

CHAPTER 7. SCHOOL-AGE CHILD CARE

1. U.S. Department of Education (2000), *After-school programs: Keeping children safe and smart* (Washington, DC: U.S. Department of Education).

2. J. Capizzano, K. Tout, and G. Adams (2000), *Child care patterns of school-age children with employed mothers* (Washington, DC: Urban Institute); L. M. Casper and K. W. Smith (2002), "Dispelling the myths: Self-care, class, and race," *Journal of Family Issues* 23(6): 716–727.

3. I. Sawhill, S. Robblee, and S. Berkowitz (2004), *Education proposals in the 2004 presidential campaign: A preliminary assessment*, working paper (Washington, DC: Brookings Institution), www.brook.edu/views/papers/sawhill/20040623.htm (accessed December 30, 2006).

4. M. Goyette-Ewing (2000), "Children's afterschool arrangements: A study of self-care and developmental outcomes," *Journal of Prevention and Intervention in the Community* 20:55–67; S. M. McHale, A. C. Crouter, and C. J. Tucker (2001), "Free-time activities in middle childhood: Links with adjustment in early adolescence," *Child Development* 72(6): 1764–1778; E. Smolensky and J. A. Gootman, eds. (2003), *Working families and growing kids: Caring for children and adolescents* (Washington, DC: National Academies Press); D. L. Vandell and L. Shumow (1999), "After-school child care programs," *Future of Children* 9(2): 64–80.

5. T. J. Dishion and R. J. McMahon (1998), "Parental monitoring and the

prevention of child and adolescent problem behavior: A conceptual and empirical formulation," *Clinical Child and Family Psychology Review* 1(1): 61–75; J. L. Mahoney, H. Stattin, and D. Magnusson (2001), "Youth recreation center participation and criminal offending: A 20-year longitudinal study of Swedish boys," *International Journal of Behavioral Development* 25:509–520; L. Steinberg (1986), "Latchkey children and susceptibility to peer pressure: An ecological analysis," *Developmental Psychology* 22(4): 433–439.

6. J. S. Eccles and J. L. Templeton (2005), "Building a bridge between theory and practice in the study of service learning" (unpublished manuscript); J. L. Mahoney, R. W. Larson, and J. S. Eccles, eds. (2005), *Organized activities as contexts of development: Extracurricular activities, after-school, and community programs* (Mahwah, NJ: Lawrence Erlbaum); Committee on Community-Level Programs for Youth, J. Eccles and J. A. Gootman, eds. (2002), *Community programs to promote youth development* (Washington, DC: National Academy Press).

7. Afterschool Alliance (2003), "Afterschool programs help working families," *Afterschool Alert Issue Brief* 16; S. L. Hofferth, A. A. Brayfield, S. G. Deich, and P. A. Holcomb (1991), *National Child Care Survey, 1990* (Washington, DC: Urban Institute); D. L. Vandell and J. K. Posner (1999), "Conceptualization and measurement of children's after-school environments," in S. L. Friedman and T. D. Wachs, eds., *Assessment of the environment across the lifespan* (Washington, DC: American Psychological Association).

8. Capizzano, Tout, and Adams, *Child care patterns.*

9. Smolensky and Gootman, *Working families and growing kids.*

10. Capizzano, Tout, and Adams, *Child care patterns;* P. S. Seppanen, J. M. Love, D. K. deVries, L. Bernstein, M. Seligson, F. Marx, and E. E. Kisker (1993), *National study of before- and after-school programs: Final report* (Portsmouth, NH: RMC Research Corporation); T. J. Kane (2004), "The impact of after-school programs: Interpreting the results of four recent evaluations" (working paper, William T. Grant Foundation), www.wtgrantfoundation.org/usr_doc/After-school_paper.pdf (accessed December 10, 2006).

11. Capizzano, Tout, and Adams, *Child care patterns.*

12. R. D. Laird, G. S. Pettit, K. A. Dodge, and J. E. Bates (1999), "Best friendships, group relationships, and antisocial behavior in early adolescence," *Journal of Early Adolescence* 19(4): 413–437.

13. Mahoney, Larson, and Eccles, *Organized activities;* Eccles and Gootman, *Community programs;* Vandell and Posner, "Conceptualization and measurement."

14. D. Belle (1997), "Varieties of self-care: A qualitative look at children's experiences in the after-school hours," *Merrill-Palmer Quarterly* 43(3): 478–496; N. L. Galambos and J. L. Maggs (1991), "Out-of-school care of young adolescents and self-reported behavior," *Developmental Psychology* 27(4): 644–

655; D. L. Vandell and H. Su (1999), "Child care and school-age children," *Young Children* 54(6): 62–71.

15. Capizzano, Tout, and Adams, *Child care patterns;* Casper and Smith, "Dispelling the myths."
16. Smolensky and Gootman, *Working families and growing kids;* G. S. Pettit, J. E. Bates, K. A. Dodge, and D. W. Meece (1999), "The impact of after-school peer contact on early adolescent externalizing problems is moderated by parental monitoring perceived neighborhood safety, and prior adjustment," *Child Development* 70(3): 768–778; G. S. Pettit, R. D. Laird, J. E. Bates, and K. A. Dodge (1997), "Patterns of afterschool care in middle childhood: Risk factors and developmental outcomes," *Merrill-Palmer Quarterly* 43(3): 515–538; N. Marshall, C. Garcia-Coll, F. Marx, K. McCartney, N. Keefer, and J. Ruh (1997), "After-school time and children's behavioral adjustment," *Merrill-Palmer Quarterly* 43(3): 498–514; Galambos and Maggs, "Out-of-school care"; H. Lord and J. L. Mahoney (2007), "Neighborhood crime and self-care: Risks for aggression and lower academic performance," *Developmental Psychology* 43(6): 1321–1333; Steinberg, "Latchkey children."
17. E. F. Zigler and N. W. Hall (2000), *Child development and social policy: Theory and applications* (Boston: McGraw-Hill); J. Brooks-Gunn, G. Duncan, and J. L. Aber, eds. (1997), *Neighborhood poverty* (New York: Russell Sage Foundation); J. L. Richardson, B. Radziszewska, C. W. Dent, and B. R. Flay (1993), "Relationship between after-school care of adolescents and substance use, risk taking, depressed mood, and academic achievement," *Pediatrics* 92(1): 32–38.
18. L. Long and T. Long (1983), *The handbook for latchkey children and their parents* (New York: Arbor House); McHale, Crouter, and Tucker, "Free-time activities"; E. F. Zigler and M. E. Lang (1991), *Child care choices: Balancing the needs of children, families, and society* (New York: Free Press).
19. H. N. Snyder and M. Sickmund (1999), *Juvenile offenders and victims: 1999 national report* (Washington, DC: U.S. Department of Justice, Office of Juvenile Justice and Delinquency Prevention).
20. M. Sickmund, H. N. Snyder, and E. Poe-Yamagata (1997), *Juvenile offenders and victims: 1997 update on violence—Statistics summary* (Washington, DC: U.S. Department of Justice, Office of Juvenile Justice and Delinquency Prevention).
21. *Congressional Record* (1983), 98th Congress, 1st session, 16455.
22. L. Greenhouse (1987), "Washington talk: The Senate," *New York Times,* July 1.
23. S. Cohen (2001), *Championing child care* (New York: Columbia University Press), xi.
24. *Congressional Record* (1983), 16455.
25. Long and Long, *Handbook for latchkey children.*

26. U.S. House of Representatives, Select Committee on Children, Youth, and Families (1984), Hearings before Select Committee.

27. Ibid.

28. M. H. Kimmich (1985), *America's children, who cares? Growing needs and declining assistance in the Reagan era* (Washington, DC: Urban Institute); E. F. Zigler and E. Gilman (1996), "Not just any care: Shaping a coherent child care policy," in E. F. Zigler, S. L. Kagan, and N. W. Hall, eds., *Children, families and government: Preparing for the twenty-first century* (New York: Cambridge University Press), 94–116.

29. M. Schmitt (2004), "Kids aren't us," *American Prospect,* June 29.

30. N. Kerrebrock and E. M. Lewit (1999), "Children in self-care," *Future of Children* 9(2): 151–160.

31. *Congressional Record* (1983), 16455.

32. Afterschool Alliance, "Afterschool programs"; Afterschool Alliance (2001), *Afterschool alert: Poll report 4* (Washington, DC: Afterschool Alliance).

33. Cohen, *Championing child care.*

34. See Fight Crime: Invest in Kids, www.fightcrime.org.

35. See Afterschool Alliance, www.afterschoolalliance.org.

36. W. J. Clinton (1998), "Address before a joint Session of Congress on the state of the union," in *Public papers of the presidents of the United States: William J. Clinton* book 1, pp. 112–123.

37. J. L. Mahoney and E. Zigler (2006), "Translating science to policy under the No Child Left Behind Act of 2001: Lessons from the national evaluation of the 21st Century Community Learning Centers," *Journal of Applied Developmental Psychology* 27:282–294.

38. J. Samelson (2003), *Afterschool in America: The state of afterschool in 2003* (Washington, DC: Afterschool Alliance).

39. Mahoney and Zigler, "Translating science to policy."

40. M. Dynarski, S. James-Burdumy, W. Mansfield, D. Mayer, M. Moore, J. Mullens, and T. Silva (2001), *A broader view: The national evaluation of the 21st Century Community Learning Center Program: Design report,* vol. 1 (Princeton, NJ: Mathematica Policy Research), 47.

41. Mahoney and Zigler, "Translating science to policy."

42. J. S. Bissell, C. Cross, K. Mapp, E. Reisner, D. L. Vandell, C. Warren, and R. Weissbourd (2003), Statement released by members of the Scientific Advisory Board for the 21st Century Community Learning Center Evaluation, May 10.

43. Mahoney and Zigler, "Translating science to policy."

44. D. T. Campbell and J. C. Stanley (1966), *Experimental and quasi-experimental designs for research* (Chicago: Rand McNally).

45. Sawhill, Robblee, and Berkowitz, *Education proposals.*

46. U.S. Senate (2003), *Investment in after-school programs: Hearing before a Subcommittee of the Committee on Appropriations,* 108th Congress, 7, http://eric.ed.gov/ERICWebPortal/custom/portlets/recordDetails/

detailmini.jsp?_nfpb=true&_&ERICExtSearch_SearchValue_0=ED483012 &ERICExtSearch_SearchType_0=no&accno=ED483012.

47. Ibid., 9.
48. Ibid., 40.
49. Ibid., 28.
50. Ibid., 29.
51. Mahoney and Zigler, "Translating science to policy."
52. Sawhill, Robblee, and Berkowitz, *Education proposals.*
53. R. Hollister (2003), *The growth in after-school programs and their impact* (Washington, DC: Brookings Institution).
54. Mahoney, Stattin, and Magnusson, "Youth recreation center participation"; J. L. Mahoney, H. Stattin, and H. Lord (2004), "Participation in unstructured youth recreation centers and the development of antisocial behavior: Selection processes and the moderating role of deviant peers," *International Journal of Behavioral Development* 28:553–560.
55. J. L. Mahoney (2003), "After-school activities as contexts for the development of peer relationships and interpersonal competence," (presentation, Learning with Excitement Conference, Harvard University, Cambridge, MA, October 3), www.pearweb.org/conferences/pear/old/pdfs/mahoney.ppt (accessed December 30, 2006).
56. J. L. Mahoney and H. Stattin (2000), "Leisure activities and adolescent antisocial behavior: The role of structure and social context," *Journal of Adolescence* 23(2): 113–127; Mahoney, Stattin, and Lord, "Participation in unstructured youth recreation centers."
57. T. J. Dishion, J. McCord, and F. Poulin (1999), "When interventions harm: Peer groups and problem behavior," *American Psychologist* 54(9): 755–764; T. J. Dishion, D. Capaldi, K. M. Spracklen, and F. Li (1995), "Peer ecology of male adolescent drug use," *Development and Psychopathology* 7(4): 803–824; T. J. Dishion, K. M. Spracklen, D. W. Andrews, and G. R. Patterson (1996), "Deviancy training in male adolescent friendships," *Behavior Therapy* 27(3): 373–390; T. J. Dishion, J. M. Eddy, E. Haas, F. Li, and K. Spracklen (1997), "Friendships and violent behavior during adolescence," *Social Development* 6(2): 207–223.
58. R. A. Feldman (1992), "The St. Louis experiment: Effective treatment of antisocial youths in prosocial peer groups," in J. McCord and R. Tremblay, eds., *Preventing antisocial behavior: Interventions from birth through adolescence* (New York: Guilford), 233–252; Mahoney, Stattin, and Lord, "Participation in unstructured youth recreation centers."
59. J. Wilgoren (2000), "The bell rings but the students stay, and stay," *New York Times*, January 24.
60. Ibid.
61. B. M. Miller (2003), *Critical hours: Afterschool programs and educational success* (Quincy, MA: Nellie Mae Education Foundation), 45.
62. S. Watson (2000), *Using results to improve the lives of children and families:*

A guide for public-private child care partnerships (Washington, DC: Child Care Partnership Project).

63. E. Zigler (2003), speech presented at the Brookings Institute, "Welfare Reform and Beyond Initiative" (conference), Washington, DC, July 10.

64. Afterschool Alliance, "Afterschool programs help working families"; Mahoney, Larson, and Eccles, *Organized activities.*; J. S. Eccles and J. L. Templeton, (2005), *Building a bridge between theory and practice in the study of service learning* (unpublished manuscript).

65. Eccles and Gootman, *Community programs;* Mahoney, Larson, and Eccles, *Organized activities.*

66. J. L. Mahoney, H. Lord, and E. Carryl (2005), "After-school program participation and the development of child obesity and peer acceptance," *Applied Developmental Science* 9(4): 202–215.

67. Ibid.

68. Promising Practices in Afterschool Database (2006), www.afterschool.org.

69. Zigler and Lang, *Child care choices.*

70. *Congressional Record* (1975), 94th Congress, 1200.

71. K. DeAngelis and R. Rossi (1997), *Schools serving family needs: Extended-day programs in public and private schools* (Washington, DC: American Institutes for Research).

72. J. G. Wirt (2000), *The condition of education, 2000* (Washington, DC: U.S. Department of Education); Miller, *Critical hours.*

CHAPTER 8. MOVING FORWARD

1. S. Cohen (2001), *Championing child care* (New York: Columbia University Press), 218.

2. U.S. Department of Health and Human Services Administration for Children and Families (2006), "Child Care Bureau history," http://www.acf.hhs.gov/programs/ccb/general/ccbhist.htm.

3. C. Dodd (2006), "Senator Dodd opposes diminishing the Child Care Bureau in the Health and Human Services Department" (press release, March 16), http://dodd.senate.gov/index.php?q=node/3425.

4. P. Hopper and E. Zigler (1988), "The medical and social science basis for a national infant care leave policy," *American Journal of Orthopsychiatry* 58(3): 324–338; E. F. Zigler and S. Hunsinger (1977), "Day care policy: Some modest proposals," *Early Childhood Education Journal* 4(5): 9–11; E. F. Zigler and M. Frank, eds. (1988), *The parental leave crisis: Toward a national policy* (New Haven, CT: Yale University Press).

5. E. F. Zigler, M. Finn-Stevenson, and N. W. Hall (2002), *The first three years and beyond: Brain development and social policy* (New Haven, CT: Yale University Press).

6. S. B. Kamerman (2000), "Parental leave policies: An essential ingredient in early childhood education and care policies," *Social Policy Report* 14(2): 3–15.

7. Paid Family Leave Collaborative (2006), "California paid leave: 10 facts about the law," http://www.paidfamilyleave.org/law.html (accessed January 3, 2007).

8. S. S. Cohen and H. Lord (2005), "Implementation of the Child Care and Development Block Grant: A research synthesis," *Nursing Outlook* 53(5): 239–246.

9. J. Mezey and B. Richie (2003), *Welfare dollars no longer an increasing source of child care funding: Use of funds in FY 2002 unchanged from FY 2001, down from FY 2000*, publication no. 03–59 (Washington, DC: Center for Law and Social Policy).

10. Cohen and Lord, "Implementation of the Child Care and Development Block Grant."

11. D. J. Besharov and C. A. Higney (2005), *Federal and state child care expenditures 1997–2004: Rapid growth followed by steady spending* (Washington, DC: Maryland School of Public Policy Welfare Reform Academy).

12. H. Matthews and D. Ewen (2006), *Child care assistance in 2005: State cuts continue* (Washington, DC: Center for Law and Social Policy); J. Mezey, M. Greenberg, and R. Schumacher (2002), *The vast majority of federally eligible children did not receive child care assistance in FY 2000* (Washington, DC: Center for Law and Social Policy).

13. N. D. Campbell, J. Entmacher, A. K. Matsui, C. M. Firvida, and C. Love (2006), *Making care less taxing: Improving state child and dependent tax provisions* (Washington, DC: National Women's Law Center).

14. National Women's Law Center (2003), *Indexing DCTC is necessary to prevent further erosion of the credit's value to low-income families* (Washington, DC: National Women's Law Center).

15. National Center for Education Statistics (2003), *Pre-kindergarten in U.S. public schools, 2000–2001* (Washington, DC: National Center for Education Statistics).

16. Ibid.

17. V. Washington (2004), "Where do we go from here?" *American Prospect*, November 2.

18. D. A. Olsen (1999), "Preschool in the nanny state," *Weekly Standard*, August 9.

19. E. Zigler, W. S. Gilliam, and S. M. Jones (2006), *A vision for universal preschool education* (New York: Cambridge University Press).

20. J. L. Mahoney (2003), "A critical commentary on the national evaluation of the 21st Century Community Learning Centers," *School of the 21st Century Newsletter* 1.

21. A. Szekely and H. C. Padgette (2006), *Sustaining 21st Century Community Learning Centers: What works for programs and how policy makers can help* (Washington, DC: Finance Project), 5.

22. Ibid., 13.

23. See National Child Care Information and Technical Assistance Center, http://www.nccic.org.

24. D. Bryant, K. Maxwell, and K. Taylor (2004), *Summary of statewide findings NC early childhood needs and resources assessment: Final report—Spring 2004* (Carrboro: Frank Porter Graham Child Development Institute, University of North Carolina), http://www.fpg.unc.edu/%7ENCNR_Assessment/pdfs/ Statewide_Summary.pdf; K. W. Marsland, E. Zigler, and A. Martinez (2003), "Regulation of infant and toddler child care: Are state requirements for centers adequate?" (unpublished manuscript, Yale University).

25. W. T. Gormely (2002), *Differential reimbursement policies and child care accreditation* (unpublished manuscript, George Washington University).

26. C. C. Henrich (2004), "Head Start as a national laboratory," in E. F. Zigler and S. Styfco, eds., *The Head Start debates* (Baltimore: P. H. Brookes).

27. National Child Care Information and Technical Assistance Center (2006), *Child Care and Development Fund: Report of state and territory plans FY 2006–2007* (Washington, DC: Administration for Children and Families).

28. National Association of Child Care Resource and Referral Agencies (2006), *NACCRRA Strategic Plan 2006–2011* (Washington, DC: NACCRRA), 2, http://www.naccrra.org/docs/about/2006_strategicplan.pdf.

29. Ibid., 9.

30. Bright Horizons Family Solutions website, www.brighthorizons.com (accessed March 21, 2006).

31. Ibid.

32. Ibid.

33. E. Zigler and M. Lang (1991), *Child care choices: Balancing the needs of children, families, and society* (New York: Free Press).

34. N. D. Campbell, J. C. Appelbaum, K. Martinson, and E. Martin (2000), *Be all that we can be: Lessons from the military for improving our nation's child care system* (Washington, DC: National Women's Law Center); K. T. Young, K. W. Marsland, and E. Zigler (1997), "The regulatory status of center-based infant and toddler child care," *American Journal of Orthopsychiatry* 67(4): 535–544; U.S. Government Accountability Office (1999), *Child care: How do military and civilian center costs compare?* (Washington, DC: U.S. Government Accountability Office).

35. Trible Amendment, 40 U.S.C. 590 (formerly 490b).

36. U.S. Government Services Administration (2007), "GSA child care centers: Annual profile," http://www.gsa.gov/gsa/cm_attachments/GSA _DOCUMENT/227profile_R2-u-fV_oZ5RDZ-i34K-pR.pdf.

37. L. Miller, A. Melaville, and H. Blank (2002), *Bringing it together: State-driven community early childhood initiatives* (Washington, DC: Children's Defense Fund).

38. M. Finn-Stevenson and E. Lapin (2006), personal communication, December.

39. J. Gottesman (2006), personal communication, December.

CHAPTER 9. ENVISIONING A SOLUTION

1. S. W. Helburn (1999), "Preface," in S. W. Helburn, ed., "The silent crisis in U.S. child care," *Annals of the American Academy of Political and Social Sciences* 563: 8–19.
2. K. Morgan (2001), "A child of the sixties: The great society, the new right, and the politics of child care," *Journal of Policy History* 13(2): 238.
3. E. Zigler and M. Frank, eds. (1988), *The parental leave crisis: Toward a national policy* (New Haven, CT: Yale University Press).
4. P. LeFebevre (2004), "Quebec's innovative early childhood education and care policy and its weaknesses," *Policy Options* 25(3): 52–57, http://www .irpp.org/po/archive/maro4/lefebvre.pdf.
5. M. Baker, J. Gruber, and K. Milligan (2005), *Universal child care, maternal labor supply, and family well-being* (NBER Working Paper No. 11832).
6. S. Helburn and B. Bergmann (2002), *America's child care problem: The way out* (New York: Palgrave for St. Martin's).
7. J. Sugarman (1989), *The children's investment trust: For America's future* (working paper, Washington, DC).
8. E. F. Zigler and M. E. Lang (1991), *Child care choices: Balancing the needs of children, families, and society* (New York: Free Press).
9. Ibid.
10. J. R. Walker (1996), "Funding child rearing: Child allowance and parental leave," *Future of Children* 6(2): 122–136.
11. E. Zigler, W. S. Gilliam, and S. M. Jones (2006), *A vision for universal preschool education* (New York: Cambridge University Press).
12. Ibid.
13. A. Raden (2003), "Universal access to pre-kindergarten: A Georgia case study," in A. Reynolds, M. Wang, and H. Walberg, eds., *Early childhood programs for a new century* (Washington, DC: CWLA Press), 99.
14. B. T. Bowman, S. Donovan, and M. S. Burns, eds. (2001), *Eager to learn: Educating our preschoolers* (Washington, DC: National Academy Press).
15. U.S. Department of Education and Learning Point (2005), *21CCLC performance and profile information collection system* (Washington, DC: U.S. Department of Education and Learning Point).
16. D. M. Blau (2001), *The child care problem: An economic analysis* (New York: Russell Sage Foundation).
17. Child Care Bureau history retrieved from http://web.archive.org/web/ 20020802215641/http://www.acf.hhs.gov/programs/ccb/.
18. National Association of Child Care Resource and Referral Agencies (2006), *NACCRRA Strategic Plan 2006–2011* (Washington, DC: NACCRRA), 397, http://www.naccrra.org/docs/about/2006_strategicplan.pdf.
19. L. Smith, Y. Vinci, and M. Galvan (2003), *Poised for shaping results-based early learning systems: A report on child care resource and referral in the United States* (Washington, DC: NACCRRA).
20. NACCRRA, *Strategic Plan 2006–2011*, 4.

21. Ibid., 20.
22. G. Westervelt (2007), personal communication, January.
23. "Moms Rising," http://www.momsrising.org (accessed March 14, 2007).

INDEX